On the Art of Designing Cities:
Selected Essays of Elbert Peets

On the Art of Designing Cities:
Selected Essays of Elbert Peets

Edited by *Paul D. Spreiregen*

The M.I.T. Press
Massachusetts Institute of Technology
Cambridge, Massachusetts, and London, England

NA 9127
W2
P4
1968

7H
P375

Foreword

Designing cities is possibly the most difficult of society's tasks. No one generation can learn by itself all that it needs to know about the job. It is too complex and depends on far more subtleties than one generation can recognize.

However, everyone participates in the job, if only by exercise of preference. In well-planned cities everyone benefits, if only by the joy derived from the pleasure of little accommodations. As in other endeavors the designing itself may be assigned to experts. But that assignment is not a surrender of responsibility, only a directive from the people. "What is a city but its people?" asked and answered William Shakespeare.

Our collective knowledge of urban design is not exactly reassuring at the present time. The books and articles in this field dwell largely on dissecting the problems. But what can we actually do? How should we design our cities?

We might start by learning from the best that has been done. Some would object, claiming the past has little to teach in a period of rapid social change. For those people the answer lies obscured in the future, to be glimpsed by probing minds. Such an argument, however, is academic. Ideas are important if they are useful; their pedigree is secondary.

This book is made up of the observations of a now elderly American landscape architect, Elbert Peets, written over a period of a third of a century. Peets's active career spanned a period no less tumultuous than the present.

Peets was born toward the end of the last century and, as a young man, found himself at the zenith of the American park movement as well as a moment of rebirth in American city planning. The air of the first quarter of this century was charged with a certain optimism. Urban population was growing, swelled by foreign immigration and a population surplus from America's farms. American industrial growth needed growing cities, and growing cities needed growing population—which all added up to a need for designing cities.

The opportunity attracted great minds, many from abroad. America in the early part of this century was one of the most hopeful places for urban planning. With the advantage of perspective we can now judge just how much we accomplished, perhaps in terms of the ratio between ideas offered and accomplishments realized. We should also consider the whole spectrum of ideas then at hand. Few can tell us more about this than Peets, who lived it and practiced it.

No less vital to Peets's experience was the fact that ideas for designing cities had a ready market— in government and in many quarters of the real estate world. Before and long after World War I it was a rule rather than an exception for cities to be engaged in ambitious public works programs that heavily involved design, whether in parks or in groups of civic buildings. Many of our college campusus found their characteristic forms in this period. Garden suburbs and developments, even new towns, were built by private enterprise to a far greater extent than they are today. States were acquiring parkland, and some were formulating state-wide plans. The depression saw a transfer in the initiative of such efforts rather than a diminution.

That the propositions of this era did not evolve into the characteristic methodology or style of development for America is no small tragedy. To investigate the reasons for this failure is not the subject of this book. Rather, the intention is to offer the propositions themselves as seen through the eyes of one of the period's outstanding practitioners and conveyed through his flowing prose.

Specifically, Elbert Peets practiced as a landscape architect, site designer, and town planner. His early work was done in collaboration with Werner Hegemann, with whom he coauthored the monumental book *Civic Art: The American Vitruvius,* published in 1922. Peets spent many years in private practice, in a city planning department, and in a planning section of the federal government. He also served as a consultant, and he taught at Harvard and Yale. Throughout his career he had only distant relations with professional associations. He seems to have preferred perspective to position. But he wrote constantly, as much for professional journals as for the popular press.

His writing takes us through much of the heritage of Western planning experience, and his work reflects that experience. To our good fortune, his skill with a pen matches his observations. His words reveal him as a man of taste, elegance, wit, and a readiness to swipe at the pompous or the banal. That H. L. Mencken was one of his frequent editors is therefore not surprising.

His particular love was the design of Washington, to which much of his writing is devoted. As a lover, he was not blind; he saw the flaws of human failure as often as the gleams of unfulfilled possibilities in that near-gem of civic design.

Assembled here are twenty-six of Peets's published essays and one not published before, constituting a large part of his literary output. They are arranged in seven sections, but their order need not restrict the reader. Any chapter can be read independently.

Of the seven sections the first three deal with Washington, D.C. The fourth concerns other town planners and other town plans. The fifth looks at two old friends of design, domes and water. Landscape architecture fills the sixth section, and observations on site planning complete the book as the seventh section. This section should be of very real use to residential site planners.

Collections of essays frequently contain repetitions, and some will be found here. It seemed wiser to preserve the integrity of the individual pieces. For those wishing to delve further, all of the papers that came into my hands as editor have been given to the Collection of Regional History and University Archives at Cornell University.

These essays were assembled with a single view in mind—to focus attention on a body of useful information regarding the design of cities. Not a small part of its usefulness is the humane attitude toward cities—their people—which motivated the author. May that attitude grow.

The collection and preparation of these essays for publication was made possible by a grant-in-aid awarded in 1965 from the Arnold W. Brunner Scholarship Fund, administered by the New York chapter of the American Institute of Architects. The editor is deeply grateful for that vital and timely assistance.

The personal contributions that supported this edition of Elbert Peet's essays were no less essential. For the preservation of the essays the editor is grateful to Miss Elisabeth Coit, FAIA, of New York City, Mrs. Helena Newman of Washington, D.C., Mrs. Blossom van Bergen of Austinberg, Ohio, and Mr. Orville Peets of Millsboro, Delaware.

Finally, it is obvious though not always mentioned that a book is produced by many people at various moments of its preparation. In this case, they include the members of the Brunner Scholarship Committee—in particular, Mr. Dean McClure, Mr. Lawrence Litchfield, Mr. Owen Delevante, and Mrs. Margot Henkel, who serves the New York AIA chapter. Too numerous to mention are the editor's colleagues, whose perspicacity sets a standard of performance one can but strive to attain.

PAUL D. SPREIREGEN, AIA

Washington, D.C.
October 1967

Contents

I L'ENFANT'S PLAN FOR WASHINGTON

1. The Background of L'Enfant's Plan   *3*

"Famous Town Planners III—L'Enfant," *The Town Planning Review*, July 1928, pp. 30–49.

2. The Genealogy of L'Enfant's Washington   *19*

"Ancestry of the Washington Plan," *The Sunday Sun Magazine*, Baltimore, February 10, 1929, pp. 2–3.

3. Washington as L'Enfant Intended It   *26*

"The Lost Plazas of Washington," *The Sunday Sun Magazine*, Baltimore, April 24, 1932, pp. 4–5.

4. Critique of L'Enfant's Plan   *37*

"The Plan of Washington," *Civic Art, the American Vitruvius*, by Werner Hegemann and Elbert Peets (New York: Architectural Book Publishing Co., 1922), pp. 285–293.

II CRITIQUES OF PLANNING IN WASHINGTON

5. On the Concentration and Design of Federal Buildings   61

"The New Washington," *The American Mercury*, August 1926, pp. 449–452.

6. On the Plans for Washington   67

"Washington," *City Planning and Housing*, by Werner Hegemann *et al.* (New York: Architectural Book Publishing Co., 1937), Chapter 27, pp. 382–394.

7. On the Mutilations of L'Enfant's Plan   79

"The New Washington—A Sharp Complaint," *The Sunday Sun Magazine*, Baltimore, January 26, 1930, pp. 1–2.

8. On the Rebuilding of the Mall in the 1930's   88

"New Plans for the Uncompleted Mall," *The Sunday Sun Magazine*, Baltimore, March 3, 1935, pp. 1–2.

III MONUMENTS IN WASHINGTON

9. The Interior of the Lincoln Memorial   101

The American Mercury, June 1925, pp. 194–196.

10. The Jefferson Memorial and Blocked Vistas   105

"City Planner Believes John Russell Pope Did Job He Was Employed to Do," *Washington Daily News*, April 7, 1937, p. 10.

11. The Golden Horses and Civic Art   107

"The Golden Horses," *City Planning at Yale*, edited by Christopher Tunnard and John N. Pearce (New Haven: Yale University Press, 1954), pp. 44–48.

IV OTHER TIMES, OTHER PLANS, AND OTHER PLANNERS

12. *Plans for Rebuilding London in 1666*   *115*

"Famous Town Planners IV—Plans for Rebuilding London in 1666," *The Town Planning Review*, May 1930, pp. 12–30.

13. *Haussmann and the Rebuilding of Paris*   *133*

"Famous Town Planners I—Haussmann," *The Town Planning Review*, June 1927, pp. 180–190.

14. *Camillo Sitte*   *143*

"Famous Town Planners II—Camillo Sitte," *The Town Planning Review*, December 1927, pp. 249–259.

15. *Mussolini, Haussmann, and Company*   *151*

The New Republic, February 3, 1926, pp. 295–296.

16. *The Restoration of Rome*   *154*

Catholic World, January 1927, pp. 451–456.

17. *Williamsburg*   *160*

City Planning and Housing, by Werner Hegemann *et al.* (New York, Architectural Book Publishing Co., 1937), Chapter 27, pp. 395–400.

18. *The Century of Progress*   *165*

City Planning and Housing, by Werner Hegemann *et al.* (New York, Architectural Book Publishing Co., 1937), Chapter 27, pp. 401–406.

V ON DOMES AND WATER

19. *The Reign of the Masonry Dome*   *173*

    The Nation, June 8, 1927, pp. 632–633.

20. *The Cleveland Reservoir*   *176*

    The Nation, February 9, 1927, p. 145.

VI CRITIQUES OF LANDSCAPE ARCHITECTURE

21. *Central Park*   *181*

    The American Mercury, March 1925, pp. 339–341.

22. *The Landscape Priesthood*   *186*

    The American Mercury, January 1927, pp. 94–100.

VII RESIDENTIAL SITE PLANNING

23. *The Neighborhood Concept*   *197*

    A series of responses to Reginald Isaacs' critique of the "neighborhood concept" published in *The Journal of Housing,* December 1948, pp. 300–301.

24. *The Orientation of Row Houses*   *199*

    Unpublished previously.

25. *Residential Site Planning Texture*   *202*

    "Studies in Planning Texture—for Housing in a Greenbelt Town," *Architectural Record,* September 1949, pp. 131–137.

26. *Greendale*   *216*

City Planning and Housing, by Werner Hegemann *et al.* (New York: Architectural Book Publishing Co., 1937), Chapter 27, pp. 407–414.

27. *A Concluding Thought*   *223*

City Planning and Housing, by Werner Hegemann *et al.* (New York: Architectural Book Publishing Co., 1937), Chapter 27, pp. 414–416.

APPENDIX A
Other Articles by Elbert Peets   *225*

APPENDIX B
Biographical Résumé of Elbert Peets   *226*

INDEX   *229*

Part I

L'Enfant's Plan for Washington

I

The Background of L'Enfant's Plan

The story of Pierre Charles L'Enfant as town planner is interwoven with the story of the founding of the capital of the United States. I shall not try to separate completely the two themes or to give a full chronological narration of either. Our present purpose will be better met by grouping the facts. The earlier paragraphs will concern the beginning of the city, the later ones L'Enfant and his plan.

The idea of a capital city whose name should stand for all the colonies, not merely for one, took form even before the treaty of 1783 was signed. Kingston, a hundred miles up the Hudson, offered itself and three hundred acres for the federal buildings, the whole to be ceded to and governed by the National Congress. The good sense of this last proposal, to save Congress from dependence upon the hospitality of any one state, made it an accepted part of the capital conception. Maryland offered Annapolis, with the state house and "public circle" and thirty thousand pounds in Maryland currency. Virginia offered Williamsburg, with thirteen mansions for the state delegates—or twenty-five square miles anywhere in the state. New Jersey offered a site. Pennsylvania urged Philadelphia, where the Continental Congress had met.

Philadelphia's claim was strong, but one day in June 1783 it suffered a fatal hurt. Congress was in session when a battalion of infantry, tired of waiting for their pay, marched from Lancaster and surrounded Independence Hall. They were dissuaded from their minatory purpose, but the delegates claimed that the state officials should have called out a guard. That they did next day, but Congress had adjourned to Princeton, New Jersey. Later, by way of Annapolis and Trenton, it moved to New York. It provided, too, by law, for the creation of a federal district two or three miles square—but no location was fixed.

Another line must be traced. In 1784 the Company of the Potomac was formed to build a canal from tidewater to the Ohio—for the Potomac follows one of the few clefts in the mountain range that bars the central valleys from the Atlantic. George Washington was president of the company. Great areas of land were involved, and the co-operation of three states was needed. The negotiations showed that for such a project the loose "Articles of Confederation" then uniting the states offered no security. Step followed step, and the Constitutional Convention of 1787 formulated a strong central government, clearing the way for large interstate undertakings. It gave to Congress, too, "exclusive legislation over such district (not exceeding ten miles square) as may, by the cession of particular States ... become the seat of the government of the United States."

The new Congress met at New York. To house it the city hastily rebuilt its city hall, the architect being L'Enfant. His Federal Hall was much admired. On its "grand balcony" President Washington took the oath of office, and in its halls, during 1789 and 1790, a question full of fate for the young architect was sharply debated. The North and the South could not agree on the location of the capital. One faction favored the region of the falls of the Delaware, above Trenton, the other a site on the Potomac.

By sharp bargaining, with the temporary capital as one of the pawns, the North won, and a committee was named to inspect the Trenton site. Two weeks later, by a chance majority, the southerners put through a law creating a second capital, on the Potomac. The temporary capital was also to oscillate. The country sensed a lack of dignity in this procedure, and the inevitable wag proposed that the seat of government should be of vehicular construction and that the proposed equestrian statue of General Washington should also be built with wheels, since no capital is complete without a monument.

But another question divided the country. The North wanted the nation to assume the war debts of the states in exchange for their western territories.

FIGURE I. The site of Washington, showing the ten-mile square, topography, and the relatively flat central triangle with L'Enfant's plan indicated. This map was made by Major Andrew Ellicott, L'Enfant's assistant.

Hamilton sounded both sides, Jefferson persuaded the Virginian members, the Funding Bill was passed, and a few days later the Residence Law gave the seat of government definitively to the Potomac. The temporary capital, until 1800, was to be Philadelphia.

The location thus determined has some likeness to the geographical situation of London. It resulted from the theoretical application of principles which in practice had formed the English metropolis. It was at the head of a tidal estuary, giving it accessibility to the sea yet relative safety from sea attack, the river above the site gave access to the hinterland, it was at the first bridge or ford, and it was on the principal north-south national highway. The site was thus by no means an arbitrary one. Its proximity to Washington's estates at Mount Vernon can fairly be taken as nine parts happy coincidence. Another factor, likely to be underestimated by Europeans, is that nothing was then commoner in North America than founding towns, drafting plots, and selling lots. The "fiat city" and the mushroom town were part of the colonial ideology.

In October 1790, President Washington visited the reach of the Potomac specified in the law and selected the most southerly part, between Georgetown and the Eastern Branch. By proclamation he *Fig. 1* defined the federal district, giving distances and *Fig. 2* bearings from the courthouse in Alexandria. He also, as the law required, named three commissioners to manage, with his approval, the whole undertaking. One of these was a doctor, one a lawyer and later justice of the Supreme Court, and the third was just leaving Congress. The commissioners received a per diem allowance, afterwards made a salary of sixteen hundred dollars a year with the requirement that

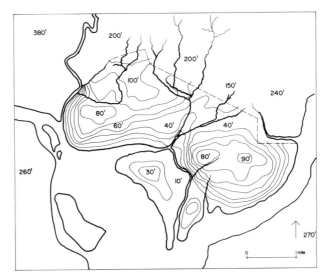

FIGURE 2. Topography of Washington. (*Editor's note:* Figures 2–6 show general intentions only.)

they reside in the city. This last arrangement was intended to keep down the cost of superintendence and to enable the commissioners to show lots to visitors. There were changes of personnel, one of the later commissioners being Thornton, the principal architect of the Capitol.

The land Washington wished to include in the *Fig. 3* city was owned by some nineteen proprietors and by numerous holders of lots in two small paper towns. The President asked two friends at Georgetown secretly to get options on these lots and on certain areas whose owners he thought might make trouble. Later, but before revealing just where in the district the city would lie or at least would center, Washington induced the proprietors to accede to this program: the land to be deeded to two trustees; the city to be laid out in streets, lots, and public areas; the proprietors to receive back half the lots and to be

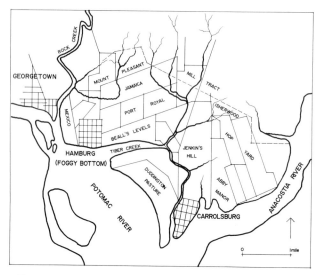

FIGURE 3. Original property lines.

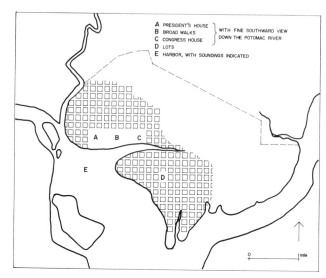

FIGURE 4. Jefferson's checkerboard plan.

paid sixty-six dollars an acre for land taken for public buildings and parks but to receive nothing for the land taken for streets. This obviously disposed the authorities toward liberality in the number and width of streets. As it worked out, of the total 6,111 acres, 3,606—or 59 per cent—were used for streets, 541 acres were bought for public use, 982 acres represented the lots sold by the government, and 982 acres—about 16 per cent—were returned to the grantors. There were in all 20,272 lots, about ten to the net acre. After being subdivided each block was divided into quarters, which were allotted by chance to the government and the proprietors.

Most of the proprietors liked L'Enfant's plan. Doubtless the reason for this somewhat surprising fact was that reducing the proportion of each acre available for building meant that the city would spread over a larger number of acres, a condition which would profit the outlying proprietors.

The commissioners took no land by eminent domain. Maryland had provided by law that a certain acreage could be taken without compensation, but this power was used only as a threat. In 1797 the President notified the city trustees to deed to the commissioners, in fee simple, the streets and public areas. They did not do so, and the public ownership of these areas is not recorded, the attorney general holding that the original agreement with the proprietors was sufficient title.

Having fixed the location of the federal district and named the commissioners, Washington engaged Major Ellicott to mark the boundaries of the district. He also appointed Major L'Enfant to survey the site of the city and to make a plan for it. Three days after his arrival on the Potomac, L'Enfant wrote Jefferson enthusiastically about the site, and three

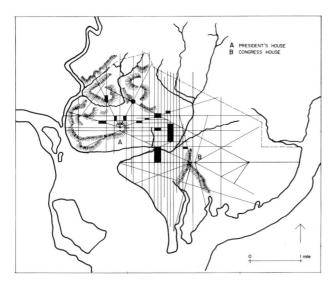

FIGURE 5. A rendition of L'Enfant's first draft plan, showing his careful regard for topography.

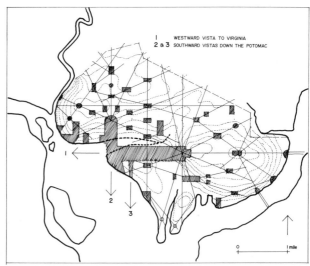

FIGURE 6. A comparative study of the relation between topography and the principal elements of L'Enfant's design—avenues, plazas, and major central axes.

weeks later he sent the President a report outlining in a very general way the plan as it was later drawn. Washington visited the site with L'Enfant and shortly afterwards sent him a sketch of his own (he was an experienced land surveyor) and one by Jefferson. The latter was a simple chessboard, as probably was Washington's. In June, not four months after his first view of the site, L'Enfant sent Washington a complete draft. There was another conference on the site, and changes were made—the number of diagonals was reduced, and the President's house was moved a little west to higher ground. The revised plan, with a long report, was finished in August. An auction of lots was held in October. The commissioners now pressed L'Enfant for a complete plan from which an engraving could be made. The burden of all this on L'Enfant can be judged from the facts that he had to do a considerable amount of

surveying of land in large part wooded and rendered almost impassable by recent lumbering operations, that he was doing at least a certain amount of superintendence of construction, that he was making detailed studies for canals, bridges, parks, and the public buildings, and that his plan was not worked out on paper merely nor from a good topographic map but was in part adjusted to points on the ground of which the exact location was not known. Difficulties between L'Enfant and the commissioners began during the autumn, later centering on the delay in the engraving of the map. A final rupture, which the President greatly deplored but in which he supported the commissioners, came almost exactly a year after L'Enfant's appointment.

The preparation of plans from which sales could be made had been begun by Ellicott and several assistants, and continued under these men and their

Fig. 4

Fig. 5
Fig. 6

Fig. 7

Fig. 8

numerous successors. The survey was not finished until June 1795.

The law provided that Congress should convene in the new capital in December 1800. The commissioners had not merely to plan the city but to prepare buildings for Congress and the President and to induce private persons to erect hotels and houses. Clearing and grading streets, building bridges, digging canals to facilitate bringing in materials for the Capitol, raising wharves—these were typical undertakings. In 1791, L'Enfant selected a quarry of foundation stone. The following year competitions for the design of the Capitol and President's house were held or begun, but there was great difficulty in getting plans worthy of the purpose and within the limitations of cost and time. There were endless bickerings with and among architects, trouble in finding workmen and in making payments. When 1800 came, one wing of the Capitol was ready, part of the President's house was habitable. There were in the city 109 buildings of brick and 263 of wood, housing some three thousand souls.

The Residence Law made no appropriation. It merely empowered the President to receive and expend money. The Virginia legislature gave $120,000 for the erection of public buildings, and Maryland gave $72,000, these sums becoming available as the states had funds. When they were exhausted, unsuccessful efforts were made to arrange foreign loans on the public share of the lots. Washington then appealed to Maryland, and the state lent its credit to mortgage bonds to the par value of two hundred thousand dollars. Maryland's help was due to the hope of the western part of the state that land values would be raised by the canalization of the Potomac and the growth of a populous market city.

Congress underwrote a hundred thousand. After the government moved to Washington, it assumed all expenses.

As a real estate development the city was hardly a success. Lot sales were fair, over half the government's share being gone in five years, but the prices were disappointing, and payments were often deferred. The government got its land at a low price, but it did not share largely in the expected increment. Several private owners and speculators lost heavily. There is a tradition, doubtfully founded, that business did not locate southeast of the Capitol because of the speculative increase in values on the supposition that it would do so. A syndicate took six thousand lots at eighty dollars in this district and as many more from the proprietors. It sold five hundred a year later at $266; but this price was not sustained, and the syndicate failed. To reduce speculation later sales by the commissioners were of limited areas to persons promising early building. The gross paper selling price of the public share of lots was $850,000.

In pooling their land the proprietors agreed to accept such building regulations as the President might think wise. A schedule of "terms and conditions" was "declared" by President Washington. The first article provided that "the outer and party walls of all houses shall be built of brick or stone." By the third, "the walls of no house shall be higher than forty feet to the roof in any part of the City, nor shall any be lower than thirty-five feet on any of the Avenues." These articles were found to hinder building, and in 1796 the President suspended them until December 1800. The suspension was renewed until it was made permanent in 1818.

It will be seen from these regulations that the city

was intended to be built in close rows of houses in the manner of English and Colonial towns. The freestanding wood frame house, which was shortly to facilitate the rapid rise of the western cities, though not then unknown, was probably thought to want civility.

By the Residence Law, the laws of Maryland and Virginia were to continue in force until Congress assumed jurisdiction. Maryland gave the commissioners certain powers, such as to regulate building and to record land deeds. The officials of the county in which the city was located continued to exercise the right of taxation and cared for the old highways until 1800. The city was not incorporated. The complicated status of law and tenure is illustrated by the fact that the United States, wanting land for a navy yard, purchased it from the commissioners.

When the commissioners named the capital the City of Washington, they honored not only the *pater patriae* but also the *pater urbis*. Washington fixed on the precise site of the city, determined its extent, chose its designer, and by his constant tactful oversight carried it through the excessively difficult first half decade. He had an extraordinary capacity for settling differences and handling men. Without the vision and supreme administrative power of President Washington, L'Enfant's dream would never have come to the degree of realization it did. He made changes in L'Enfant's plan, but he liked it and was loyal to it. Yet practical matters were his nearest concern. During the first five years of the city there was danger that a new alignment in Congress would cause the project to be abandoned. Washington constantly insisted to the commissioners on the need of haste in the sale of lots, the circulation of engravings and advertisements, the erec-

tion of the Capitol, of private houses—everything that would make the project irrevocable. His realistic attitude was in sharp contrast to that of his town planner. L'Enfant wanted to borrow money at low interest—apparently from the companies which should be employed to build the city!—cut the streets, put up the public buildings, lay out parks, build wharves and canals. When everything was shipshape, the lots would be sold—at high prices. That is the way large land subdivisions are now developed, but it requires plenty of capital and an assured market. The truth of the matter is that the city was begun on a larger scale than its economic basis justified. But perhaps there was no better way to control so large an area with such narrow means.

Washington's chief secretary, Jefferson, who had traveled and studied architecture, took a keen interest in the new city. When the site was selected, he made suggestions regarding the taking of the land and proposed a rectangular plan like "that Babylon revived in Philadelphia," the streets to be a hundred and a hundred and twenty feet wide. He condemned the "disgusting monotony" of Philadelphia's uniform building line but favored the Parisian restriction of height. He made a sketch plan, argued against sharp street intersections, and made studies showing how buildings on such points could be adapted to them.

L'Enfant was born in Paris, August 2, 1754, son *Fig. 9* of Pierre L'Enfant, painter at the Gobelins, and a member of the Academy of Fine Arts. L'Enfant was lieutenant of engineers when he came to America in 1777. He fought, was wounded, and captured. Exchanged, he designed forts and was made major. In 1783 France gave him a pension of 300 livres. He also had an income from his family until the Rev-

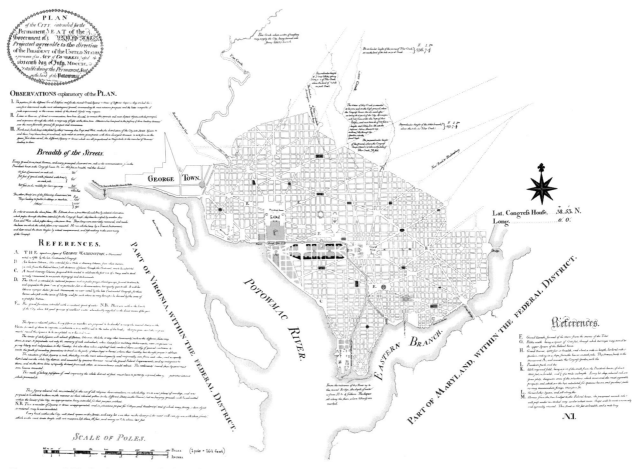

FIGURE 7. L'Enfant's engraved plan. One pole equals 16½ feet.

olution. After a brief return home he set up as engineer and architect in New York. He was called on to arrange a patriotic pageant, to design a medal for a society of veteran officers. The Federal Hall, which has already been mentioned, was carried out in a hurried manner, and cost more than was expected. L'Enfant quarreled with the contractors and

refused as insufficient the payment offered by the town. About the first of March, 1791, he was requested—no stipulation of terms accompanied the appointment—to go to the federal district and make surveys leading to the design of the new city. On the day that L'Enfant submitted his first plan to Washington, Louis XVI, seeking to escape from France,

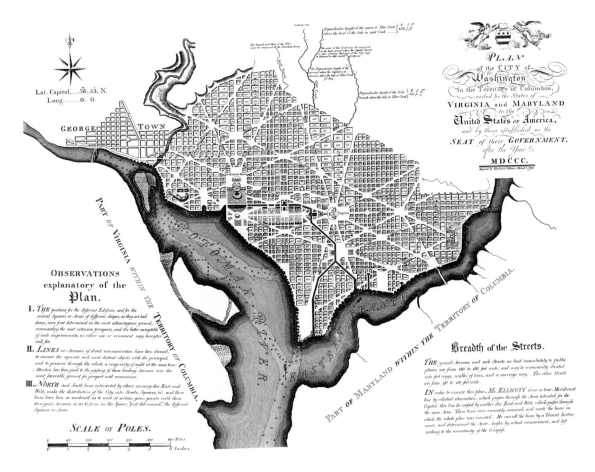

FIGURE 8. The final plan by Major Ellicott.

was brought back to Paris. The tragic occurrences in his native country added to the strain on L'Enfant; they also reduced him from financial independence to ultimate penury. Late in 1791 he was in Philadelphia, occupied with getting his plan ready for engraving, working on designs for the public buildings, quarreling with Ellicott and others. He

was discharged at the end of February 1792, having answered in the negative an inquiry whether he would subordinate himself to the commissioners. At Washington's suggestion he was offered $2,500 as payment for his work, but he refused it. He undertook to build the town of Paterson, in New Jersey, and buildings for a factory, but the owners found his ideas too grandiose. He designed a large house in Philadelphia—his client failed, and L'Enfant was left with a promissory note.

He lived at Washington during his later life, employed largely in soliciting from Congress payment for his services and losses. He asked nearly a hundred thousand dollars—Congress gave him about three thousand. During the War of 1812 he declined a professorship at the military academy. He built some fortifications near the city and is mentioned in the accounts of the visit of the British military in 1814. His last year was spent at the home of a country gentleman near Washington. He died in 1825. No authentic portrait survives, but he is described as tall and of good figure, with courtly manners.

FIGURE 9. An unauthenticated portrait of L'Enfant.

L'Enfant suffered many distressing injustices, but there must have been something in his personality that made those injuries so disastrous. His leading mental quality—both a weakness and a strength— was a frenzied desire to do things *en grand*. Indubitably he was erratic. Heroic visions and inexplicable blindness could exist together in him. His stupendous plan is full of exasperating, almost impudently willful, absurdities. His reports reveal an overflowing enthusiasm for his conceptions: he gloried in being an artist. Those reports reveal much sense, but the moment after giving sound reasons for his location of the Capitol he proposes a cascade a hundred feet wide and forty feet high, issuing from the base of the building. He knew no restraint in financial matters: if given free rein he would undoubtedly have bankrupted the United States. His writing is vivid but very inexact, whether in English or French. L'Enfant's artistic imagination may not have been well served by his training as a military engineer. He was almost wholly without experience in architecture and town planning when, at thirty-seven, he designed Washington. These facts, taken together, help explain the vagaries found equally in his work and his career.

As a basis from which to trace the sources or models that contributed to L'Enfant's ideas, I shall not use the present city map or the early engraved plans but instead the drawing preserved at Washington and supposed to be from L'Enfant's own hand. *Fig. 5* A lithographic copy has been issued by the U.S. Coast Survey. It is inexactly drafted and is so badly worn that parts are indecipherable, but for the present purpose it has the value of being the earliest surviving plan and the most strictly L'Enfant's work.

I have said that L'Enfant went to the Potomac

without experience as a town planner, but that does not mean that he went without preparation. Two years before his appointment he had written to Washington about the rare opportunity afforded by the proposal to create a new capital. Doubtless he took with him to Georgetown a certain amount of "professional material." While he was in Philadelphia, late in 1791, his office and living quarters were rifled of his property, including a "trunk and several boxes containing books, also collections of very costly engravings, models of architecture." These could have been procured during his earlier visit to Philadelphia, but probably not all were. While he was drafting his first plan, he wrote to Jefferson, asking to borrow plans of certain cities, including London. Jefferson sent him maps of Frankfort, Karlsruhe, Amsterdam, Strasbourg, Paris, Orléans, Bordeaux, Lyons, Montpellier, Marseilles, Turin, and Milan. From other sources he received other European plans, including London, Madrid, Florence, and Venice. He also knew or had such interesting American plans as Annapolis, Savannah, Williamsburg, and Philadelphia. The sketchy indication of docks along the river front in L'Enfant's plan comes pretty straight from a plan of New York published in 1789. There are, however, only two designs known to me that resemble the plan of Washington sufficiently to suggest that they may have been an important help to L'Enfant. They are the town and domain of Versailles and an almost forgotten plan that John Evelyn made for the rebuilding of London after the fire of 1666.

Fig. 10

Fig. 11

A general description of L'Enfant's plan is unnecessary, but some reference to its aesthetic functioning may be useful. The primary intention was, as in the French parks, to dominate a large area

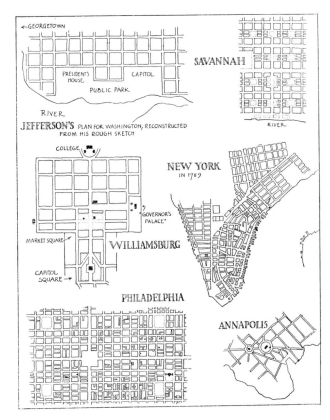

FIGURE 10. A few of the planned colonial towns extant in L'Enfant's day, and the New York waterfront.

while emphasizing its largeness. That is an aesthetic idea, but it was, in this case, also a practical benefit to have the visibility of the public buildings contribute to the finish of a maximum number of streets—which would otherwise have been green wildernesses. The plan was well adapted to the dispersion of the city, large extent disguising small population.

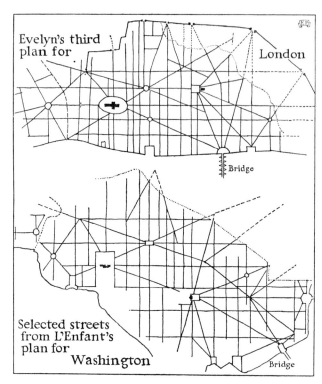

Evelyn's third
plan for

London

Bridge

Selected streets
from L'Enfant's
plan for
Washington

Bridge

FIGURE 11. A comparison of Wren's third plan for London and some major elements of L'Enfant's plan.

Fig. 12

The aesthetic driving member, so to speak, is—or was to have been—what I have called the basic triangle: Capitol, President's house, and Washington statue—for L'Enfant intended the intersection of the axes to be marked by an "equestrian figure," probably facing south. Suppose one studied this spatial integration from the Capitol. One would first look down the "grand avenue" and see the statue broadside. Its orientation would convey the impression of a spatial flow at right angles to the Capitol axis. One would then look down Pennsylvania Avenue and see the President's house. The view of its portico

and other members, lit by the southern sun, would reveal its orientation as being, like the statue, at right angles to the Capitol axis. The unifying effect of the statue, a part of both the organizations, would be felt. Normality (perpendicularity) is itself Fig. 13 a form of integration. The harmony of the two spatial flows would be sensed. In addition to the optical triangulation, there would be the common style and material of the two buildings, the perspective effect of two avenues, and similar plastic elements, all co-operating to give the spectator a sense of order in, and of tactile command over, a large organism of space and solid.

It is obvious that all this is very delicate mechanics. The want of an essential element in it would be like the omission of a transmission shaft or bearing in an engine. The difficulty of it is illustrated by the fact that if the Capitol dome covers, as actually it does, the intersection of Pennsylvania Avenue Fig. 14 and the axial avenue, then it is going to be impossible, save from the lantern, to have a perfect view of these two avenues, not to mention the third, at the left, needed to complete the *patte-d'oie*.* Except in a few parks, no such elaborate area organization as L'Enfant appears to have conceived has ever been consummated. That not a tenth part of the vital factors have been realized at Washington goes without saying.

The cost, both practical and aesthetic, of laying numerous diagonals over rectangular streets without detailed correction of their intersections, is well understood by current town planning thought. The

* A *patte-d'oie* is a goosefoot-shaped intersection of three roads, each at an angle of about 20 to 25 degrees to the others. An observer standing at the intersection can look down the three roads simultaneously since all three will be within the normal frontal field of view, about 65 degrees.

practical disadvantages are the many inconveniently shaped lots, the dangerous traffic junctions, the greater cost and maintenance. The aesthetic debits are the want of organic relation between the two sets of lines, the asymmetry of intersections, the gaping openings in the spatial boundaries of the diagonals, the disorderly relation of wall planes, the ugly flatiron buildings, the difficulty of contriving open spaces in satisfactory relation to the diagonals, and a similar difficulty in the placing of monumental buildings, save the few that can stand at the centers of radiation. The practical advantage of the diagonals is often overestimated, few distances being shortened more than one fifth. The average minor angle of divergence is only about twenty-five degrees.

Fig. 16   The irregular street and avenue intersections that L'Enfant called squares and intended as the sites of churches, monuments, and the like, are shockingly unexpected in the work of a Frenchman of the eighteenth century. Perhaps L'Enfant knew they were bad and simply had no time to work them out. Or, working from Versailles, he may have been misled by the fact that irregular intersections are not unpleasant in a hunting forest but are ugly in a city. This difference is acutely stated in the travel diary of Francis Baily, later F.R.S., who visited the city in 1796:

> The truth is that not more than half the city is cleared. The rest is in woods, and most of the streets which were laid out are cut through these woods, and have a much more pleasing effect now than I think they will have when they shall be built. Now they appear like broad avenues in a park, bounded on each side by thick woods, and there being so many of them, and proceeding in so many directions, they have a certain wild yet uniform and regular appearance which they will lose when confined on each side by brick walls.

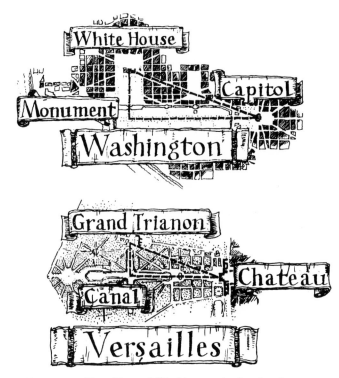

FIGURE 12. Versailles and Washington, basic triangles compared.

As L'Enfant's sources I have named only Versailles and a plan for London, but these must be taken also as the representatives of types, standing for the traditional chessboard pattern, the star of forest avenues, and the straight streets of ancient and Renaissance Rome. The plan of Washington is not an independent phenomenon. Though made in the backwoods of America it was part of the flow of European thought. The great scale of L'Enfant's plan was due not merely to a premonition of the empire the then young industrialism was to create in the central valleys of the continent; it was also a

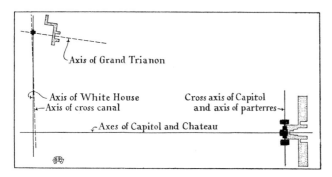

FIGURE 13. Distances of the two basic triangles compared. The Versailles dimensions are enlarged 50 per cent and superimposed on Washington as actually built.

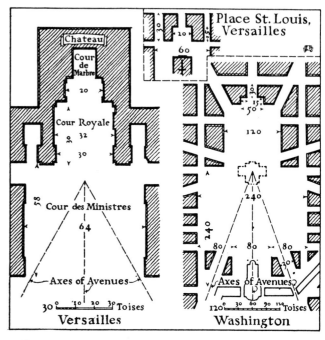

FIGURE 14. Comparison between the Cour Royale at Versailles and the Capitol Grounds at Washington (as L'Enfant designed them).

heritage from three centuries of European despotism, wealth, and art. So truly indeed was it a product of its time that it was a harbinger of certain decadent tendencies in the art of town planning. L'Enfant had a superlative sense of breadth, and he knew the avenue as a route and as a vista, but the street as a controlled composition of planes he did not know, nor the plaza as a spatial reservoir. That the maps recording the growth of European cities during the century after L'Enfant seem to contain many wrecked passages from the plan of Washington is not to be blamed on L'Enfant any more than one can blame the first stone that falls for the ruin of the building. He has had few imitators. The difficulty of carrying out such a plan has prevented its use in new projects. For the relief of overgrown chessboards it has furnished a convenient formula. Burnham's plans for Chicago, Manila, and San Francisco record his understanding of L'Enfant and Haussmann. Though generally admired they still await realization.

Innumerable changes, most of them small but some of them important aesthetically, were made during Ellicott's redrafting of the plan and afterwards. It is unlikely that Washington, though he shared the dignified architectural taste of the time, had any full comprehension of L'Enfant's aesthetic objectives. When Jefferson criticized acute lots produced by sharp intersections, L'Enfant made little parks out of these points. But Washington permitted their sale as lots. All of Ellicott's changes were approved by the President. L'Enfant later protested bitterly against some of them, particularly the failure to apply his principle of offsetting the sections of a street severed by a sharp-angled avenue, whereby he would make the carriage way of the street turn and cross the avenue at right angles. It is

Fig. 16

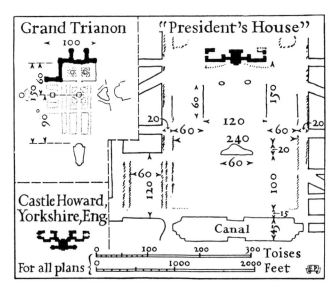

FIGURE 15. Comparison of L'Enfant's design for the President's house setting with the Grand Trianon and Castle Howard.

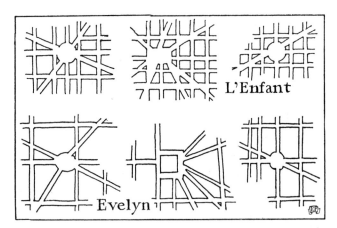

FIGURE 16. The awkward intersection of squares and diagonals—from the hand of L'Enfant and Christopher Wren.

not easy to detect the changes from his plan or to appraise them. Take the White House, for instance. L'Enfant made a great point of having the two public buildings harmonize, that being a part of his conception of the city—"to whose peculiar division those Edifices were in Configuration essential to have exactly corresponded." He wanted to plan both—he claimed afterwards that it was only with this expectation that he had consented to plan the city—and I feel sure that he would have wished to make the White House another Castle Howard, dome and all. It seems unquestionable that he would have laid Pennsylvania Avenue on the line between the two domes. Actually, however, the avenue shoots past the White House, south of it, and would barely touch one corner if cut through. We do not know whether he wished it thus or Washington made the change. But it is pretty certain that he would not willingly

have placed the White House so far from the Capitol if he had anticipated that it would be so small a building. In almost everything that concerns the relation of these two buildings, the heart of his plan, L'Enfant's purpose seems to have been wholly frustrated.

It was not my intention to refer to the present conditions at Washington, but for L'Enfant's protection it is necessary to warn the traveling town planner that he will meet with some cruel surprises. All Americans are proud of their unique capital, but it is not to be expected that there will be found, and least of all among persons in authority, an appreciation of the less obvious architectural implications of L'Enfant's design. We moderns, everywhere, tend to deal with ideas, not with concrete experiences. A typical Washingtonian will name with effusive pride the avenues that radiate from the White House. The fact that those avenues, instead of commanding views of that building, terminate in masses of thick foliage indistinguishable from any other masses of deciduous arborescent vegetation in the

FIGURE 17. A sketch of Pennsylvania Avenue, according to L'Enfant's precepts, but with a few of the more awkward short-comings corrected.

temperate zone does not bother him in the least. He is certain, too, that the Senate and House office buildings on Capitol Square "balance each other." The seventeen hundred feet of wood and meadow between them is not the least barrier to the thought that their aesthetic marriage is as firm as that of their architectural engenderers on the Place de la Concorde.

The art of architectural town planning has created three aesthetic forms: the plaza, the monumental street, and the inadequately named *patte-d'oie*. A synthesis of all three makes the Piazza del Popolo the glory of civic art. In the plan of Washington you will find twenty-five or thirty groups of three streets. But in not a single case is the center of divergence open so that one may actually experience this moving and beautiful discovery of Renaissance spatial art. For that one must still go to Rome, Versailles, and Hampton Court. It is quite likely that for pure beauty the Washington that Francis Baily saw was a finer thing than has existed there since.

Fig. 17 Pennsylvania Avenue can be taken as an example of what L'Enfant hoped to do, what he failed to do, or what was done to him—but also of what he did. It was to be the fine street of the town, the dome of the Capitol at one end, that of the President's house at the other, a "grand fountain" halfway between them, double rows of trees, and rows of stately houses. Alas, the reality is very different. Because the avenue never shot at the White House, the Treasury Building was permitted to jut far into its course and now forms such western terminus as it has. The result is picturesque but not what was wanted. Two squares or small parks ornament the avenue, but their lines are fixed by the co-ordinate streets, and the avenue cuts through them diagonally. From one end of the avenue to the other, not a single intersecting street is at right angles to it. In its western portion about half the lateral walls bounding the course of the avenue are not parallel to it but diverge at an angle of twenty degrees. Yet, with all its faults, Pennsylvania Avenue is a glorious street. It has length, breadth, perfect profile, and a fine terminal feature. There is not the absolute perfection of the Avenue Alexandre III and the Invalides, or the charm of Via Condotti and Trinità de' Monti, but it is, nevertheless, a giant of a street. One weeps because it is not better, but one gives thanks for what it is. . . . Perhaps just that is the thing to say of the whole city—and of Pierre Charles L'Enfant.

Yes, there is a breath of the atmosphere of Versailles at Washington. Splendid expansiveness, light, great and indeterminate extent, luxurious planning —these in some degree the far-from-perfect modern city has, thanks to L'Enfant and to the magnanimous art of the French Renaissance.

2

The Genealogy of L'Enfant's Washington

The plan of the American capital is unlike the plan of any other city in the world. It is unique, taken as a whole. Still, like almost everything in this country, its ancestors must have "come from" somewhere. Writers on the history of cities agree that the plan of our capital is an extraordinary phenomenon in the evolution of civic art, but they have not been quite sure where to look for the original stock which the genius of the young French engineer L'Enfant grafted and hybridized to form his magnificent creation.

It is a kind of detective work, this tracing down the original habitats of city planning forms and motives—for in civic art, as in religions, governments, and candlesticks, forms become traditional and spread from land to land. The detective searches over the plan in question with a microscope, so to speak, looking for fingerprints and clues. He investigates the education of the designer, his travels, his books, his earlier work. And often, when all the evidence is in, it is mostly circumstantial. That makes the decision a matter of individual reasoning—anyone can listen to the evidence and vote with the jury.

Perhaps the best way to present the evidence, as I see it, regarding the genealogy of the Washington plan, is to tell briefly the story of my own diggings in this corner of the field of city planning history.

The problem, in a word, is to account for the two conspicuous distinctions of the Washington plan. The first of these, and the most obvious, is that it comprises a system of diagonal streets laid over a plaid or irregular gridiron of rectangular streets. The second is that the plan has a central controlling axis scheme or organization, intended primarily to

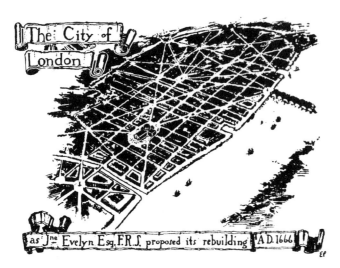

FIGURE 18. Evelyn's plan for rebuilding London, 1666.

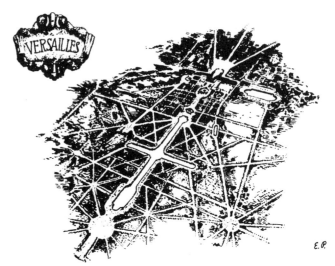

FIGURE 19. The general plan for the great French palace park, based on the original Blondel design.

give the Capitol and the President's residence effective places in the design and to enable them to dominate it. These two conspicuous elements were derived, I believe, from separate sources.

A few years ago I was in Europe on a Harvard traveling fellowship, studying the history of city planning. Winter found me in London, and naturally I spent much time in that most blessed place —the great round reading room of the British Museum. Among other things, I looked up all the plans that were made for the rebuilding of London after the Great Fire that destroyed the city in 1666. One of those plans, by Sir Christopher Wren, the architect of St. Paul's and a dozen other London churches, is quite well known. Another, by John Evelyn, a *Fig. 18* simple diamond- or kite-shaped layout, is occasionally reproduced. But greatly to my surprise I found two other "projections" by Evelyn, revisions of this first study. I found them—or copperplate engrav-

ings of them, dated 1748—in an old book bound in red morocco, published by the London Society of Antiquaries. It appears that objection was made to Evelyn's first plan and to Wren's because they would involve the moving of all the parish churches. So the ingenious Evelyn contrived a plan which would permit the re-erection of the churches on their old foundations. He gave up his simple diamond plan, but he held to his long, straight streets, and the plan that resulted was a gridiron overlaid with diagonals connecting such focal points as St. Paul's, London Bridge, the Royal Exchange, and the city gates.

A word about this John Evelyn. He was a solid, well-educated, curious-minded gentleman, the type that preceded our professional scientists. He interested himself in farming and forestry and building, traveled a good deal, knew everyone, and when the Royal Society was founded, he was made a charter

FIGURE 20. L'Enfant's plan for Washington, 1791.

member. He served on a primitive sort of city planning commission for London. As you might suspect, he kept a voluminous diary, his principal claim to present-day fame. It is more useful to historians than that of his friend Pepys, though vastly less racy to read.

Well, the moment I saw this revised plan of Evelyn's I thought of Washington. Without hesitating, you can pick out on it streets that correspond to Massachusetts, New York, and Pennsylvania Avenues.

But did L'Enfant have Evelyn's plan? That question cannot be answered with certainty either way. The only evidence lies in the similarity of the plans. But it is not at all impossible that L'Enfant had a copy of the Evelyn plan. He had a large collection of architectural books and engravings, all of them stolen, the winter after he planned Washington. Two years before he was asked to lay out the capital—in 1789, that is—the volume I ran across

at the British Museum had been published, including reprints of the engravings the antiquarians had issued forty years before. The studious and then prosperous L'Enfant was a leading architect of New York and was already interested in the talk of a new capital, but I have not been able to connect with him any of the three copies of the antiquarian volume which I have found in this country—one of them, by the way, in the library of the Peabody Institute. Yet it seems not at all unlikely that he saw these interesting London plans in 1789 or 1790, in New York or Philadelphia. I believe that he did see them and that it was Evelyn's plan that emboldened him to combine the stars of radiating avenues which he wanted to borrow from the French parks and cities with the rectangular plan required by American tradition and expected, certainly, by Washington and Jefferson, both of whom were enthusiastic devotees of the checkerboard plan.

And back to Evelyn? There were various things —the royal parks of Hampton Court and Greenwich with their divergent straight avenues, the geometric plans of the fortification engineers, and the good old gridiron or checkerboard plan which most American cities know so well. The idea of cutting long, straight streets from one traffic center to another Evelyn pretty certainly got from Rome. Pope Sixtus V in the sixteenth century built straight streets —the Via Sistina, Via Merulana, and others, through the deserted higher parts of Rome, for the convenience of pilgrims coming in by the Porta del Popolo and the Porta Pia to visit the sacred places. Evelyn had seen these streets in 1644 and had written enthusiastically in his diary of their "state and magnificence."

But if L'Enfant got any help from Evelyn, it

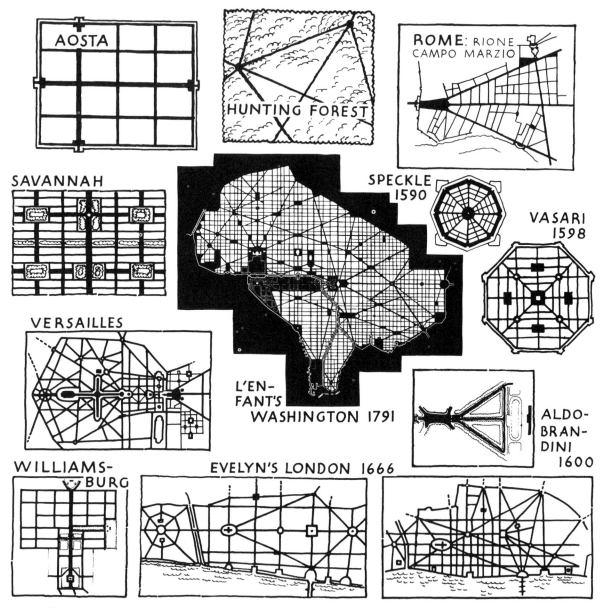

FIGURE 21. The types of planning that formed the background for the Washington plan. Aosta, based on a Roman legionary camp, illustrates the ancient use of the gridiron. The Speckle and Vasari plans are from books on fortifications. John Evelyn's proposed plans for rebuilding London, 1666, were published by the London Society of Antiquaries in 1789.

FIGURE 22. A hunting party in a forest, with converging avenues, from a French tapestry, 1734–1735.

could only have been in the general texture or type of the Washington plan, the combination of diagonal and rectangular streets—the first of the two novel features of the plan. The second feature which I mentioned, the architectural organization of the plan—the relation in particular of the Capitol and the White House to the Mall—all this came mainly *Fig. 19* from French ideas, and that means from Versailles, the château, park, and town of Louis XIV. L'Enfant was a Parisian, son of a famous painter, and must have had personal knowledge of the glories of Versailles. That he applied at Washington the principles embodied in Versailles has long been recognized. As a step in my study of the genealogy of the *Fig. 20* plan of Washington, I set out to determine precisely what were the resemblances between Washington and Versailles. To that end I made a careful comparison of old plans of the park, Blondel's in

particular, with a copy of the original autographic L'Enfant plan, preserved at the Library of Congress.

The most important correspondence between the places relates to the basic triangles of the two designs. At Washington the basic triangle is clearly marked, Pennsylvania Avenue being the hypotenuse, the Mall being one of the legs, and the three corners being at the Capitol, the White House, and the Washington Monument. (The last was built some four hundred feet from its true corner, instead of at the point L'Enfant designed as the site of the proposed "Equestrian Figure of George Washington.") At Versailles the triangle is less exact. Its corners are the Château, the Grand Trianon, and the intersection of the cross canal with the long or Grand Canal. I found that in linear dimensions the Washington triangle was just half again as large as the Versailles triangle.

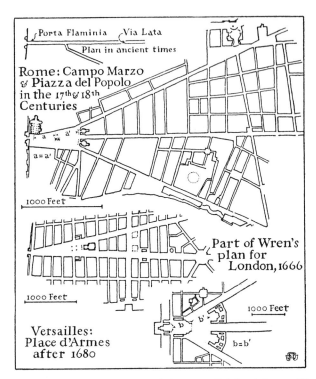

FIGURE 23. The ancestry of the *patte-d'oie* in civic art. The Campo Marzo *patte-d'oie* in Rome was partly the result of a happy alignment of streets at a key entrance. Wren utilized the concept of an acute intersection in his plan for London, and the Place d'Armes of Versailles employed the *patte-d'oie* concept in its full artistic development.

FIGURE 24. The Piazza del Popolo, Rome.

Fig. 21
Fig. 22
Back from Versailles run many tempting trails— or formal walks—into the city planning and garden history. Stars of long, straight avenues, for example, had long been the established means of opening up a hunting forest, so that the course of game could be observed and poachers could be caught. The type of gardening one sees at Versailles is the Italian style, modified by a century of French experience. The three approach avenues east of the Château, of which the middle one is the usual route from Paris, form the most famous French *patte-d'oie*—the French say goose-foot where we say turkey-foot. This Versailles *patte-d'oie* was probably the principal suggestion for the many groups of three avenues radiating from the Capitol and the White House. And the *patte-d'oie*, as a city planning feature, was brought to Versailles from Rome. The three streets that spread into the Campo Marzo from the Porta del Popolo formed the jewel of Roman civic art. That jewel was imitated everywhere—the Versailles avenues closely resemble the version used at the Villa Aldobrandini at Frascati.

Fig. 23
Fig. 24

So we come back, by way of Versailles as by way of London, to Rome, mother of the cities as of arts and laws. Nothing is more natural, for Rome was the deep soil from which grew the many-branched Renaissance. And L'Enfant's plan for Washington is one of the masterpieces of Renaissance art.

Fig. 25

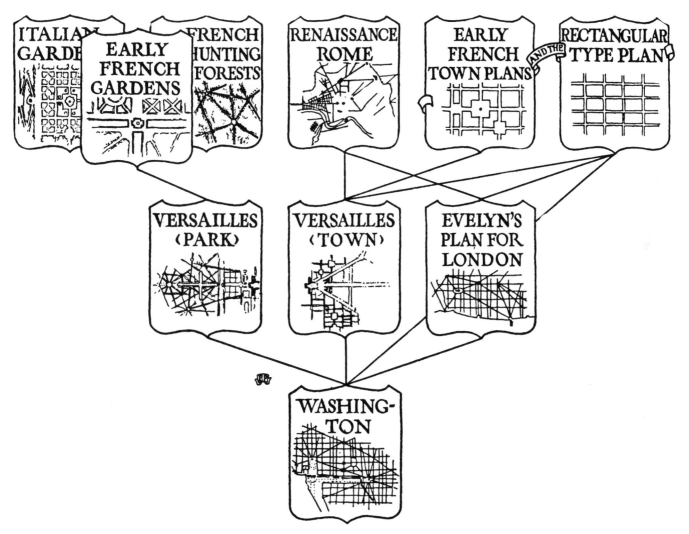

FIGURE 25. The family tree of Washington, D.C.

3

Washington as L'Enfant Intended It

While the George Washington Bicentennial is bringing to all Americans a new sense of the multiple accomplishments of our *pater patriae,* Baltimore's neighbor city to the south is honoring George Washington as its *pater urbis.* Never, surely, has the paternal relation of one man to a great city been clearer. And, very appropriately, the architects and city planners who are meeting in Washington will make their study of the civic art of the capital a public recognition of George Washington's great work as a city builder. They will doubtless honor our first President particularly for his wise selection of a designer and for the loyal support he gave to the superb conception of their gifted fellow artist, Pierre Charles L'Enfant.

Therefore, along with their celebration of the present rapid development of the capital, the archi-tects will retell the story of Washington's farsighted control of the city's founding and the story of L'Enfant's inspired design. They will ask, inevitably, just how far the anticipations of founder and designer have been realized. The answer will be, at least in the celebratory orations, that the city is a finer one than Washington and L'Enfant could have imagined. In such respects as the size of the capital and the smoothness of the asphalted streets, there is no questioning this.

But is it true in regard to the total aesthetic effect? I have doubts of that when I study L'Enfant's plan and think of the vision of beauty that intoxicated him during his one great year. I try to recapture that vision, summoning to my aid memories of Paris and Versailles and of the delightful provincial towns in which the eighteenth century survives—memories also of old streets in Baltimore, Annapolis, and Georgetown. I try to see his city as a whole, as the intellectual mastery and visual unification of a great area; I try also to see the charming details, the plazas, avenues, and "public walks." And the city my imagination builds is so unlike the one that exists—inevitably, since it is a city of the eighteenth century and not of the nineteenth or twentieth—that I think L'Enfant would say that *his* city of Washington was never built.

Of the big aesthetic structure of the L'Enfant plan, unquestionably, only a few parts were executed, and only a few fragments have survived. It is not, however, these features of the first rank that are most useful in summoning up an impression of the charm of L'Enfant's city. I shall depend, rather, on certain minor passages, especially the market places and plazas. A few of these charming sections of L'Enfant's city I have rendered in the form of pen-and-ink air views—slight sketches, meant only as points of departure for your imagination.

In making them I have followed either L'Enfant's "autograph" plan of 1791 or the Philadelphia engraving, dated 1792, doubtless in the main a copy of a revised plan by L'Enfant. In locating trees I have intended to adhere to the customs of the style L'Enfant was using. In sketching the buildings and monuments, for which there is little or no help in the plans, I have tried to be safely commonplace. The houses are in uniform rows because it is easier to draw them that way, and uniformity happens also to accord with the spirit of French civic art.

Cities, by our standards, were very primitive affairs in 1790. You will notice, for instance, what an important place the canal has in several of the sketches. We must not forget that Washington was built as a canal city and indeed was such for forty or fifty years. The Chesapeake and Ohio Canal was counted on to make Washington one of the busiest ports and commercial cities of the seaboard. L'Enfant's plan is a canal plan. That is one of its most endearing qualities, for what is there, with one or two exceptions, more adorable than a canal? It is at once serene, romantic, picturesque, entertaining, and economical.

L'Enfant knew this very well. With fine French practicality and dramatic sense, he carries his canal right through the monumental heart of his city. With no apologies for its slow loads of food, fodder, and cordwood, he broadens it into an ornamental basin as it skirts the President's estate and again at the foot of Capitol Hill. One can imagine what splendid water pageants and gay illuminations L'Enfant dreamed of, for, like a true architect, he had a flair for parades—he had, in fact, directed a patriotic pageant in New York.

Closely integrated with this canal is L'Enfant's very commodious series of market places. Besides the many little ones that must have been strung along the canal and river quays, five large markets are recognizable in the 1792 engraving. Three of these seem adapted to the handling of general produce—one became old Center Market—but there *Fig. 26* must also have been provision for special commodities, such as fuel, building materials, cattle, and hay. One of the bird's-eye sketches represents a market port which, I suppose, was intended for heavy materials or for the transshipment of goods between sailing vessels and canal boats. It is shown in the engraved plan as a long basin or dock cut in from the eastern branch of the Potomac at Fifth Street SE. There is an enlargement at the head of the ba- *Fig. 27*

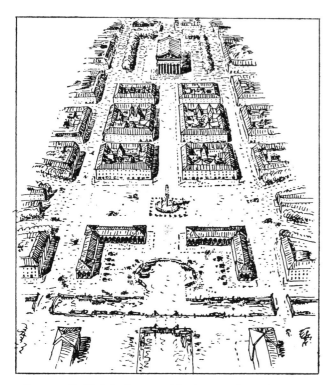

FIGURE 26. Eighth Street, with the canal, market, plaza, and "Pantheon."

develop a civic pride only if they had a worthy setting for their corporate life, the city's own Capitol. So we find, at first tentatively in the 1791 plan and then pretty well digested in the Philadelphia engraving, a huge plaza space south of Capitol Hill in the area now occupied by Garfield Park and the Capitol powerhouse. The area is truly enormous—about 2,400 feet long and about 1,400 feet broad at the widest part. My sketch of this vast civic center may carry the regularization of the layout, at one or two points, beyond the authority of the engraving, but if so, I am sure it does no more than to anticipate L'Enfant's next revision.

Here we have conspicuously that integration of the commercial life of the city with the official corporate life, a quality characteristically French and L'Enfantian, the mark of an easy and delightful urbanity—and of sound sense. In the foreground of the view we have the canal, that life channel of the city, and a public market, set with decent dignity on the main axis of the composition and lending, as contemporary writers might have said, a welcome animation to the scene. Beyond the canal is a very large open space where the civic constabulary and the volunteer fire companies might hold their Saturday night band concerts and their annual reviews. Beyond, at the intersection of five avenues and streets—one of them is an avenue radiating from the Capitol, thus linking up this plaza with the major framework of the city—stands one of the five "Grand Fountains" with which L'Enfant, in the plan of 1791, ornaments his city. At the head of the plaza, in the situation of most concentrated interests, rises the city hall. Behind it, finally, in the plan of 1791, we find a little *piazzetta* formed by notching out the corners of G Street.

sin, flanked by two large buildings. Whether this basin was ever built I cannot say, but a space 240 feet wide was left for it at the foot of Sixth Street. This was subsequently absorbed by the Navy Yard, and the wireless towers now stand on the site.

All this southern and eastern part of the city was intended to become the business district. And, quite logically, it was well south of the Capitol that

Fig. 28

L'Enfant wished to see developed a civic center quite detached from the environment of the national government.

He knew that the merchants of the city could

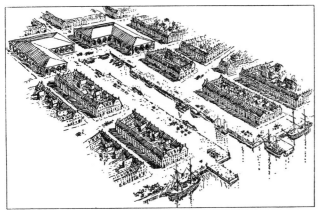

FIGURE 27. The basin and market at the east branch of the Potomac.

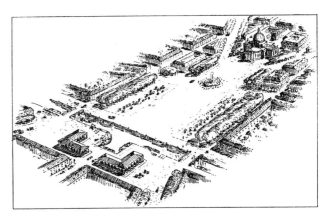

FIGURE 28. The civic center.

All this shows careful planning. If this complex plaza had had as many breaks of good luck as it actually has had of bad luck—and luck plays a big part in the growth of a city—it would now be one of the beautiful pieces of civic art of the world, and L'Enfant's reputation as a designer of plazas would stand higher than it does.

This is a lost plaza, a lost work of art, for there is an art of plazas, and this is perhaps a proper place to discourse a little upon it. In our modern day of corruption in civic art—due, I shall casually hint, to the supremacy of the kinetic over the static —any sort of sprawling open space where streets and traffic flow together is called a plaza. This can only make the judicious grieve, for in the good old days of city planning the plaza—"square" is the best-accredited English word—was a definitely marked open space, a commodious enclosed room flooded with light and sharply differentiated from the narrow streets that gave access to it. The square in front of St. Mark's Church in Venice is perhaps the loveliest plaza in the world.

Never to have had such a thrill as plazas of that sort can give one, such a feeling of life, and such a full and pleasant perception of the three dimensions of space—not to have had that experience may be likened to not having heard symphonic music. The comparison is inane, of course, but the citation of another art is almost necessary in order to express the importance of the plaza as one of the types of aesthetic composition used in civic art.

Now, surprisingly, in Washington at this moment there is not a single good example of the plaza in the historical sense of the term. Baltimore's Mount Vernon Place and such city squares as there are at the center of Reading and Harrisburg have much more plaza beauty than you can find in Washington. The fact that makes this a surprising circumstance is that the heyday of plaza design came after the middle of the eighteenth century and in France, precisely the time and place that might be supposed to have formed L'Enfant's taste.

There are various, perhaps partial, explanations. L'Enfant obviously hitched his wagon to the star of wide avenues, and it is precisely the wide avenue that is the great enemy of the plaza, whose precious sense of enclosure it destroys. L'Enfant, I fancy, worked on horseback, liked to use his compass, and liked to get the bearing of long shots. You might call him a Dionysian street worshiper: I doubt whether he cared very much for the Apollonian repose of plazas. But plainly this was not an exclusive preference, for these sketches show that on occasion he could bend his hand to the design of enclosed places. There are many other instances in his plan, also, where a careful revision, which he doubtless planned to give it, could have effected some degree of plaza feeling. In most such cases the romantic "landscape" planting of the square during the post–Civil War period has effectively squashed all architectural quality.

Fig. 29   There is no more conspicuous example of such changes from L'Enfant's intention than Capitol Square. He made of the upper part, east of the Capitol, a civic square contrived as an architectural forecourt for the building. It was just half as wide as the very differently intended parklike lower square. The enlargement, in the 1860's, of the upper square and its planting as an informal park has been a jolly thing for the squirrels, but it has obliterated lines which had at least the possibility of forming a true architectural plaza.

Fig. 30   For my sketch of this square I have followed the 1791 plan because it has the pleasant notched-out corners at the opening into East Capitol Avenue. My ornamentation is hypothetical; perhaps two low fountains would be better than the columns. The arcade-covered sidewalks are specified in a note on Fig. 31   the plan: "Around this square, and all along the avenue from the two bridges to the Federal house, the pavement on each side will pass under an arched

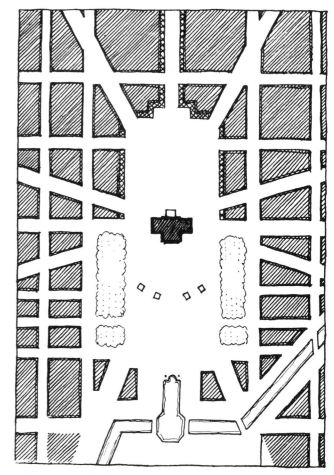

FIGURE 29. Capitol Square as L'Enfant intended it.

way, under whose cover shops will be most conveniently and agreeably situated." All architects are born with a great yearning to build arcades around squares, so there is little point in seeking the inspiration of L'Enfant's idea. The famous arcades of the Rue de Rivoli did not yet exist, but the Place Royale (now Place des Vosges) was arcaded, and

FIGURE 30. A bird's-eye view of Capitol Square, looking eastward.

FIGURE 31. A ground-level view of Capitol Square, again looking eastward. In the distance, a column acting as the "zero milestone" for the nation.

all Americans had heard of the "piazzas" of Covent Garden. The "arched ways" were never built; they rarely are. Down Pennsylvania Avenue we now stroll, and in the best tourist fashion we gather at Eighth Street to observe this part of L'Enfant's dream city. Here, remember, we are at the midpoint of the avenue, halfway from the Capitol to the White House. It is a place of importance in the composition, and L'Enfant has accordingly devel-

Fig. 32

oped Eighth Street into a brilliant subsidiary axis. At the point of intersection another of the five great fountains leaps and splashes. Up the street, on the

Fig. 33

F Street hill, rises a Grecian portico—or perhaps a Renaissance dome—for all the world like the Paris

Fig. 34

Pantheon at the top of Rue Soufflot. It is one of the fine architectural vistas of the capital. This is the national nonsectarian church, or pantheon, wherein the poetic L'Enfant thought the country would honor it heroes, and in place of which Heaven has given us the old Patent Office and the Hall of Statuary in the Capitol. At the south side of the fountain square are a market, a pair of buildings, the opening between them giving us a long view across the canal, a basin, and a broad open area, past the Grand Avenue, through another square, and so

Fig. 35

down to the Naval Column, which appears in another of the sketches.

This particular market in the plan became a market in reality and so remained continuously from the earliest times down to the happy reign of his present majesty. But the things that are now being done to this area, to the Grand Fountain Plaza, and to the vista toward the Washington Monument would give the now ecstatically praised Monsieur L'Enfant more pain than I have heart to think about.

So let us turn to something pleasant. There is a certain passage in the autograph plan that greatly mystified me when I first noticed it. It is a street— Twelfth Street SW., in the 1791 plan, Eleventh in

Fig. 36

the engraving and the present city—running south from the Mall. Though without apparent structural importance in the general scheme, it is the widest street or avenue, except the Grand Avenue of the Mall, in the whole plan. And it tapers, scaling about 250 feet wide at the Mall to about 200 at the river. Why the wide street, and why right here?

The answer appeared when I studied a map of the region. There is an exceptionally long, straight stretch in the Potomac south of Washington. One can sail in a beeline due south from the city to Fort Washington, some twelve miles. L'Enfant had noticed this on a map or had climbed a tree with his compass and had discovered that this noble view down the river could be worked into his scheme of north and south streets. Here—mon Dieu!—was a water vista that Versailles could not touch.

And I sometimes wonder whether L'Enfant did not at first intend to set the White House on this line. We know that Washington suggested, when he saw the Major's first draft, that the President's house be moved farther west to higher ground. This wide street, therefore, which in the next revision was suppressed to ordinary proportions, may be a vestige from that first draft whose differences from the later versions we understand so little.

And the taper? That may well be due to L'Enfant's inexact drafting, though I prefer to think not. When there is a wide terminal view, a street ought to spread, on the blunderbuss principle, as it recedes from the spectator. But a narrow objective may

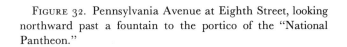

FIGURE 32. Pennsylvania Avenue at Eighth Street, looking northward past a fountain to the portico of the "National Pantheon."

FIGURE 33. The most likely model for Eighth Street—the Rue Royale, standing in the Place de la Concorde (Place Louis XV) looking toward the Church of the Madeleine.

FIGURE 34. Eighth Street as it is.

FIGURE 35. The Naval Column at the southern end of the Eighth Street axis.

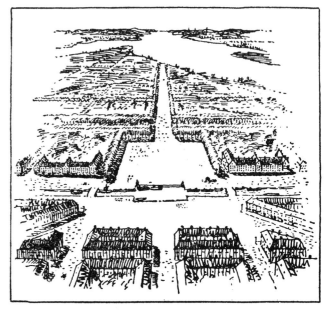

FIGURE 36. A bird's-eye view of the tapered avenue at Twelfth Street, looking southward down the Potomac.

permit a convergence, and a street that converges as it recedes seems prettier, because you see more of the side walls, than a straight or spreading street. The optical impression of distance, in one case or the other, here seems of little significance.

There are many other lost or obscured features of the L'Enfant plan that seem worthy of study and reconstruction on paper. There is the vicinity of the White House, for example, where the "autograph" plan differs from the engraving and where many subsequent changes have been made. There are the unhappy "circles" and "squares" formed by the fortuitous confluence of streets and avenues. These are a stiff challenge to the ingenuity that seeks to

bring form out of this formlessness; I suspect that L'Enfant gave up many of them in despair. And there are three or four smaller plazas that would have added pleasant touches of incident to the city plan.

There was a charm about L'Enfant's city, a charm that Washington has had to give up in paying the cost of size and engineering efficiency. His city was quieter than ours, its tempo was slower, and in color and form it was better controlled. The private *Fig. 37* buildings were low, and the monumental buildings stood out in better contrast. Thus its rhythms were *Fig. 38* more pronounced, and its architectural organization was more legible.

FIGURE 37. The President's house was intended to be a far larger building than it is, very likely with a dome such as John Vanbrugh's "Castle Howard," sketched in here against the lower vernacular buildings which L'Enfant had in mind as its architectural setting. This and Figure 38 are views looking westward along Pennsylvania Avenue toward the White House.

FIGURE 38. The same view as Figure 37, as it is today. The portico is that of the Treasury. The President's house cannot be seen.

L'Enfant's genius for amalgamating what might be called the sacred and the profane structures, for tactfully distributing his monumental elements, has the happiest effect on the feeling of his town. This is the delightful democracy, the easy civic manners of the French, accustomed for centuries to pursue their affairs, though it be no more than buying two eggs, in the shadow of a cathedral. In his manipulation of solids and voids L'Enfant was a better artist than his unruly collaborator Master Time. Though the plaza was of secondary interest to him, his plan comprises studies for many well-conceived open places, most of which, regrettably, have been lost.

Yes, on the whole, I am inclined to think that the city of L'Enfant's imagination, through which you and I have been wandering, is a finer piece of civic art than the city that has been built.

Fig. 39

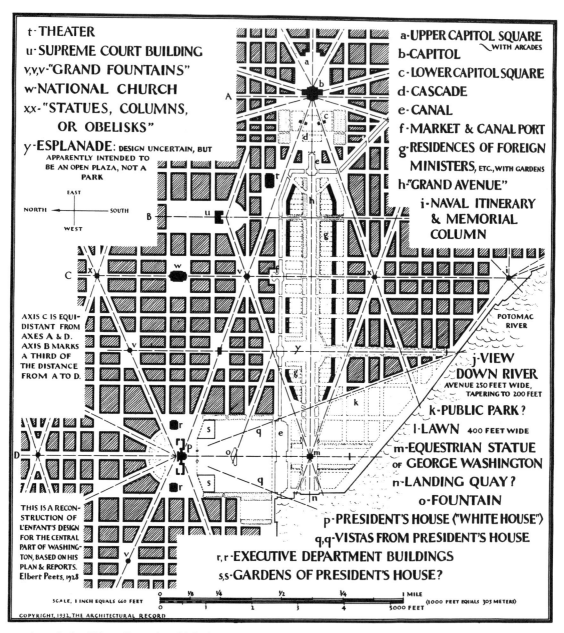

FIGURE 39. A study by Elbert Peets, in which the central part of Washington is refined and corrected. It deserves very careful examination in the mind and in the mind's eye. This drawing accompanied an article in the September 1932 issue of *Architectural Record* (pp. 158–160).

4

Critique of L'Enfant's Plan

Fig. 40

The plan of Washington is a carefully considered design. In essence, it is a design of two axes with a strongly marked intersection at right angles; on each of these axes is a building, and each of these buildings is a focus upon which a cycle of avenues is drawn together. Then, for convenience, and to give a uniform texture to the whole area of the design, a plaid of gridiron streets is laid in as background. A few secondary diagonals cut across the plaid, but each of them is at least a servant to the servant of the king—or of the queen. The plaid remains upon the plan a plaid, but for the true appreciation of the street plan of Washington the first essential is the clear recognition of the fact that Washington is not a gridiron city. Except when the gridiron streets lie upon important axes, it is not important that they do form a gridiron—not important that they are long and straight and cross each other at right angles.

This conflict, which is so obvious in the printed plan, between the "avenues" which really form the design and the streets which open up the spaces not tapped by the dominant avenues, seems to have shown itself at the very conception of the plan. L'Enfant saw the value of the star of avenues which can make a monument the master of a great area or bring into the crowded city almost a prairie spaciousness; he saw that streets ought if possible to run straight from one center of traffic to another and that they ought to be related to the natural features of the site. Jefferson felt the dignity of a simple gridiron, the beauty of a straight street with equispaced openings cut at right angles and exactly opposite each other, and he knew the architectural conven-

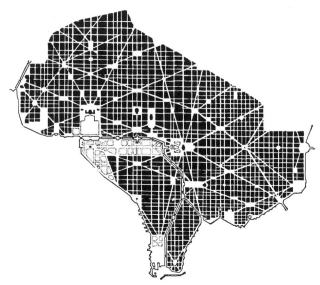

FIGURE 40. A rendering of L'Enfant's so-called "autograph plan."

ience of rectangular building plots. Whether the adopted plan was a compromise or an unfettered expression of L'Enfant's judgment we do not know. But whether the plan was a compromise between men or not, it is certainly a compromise between ideas, for in it neither the method of placing streets individually and in groups where they will create the beauty of an organized articulated design nor the method of distributing them uniformly in an orderly gridiron has attained purity, nor has either realized the full value of its type. Wren, in drafting his plan for London, employed both the gridiron and the radial motifs, but he knew that they could not both be used in same area.

As a type, the plan of Washington has two general faults, both of them the result of the application of the radial and the gridiron types of street plan to the same area without sufficient interadjust-ment. The first of these faults is that the radial and diagonal avenues have their identity, beauty, and dignity sapped away by the constant intrusion, often at very acute angles, of the gridiron streets. These streets enter the avenues at irregular intervals, often bringing one of their own right-angled intersections so close to an avenue that the area of the intersection becomes an awkward enlargement of the avenue and, even more often, marking out along the course of an avenue little triangular blocks which, being too small to build on, are freighted with clumps of trees and remain like undigested fragments of the primeval forest. Such thoroughfares may be convenient utilities, though sharp intersections are anathema to the traffic engineer; but they cannot be works of art as Pall Mall and Regent Street, the Via Nuova—yes, and Fifth Avenue—are works of art. To produce a coherent aesthetic effect a street ought to be or seem as orderly in design as a great cathedral, and surely no one would enjoy walking through a church whose nave columns were spaced with grotesque irregularity, whose walls were at intervals broken out at heterogeneous angles or cut through entirely, whose transepts stood out on the bias from a lopsided crossing, and whose choir terminated in a shrubbery bosquet.

Perhaps the best example to cite in this connection is Pennsylvania Avenue. Here, potentially, is a glorious street—broad, long, but not too long, level or just sufficiently concave in profile, and at its end the largest dome in America. But, no matter how skillfully the buildings fronting on it may be designed, Pennsylvania Avenue, with its present ground plan, will never be a really monumental street, simply because it cuts across the east-west streets of the gridiron at an angle of about fifteen degrees. As a result, between Fourteenth Street and Sixth Street some six of the little leftover slivers are moored alongside the great avenue. More than a quarter of this stretch is taken up by street openings, about as much more by the little parklets, and less than half is built-up frontage. In other words, many more than half the buildings directly in sight at either hand, as one goes from Fourteenth Street to Sixth, stand at angles of fifteen or seventy-five degrees with the avenue. Now a good street view is an orderly, concentrated composition of planes. How can this part of Pennsylvania Avenue make a monumental effect when half the planes which bound its volume of space cut into each other, now on one side and now on the other, at all sorts of unrelated angles? Above Sixth the street walls are much more continuous, but the official plan remedies this want of uniformity in the avenue by joining up the two sections of B Street, thus creating two more of the little triangles.

When a monumental building is to be built on Pennsylvania Avenue, the authorities must decide between a building of true rectangular plan, placed at an angle with the avenue, and a building of unequal sides, conforming to the avenue building line. The old post office, the District Building, and the Southern Railway Building stand square with the gridiron and hence at an angle with the avenue. A similar placing is planned for the Justice Building. Thus, at the south side of Pennsylvania, of the first five blocks east of the Treasury four will be occupied by buildings standing at an angle with the avenue and in three different planes. Particularly bad is the block between Twelfth and Thirteenth Streets. Here, where the workings of geometry have created an open parallelogram of which the avenue

Fig. 41

FIGURE 41. Pennsylvania Avenue at Fourteenth Street, looking eastward.

is a diagonal, the interruption to the spatial flow of the avenue is especially violent.

These difficulties anent the placing of buildings along Pennsylvania Avenue are not primarily due to lack of judgment on the part of individual architects. They are the inevitable result of the inelastic application of the gridiron street plan, of itself admirable, to situations for which it is not fitted. The gridiron streets which thus butcher Pennsylvania Avenue are, for the most part, not important streets. They could easily have been diverted and concentrated and brought into or across the avenue at right angles. The areas now used in planted triangles and superfluous pavement at awkward intersections could have been concentrated into plazas forming worthy sites for public buildings and adding actual beauty to the avenue. Such plazas are rare indeed in Washington, and that is the second basic shortcoming of Washington as a type plan.

Fig. 42

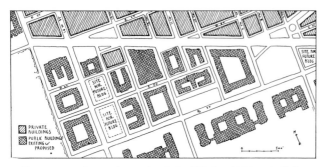

FIGURE 42. An early study of the "Federal Triangle," showing the difficulties of obtaining a uniform façade for Pennsylvania Avenue.

The map of Washington, to be sure, is dotted over with a variety of expanded street intersections bearing such labels as "square" or "circle," but these are no more plazas in the architectural sense of the word than is a pile of stones a beautiful building. That an open area is a virtue and a thing of beauty in itself, merely because it is so many square feet of space capable of growing grass or shrubs, is an idea which one can sympathetically observe in a horse or a caterpillar, but it is entirely unworthy of us human beings, to whom has been given that ultimate sense which is sensitive to form, to art. It is no more definitive praise to say of a city "square" that it has a superficies of two acres than it is to say of a piece of sculpture that it weighs a ton. The shape, enframement, and development of the open area are just as vital to its value as a work of civic art as are silhouette and modeling to the beauty of a statue. There are people who think of architecture as a thing of façades and moldings and textures, who do not feel the mass of a building and are not sensitive to rooms as shaped and proportioned volumes of space. The words "court," "plaza," and "square" can have little association with art in such minds; and yet the cult of the plaza, the feeling for enclosed space, like all the rest of art, is firmly rooted in the universal human desire for clarity, rhythm, and poise. Even the superficial madam chairman of the committee which planted the round bed in front of the court house with cannas and elephant-ears cannot help feeling a genuine thrill of joy when, having traversed the dark and tortuous Merceria, she suddenly passes under an arch and steps out into Piazza San Marco. She will come back and plant more cannas (just as her male equivalent will continue to cite Thomas Circle as one of the beauty spots of Washington), but that is because she does not know why she enjoyed the Piazza San Marco and there is no tradition, no propaganda even, to help her to do the right thing without conscious cultural training.

The years of L'Enfant's boyhood in France were the heyday years of the plaza, when the "place" was as much an accepted part of architectural thought as is the skyscraper with us. But his training was not in architecture, and he seems not to have brought to the design of the Washington plan any strong feeling for formal, enclosed, architectural areas. Perhaps he thought that such details would be worked out with the gradual execution of the plan, but it must be admitted that some of his "open spaces" at the intersections of streets and avenues seem inherently incapable of any possible hammering into aesthetically effective shapes. The few simple and regular openings which appear in his plan were mostly lost in execution.

This absence of effective plazas, and even of the sites for plazas, in L'Enfant's plan is, like the architectural imperfection of the radiating avenues, almost a necessary result of the superposition of the gridiron over the radials. The intersection of a number of streets is, in general, by no means an ideal location for a plaza, but at least it is certain that if several streets have to be brought together, their union must be contrived in some sort of orderly and dignified way. If you start with a checkerboard and lay upon it, not geometrically, but in conformity to actualities of the site or of the larger design, a system of diagonals, it is going to be mighty hard to fudge the intersections into any semblance of regularity. Take the just-mentioned Thomas Circle, for instance. It is at the intersection, at right angles, of Vermont and Massachusetts Avenues—also the intersection of M Street and Fourteenth Street. If this double intersection had produced an *étoile* with eight equispaced rays, it might with inspiration have been made into a creditable composition. But these "avenues" do not happen to lie at forty-five degrees with the "streets," and the mechanical acceptance of the gridiron principle does not permit a "street" to be bent. So the rays, besides being of unequal width, are not equally spaced; the wall of the circle is made up of four small arcs, and each of the wide spaces separating them is unequally split by knife-edge slivers of building sites, neither in the circle nor out of it.

What makes it especially surprising that L'Enfant did not, in such a case as this, bend his gridiron streets and make them bisect the angles between the avenues, is that he did not insist upon perfect continuity in the gridiron streets. Not only are many of them interrupted by sites for monuments and buildings, but a very considerable number (more in the executed plan than in L'Enfant's design) are broken at their intersection with such avenues as cut them

FIGURE 43. Looking eastward at Pennsylvania Avenue, from the terrace of the Treasury.

at sharp angles. Thus L Street, where it meets Massachusetts Avenue at Eleventh Street NW., is set over to the north rather more than its width, and at its intersection with New York Avenue at Fifth Street it is set back approximately in line with the first section. But each section of the street is bounded by perfectly straight lines—there is no angle in the street line corresponding to the angle there normally is in the track of a vehicle which makes the shift over from one section of the street to the next. These breaks were apparently motivated by a perception of the inconvenience, even to coach traffic, of extremely acute street intersections, and perhaps they were also a means of regulating the size of blocks. No aesthetic motive is distinguishable. But they have the important negative value of showing that L'Enfant was not entirely adverse to the visual and linear interruption of the gridiron streets, if only the break could be made without a change of orientation. It is regrettable that this element of ductility in his attitude toward the east-west and north-south streets was not sufficiently enlarged to permit him, when circumstances required it, to break the streets by angles as well as by offsets.

If one result of the generally uncompromising relation between the two street systems has been the destruction of the regularity of almost all of L'Enfant's avenue intersections, thus making an architectural treatment of them almost impossible, another result has been the practical impossibility of creating plazas in other situations. The avenues are the important highways as well as the dominant elements in the design of the street plan. A monumental plaza must almost necessarily relate itself to one of the avenues. But it is nearly impossible to find a practicable plaza site near an avenue, for there is not an avenue which has fronting upon it a single rectangular block, and there is not an avenue which is crossed at right angles by a single street. Under such conditions and with a public opinion which looks upon the closing of a street with almost fanatical abhorrence, what can be hoped for? Rarely in history has there been such an opportunity for architectural grouping on a grand scale as is offered by the building program proposed for the area between Pennsylvania Avenue and the Mall. Is not the plan as it now stands a sufficient proof of the inhibiting potency of the sacred system of gridiron streets?

If the thing L'Enfant produced had been no more than a type or texture of street arrangement, his plan would be worthy of little attention. What makes his vision a work of true creative imagination, compelling our homage and repaying our closest study, is that it is articulated, organized, pulled strongly yet suavely together, into a single work of art of unparalleled magnitude. But that vision was one of unprecedented daring; its author, without experience himself and with almost no opportunity to learn from the experience of others, had the most limited means of foreseeing its effect in reality; it was formulated and put on paper in a very brief time; the control of its realization, a process in which numberless refinements would have been worked out, was taken from him; the greatest part of it was embodied in brick and stone during a period and by a society probably unequaled in paucity of artistic feeling. No greater hurt could be done to L'Enfant than to accept without question every detail of his plan and to acclaim as beautiful every part of the imperfect realization of it which the vicissitudes of history have assembled.

The plan of Washington is "organized" by the vertical relation of the great meridional and longitudinal axes on which lie the White House and the Capitol. In the plan this relation is obvious and effective; in the city itself it is not easy to say how definitely it is felt, nor is it easy to determine the degree to which the perception of this relation would be facilitated by such a clarified expression of the axes as L'Enfant intended or as is proposed in the present official plan. Obviously, much depends on the treatment of the intersection of the axes, of which more will be said presently. This integration by normality of axes is supplemented by a diagonal connection, Pennsylvania Avenue. But the function of Pennsylvania Avenue in the design is not a separate one. The avenue affords, as L'Enfant expressed it, "reciprocity of sight," but plenty of buildings visible one from another create no effect of common design. As a working statement of the aesthetic

Fig. 43

Fig. 44

Fig. 45

FIGURES 44–45. Pennsylvania Avenue, from exactly halfway between the Capitol and the President's house on the Eighth Street axis. Figure 44 is looking eastward to the Capitol; Figure 45 is looking westward toward the unseen President's house.

function of Pennsylvania Avenue in relation to the White House and Capitol—taking it for granted that L'Enfant intended the White House to project well into the view down the avenue and not to stand, as it does, at one side of its course—one might say that it is an opening affording, from one building, information not merely of the existence of the other but specially of its orientation. If, for instance, one could stand on the west terrace of the Capitol and look down Pennsylvania Avenue and see the White House with sufficient clearness to detect its orientation, and if one could then turn and look down the Mall and see some conventional marker of intersecting axes, such as a fountain, a statue, or an obelisk, just a bit less distant than the White House, one's innate sense of geometry, abetted by the universal human desire to see order in the world, would at once create the conviction that the White House faced toward the statue, or whatever it might be, and that the two axes crossed at that point at right angles and were thus organized and unified. The result would be a three-dimensional, spatial, architectural composition, whereas if there were no view down the Mall and if one could not discern the orientation of the White House, one would have a pretty "vista" and nothing more—a two-dimensional, photographable picture.

Of the plan's two organizing axes the more important is the east-west axis, which is dominated by the "Congress House." Besides standing at the head of the Mall the Capitol performs various city planning functions. By its height and mass it assumes the office of presiding over the whole city; it is the center of a star of avenues; it dominates the open area immediately around it. This last role of the Capitol is the one to which the least attention has been given, but it is not unimportant. The Capitol stands, in conformity with what might be called the American tradition, in the midst of a seventy-acre park, the "Capitol Grounds." Such a situation has advantages and disadvantages; perhaps the best way to shed light on the problem from various an-

Fig. 46

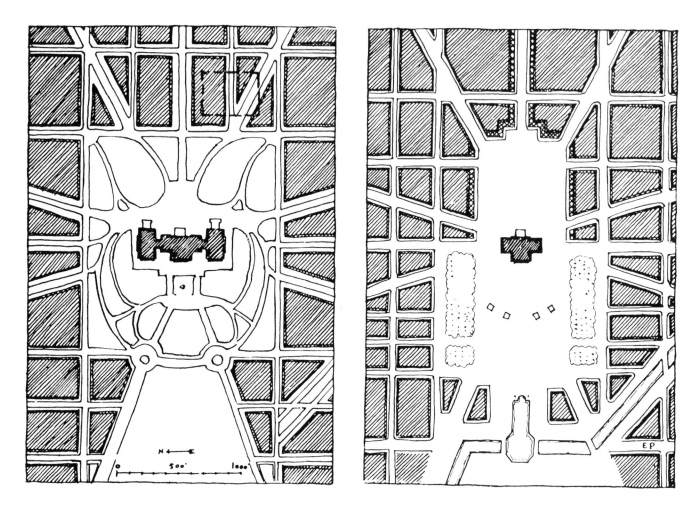

FIGURE 46. Two versions of the Capitol Grounds. At the left is the block plan as it stands, restored to symmetry by ignoring the Congressional Library; at the right is an enlargement of L'Enfant's plan, at the same scale, with street arcades indicated in accordance with his note. If one ignores the present great extent of the Capitol but remembers that the Capitol stands at a sharp break in grade, it seems obvious that L'Enfant's plan is the superior in imagination, plasticity of design, and adaptability to the site.

gles is to take the plan as it exists (perhaps to be credited to Washington or to the surveyor Ellicott— for L'Enfant, a circumstance which adds sympathy to our respect, could not agree with the commission he was serving and was dismissed soon after his plan was drafted) and compare it with L'Enfant's own version. It would seem that L'Enfant had in mind the common Renaissance motif (as at Versailles, for instance, or Karlsruhe) of a large building with the town on one side and a park on the other. One of the premises of his plan was that the business district of the city would lie east of the Capitol. Of Capitol Square he notes on his plan that "around this Square and all along the Avenue from the two bridges to the Federal House, the pavement (sidewalk, we now say) . . . will pass under an Arched way, under whose cover, Shops will be most conveniently and agreeably situated." To the west of the Capitol he intended having a cascade falling into a "reservoir," with three "fills" (whatever they may be) running to the "Grand Canal"; at each side, masses of trees. Quite naturally, this garden area is much wider than the shopping square. The resultant setting of the Capitol is strongly oriented; one might suspect, merely from an inspection of the plan, that the ground falls toward the west. But in execution this orientation was lost: the Capitol stands in the center of an area whose outline gives no hint that one side of it is some eighty feet higher *Fig. 47* than the other. The topography, certainly, is not favorable to the present program of edging the entire Capitol Grounds with public buildings. But even if the site were level and if the Capitol had been planned to stand in the center of a square, it would still be of doubtful wisdom to line the square with monumental buildings under the pretense of

FIGURE 47. The Capitol end of the Mall, as proposed by the Commission of 1901.

thereby creating an aesthetic ensemble. The area is certain always to be planted with trees; and even if "reciprocity of sight" were assured, the breadth of the area is too great to permit any feeling of architectural interdependence between its sides. It is twice as wide as the Piazza San Pietro, the Place de la Concorde, or the court of the Tuileries; take any of these, quadruple its area, plant it with an informal park, and how much architectural value would *Fig. 48* remain? Only enough to make a pretty rendered plan.

The situation of the House and Senate office buildings constitutes a sufficient proof of the difficulty of making a composite photograph of Central Park and the Place de la Concorde. Architecturally they are excellent buildings, barring the cigar store location of the entrances, but they can hardly be called an accomplishment in city planning. The streets on which they stand slope sharply across their principal façades, a condition always inimical to true monumental effect; they are so far apart, and the foliage of Capitol Square is so dense, that in sum-

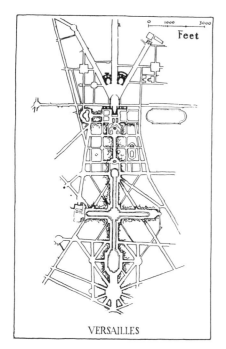
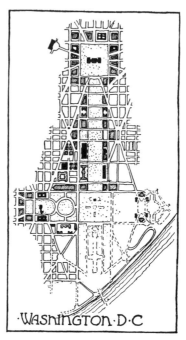
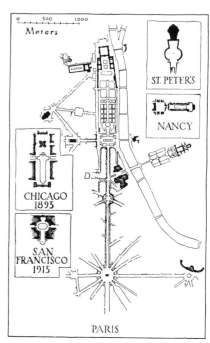

FIGURE 48. A comparison between Washington, Versailles, and Paris. Note the relative sizes of the plazas.

mer one of them can hardly be seen from the other; the ground between them is convex in profile, in defiance of the primary law of the monumental relation of buildings to grounds and of pairs of buildings to each other. All of these difficulties could have been avoided much more easily if L'Enfant's less expansive square had been built. The sloping streets, for instance, would have lain back of the framing buildings, permitting the floor of the square itself to be perfectly flat.

The reference to letter "H" on L'Enfant's plan runs "Grand Avenue, 400 feet in breadth, and about a mile in length, bordered with gardens, ending in a slope from the houses on each side." This was the inception of the "Mall," now recognized as the aesthetic backbone of the Washington plan. It would be interesting to work out in detail L'Enfant's visualization of the Mall. What, for instance, would these "Gardens" be like, and just what would the slopes be? There could hardly be a slope toward the avenue from the houses north of it because they, bordering the "Grand Canal," would certainly be lower than the avenue. And of the "houses" one would probably see the rear façades (or, more properly, the garden fronts) since these houses would face on the streets paralleling the avenue. It was perhaps on account of the topographic difficulties (for the ground is almost hilly at places, especially between Eighth and Fourteenth Streets) that the planting of the avenue was postponed, with the unfortunate results of the incorrect location of the Washington Monument, the railroad invasion, and the creation of a naturalistic park.

When Senator McMillan's commission (Burnham, McKim, Saint-Gaudens, and Olmsted) came on the ground in 1901, they rediscovered L'Enfant's "Grand Avenue" and saw that it was needed to pull together the Washington plan. Incidentally, they expanded the idea by making the avenue not merely an avenue of trees but of public buildings, and that is now the current understanding of the word "mall" in this country. L'Enfant, to be sure, had apparently intended (if one may judge from some reproductions of his plan) that there should be rows of houses about where the buildings are to stand; but red brick row houses, separated from the avenue by gardens and slopes, would produce an effect quite unlike that of widely separated (at least two hundred feet apart) and strongly membered monumental constructions of granite and marble. One can only pray for the early completion of the new Mall so that the reality, and not merely the plan, can be judged. It must be confessed that the many published ululations of the conception are disquietingly general in statement. To be told that the buildings along the Mall will be "brought into harmonious and effective relation to each other" will not calm a questioning mind. Certainly, it is a grandiose composition and, in a large way, orderly, but will it hang together? A mile long, a thousand feet wide—was there ever such a group? Can it possibly be felt as a whole? That it will not be good if it can't be sensed as a whole seems certain. That the intention was to produce "effective" situations for individual public buildings seems most unlikely since it takes much more than a general atmosphere

of monumentality to breathe architectural distinction into a building which is one of a dozen lined up like cars in an auto park. If the purpose was to create a sort of glorified avenue of sphinxes as an approach to the Capitol, the separate buildings should have been severely subordinated, made uniform, and equally spaced, as were the courtiers' residences at Marly. But if these motives have influenced the design, they must have done so secondarily, as an effort to utilize aesthetic by-products. The Mall must be primarily what L'Enfant called it, a "Grand Avenue," an open way and a channel of space, a member of the Capitol organism extended to the point of union with a similar spatial extension of the White House. In this channel the longitudinal movement is all-important—what happens at either side is as irrelevant as is the interior treatment of the bosquets which flank the Tapis Vert and the canal at Versailles. Every lateral pull upon the attention will diminish the essential value of the Mall. In detailing the buildings facing on the avenue and in arranging their settings, use should be made of every unifying device: uniform terraces and fences, hedges, and clipped trees—everything that will tighten the bounding walls of the avenue, define its channel, and facilitate its flow.

A plea for simplicity and uniformity in the Mall buildings is not likely to profit much. We Americans are too prone to feel that nothing is monumental which is not of granite and in granite scale. We do not know that good taste and fine proportion are more effective than prodigal appropriations; we forget the modest little residences of teachers and *avocats* which form the beautiful Place de la Carrière in Nancy.

This effort to sketch a critical interrogation of the

FIGURE 49. A tourist's view of the Washington Monument, close up.

Washington Mall before it is built would perhaps be unwarranted if it were not that every big idea of this sort promptly generates a flock of little progeny the study of which can only make the judicious grieve that some contraceptive measure was not employed. Cleveland made a "group plan"—the renderings were hardly dry when civic centers sprang up everywhere. Philadelphia started Fairmount Parkway, and straight edges were laid diagonally across every gridiron plan in the country. The Washington Mall was heralded, and now the air is full of malls and rumors of malls. This doing things because they are done—and designing in terms of names written on a plan, the idea that a mall must be good just because it's a mall—is as deadly to artistic creation as it is paralyzing to intelligent thought.

In L'Enfant's plan the intersection of the Capitol and White House axes, the western end of the Grand Avenue, was made the site of the proposed monument to Washington, then intended to be an equestrian statue. Instead, there now stands (some

Fig. 49

one hundred twenty feet south of the true intersection and three hundred sixty feet east of it) Robert Mills's beautiful obelisk, one of the architectural glories of America. The new Washington plan provides a formal garden to the west of the monument, with a circular pool on the White House axis. The story of this one phase of the plan of the capital could be developed into an entire theory of city planning.

L'Enfant's approach to this delicate problem was probably guided by a memory or understanding of European precedents. Perhaps the nearest parallel was the intersection in the Place Louis XV (now de la Concorde) of the Tuileries axis with the Madeleine axis. This intersection was then marked by an equestrian monument about fifty feet high facing up the longer axis—that is, toward the Tuileries. The use of a statue to mark an intersection of axes was very common in France. A statue is an object large enough to attract attention and definitely to indicate a node in the axis but not so large as to stop the view dead, and the capacity of the statue to indicate orientation is often useful in the expression of the direction of flow of the design and the relative importance of the axes.

But when, after some fifty years, work on the monument was finally begun, its function in the city plan was ignored—the site itself was doubtless lost in deep woods. In addition to the statue, plans were made for a great temple, of which the obelisk was to be part. The site chosen was probably favored on account of its elevation above the river marsh, which, besides facilitating the laying of foundations, was a clear gain in height. It is unquestionably regrettable that the obelisk was not set on the axis of the Capitol because the fudging of the Mall axis will

FIGURE 50. The sketch at the left suggests the view south from the White House as it will be after the realization of the present plan. In the other sketch the Monument is set on axis, where L'Enfant would have placed it. The proposed gardens at the intersection of the axes will be fine of themselves, but they cannot, from this viewpoint, contend against the immense size of the Monument, which will always seem inorganically situated. (*Editor's note:* Peets wrote this caption in 1922.)

FIGURE 51. The same view as above, summer 1967.

be easily discernible from various important points. The further question of whether it is to be regretted that the Monument was not set on the White House axis, exactly at the intersection, would form an interesting topic for an architectural debate. In theory, certainly, the object marking the intersection of the axes ought to be in sight along each. It is the pin at the joint, and it oughtn't to be anywhere else. The only possible doubt is whether the Monument, as it was built, would unpleasantly block, with its fifty-five feet of breadth, the view from the White House. If the mall or meadow running south from the White House were made very wide, say a thousand feet, the Monument would hide such a small part of the horizon that it would not be felt as cut-

Fig. 50
Fig. 51

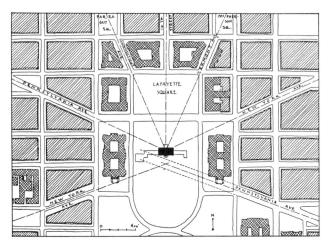

FIGURE 52. The White House. The buildings indicated by crosshatching are either existing or proposed according to the plan issued by the Public Buildings Commission in 1917. The center lines of the radiating streets are shown, as well as the curb lines (which are also the tree lines) of Pennsylvania Avenue, which clear the White House, indicating that the vista would not be perfect even if the Treasury had not been built where it is.

ting the view into halves. Such a situation woud be admirably suited to emphasize the characteristic beauty of the obelisk. The apotheosis of verticality ought surely to be enthroned amid a setting of horizontals.

An incidental regret—or, rather, a genuine tragedy—in relation to the incorrect location of the Monument is that, though supremely fitted to serve as the objective of long vistas, almost no street in Washington shoots directly at it. If L'Enfant had dreamt of any such prodigiously effective star center, he would surely have radiated additional avenues from the intersection of the axes. Whether one would want to have the Monument appear above the White House in the view south along Sixteenth

Street may be open to question. The distant views, with the Monument soaring above the converging foliage of the street trees, would be fine, but from nearby one would probably wish for a light mist to intensify the atmospheric perspective and clearly separate the Monument from the White House.

The plan for the Mall prepared by the Commission of 1901 could not avoid varying in many ways from L'Enfant's plan, as we know it, if only because of the differences in practical conditions. The most important of these was the existence and location of the Washington Monument; another was the filling of the swamp below the Monument. This last change made possible a considerable extension of the Mall axis, an extension, by the way, which cannot from every viewpoint be considered as an integral part of the Mall. From the Capitol terrace it will be an effective continuation of the Mall, but from the floor of the Mall itself the extension will not be visible, for the Mall rises toward the south. It will be interesting to see how this will affect views from the Mall of the Lincoln Memorial, which is raised, for this reason, on a fifty-foot platform. It may be desirable to block the ground view south along the Mall by introducing a low screen of some sort near the Monument. That would make of the Monument the unquestioned terminal feature of the eastern section of the Mall and, saving the spectator from imperfect glimpses of the Memorial and the intervening gardens, would give him a sudden and dramatically comprehensive view of them as he passed through the screen and came out onto the high terrace on which the Monument will stand. That view will in any case be a fine one, for the gardens between the Monument and the Memorial promise to be very beautiful indeed.

FIGURE 53. Hypothetical view looking northward from the White House at a *patte-d'oie* of three streets—had L'Enfant's design been carried through.

The intersection of the axes, where L'Enfant intended an equestrian statue, is to be occupied by a large circular pool. The function of expressing the axial intersection, which could hardly be performed by a flat water surface, is tranferred to the garden as a whole with its surrounding tree masses which, by the clearing of the "Oval," will be brought into view from the White House. The plan of the garden is a Greek cross; the Monument, at the top of a flight of steps, like the Duke of York column in London, is in the eastern arm of the cross. The cross is bounded by a heavy band of trees. This band is arranged symmetrically on the north-south as well as on the east-west axis, in spite of the fact that the ground rises abruptly at the east side. One must suppose that Le Nôtre, innocent of the temptations of rendered show plans, would hardly have combined an asymmetrical section with a symmetrical plan.

The changes which have come to the passage in L'Enfant's plan represented by the Monument are hardly greater, though perhaps more conspicuous, than the changes which have come in the vicinity of the White House. L'Enfant's street plan has been followed very closely, but in the third dimension, if the expression may be used, his intentions have been forgotten and nullified. To him the White House appeared, perhaps, at the end of the north-south arm of the central axis scheme, as a fist gripping firmly the radiating reins which should hold in subjection all that part of the city. And we may be sure that as a son of France and the Renaissance he intended that dominance to be a real one, a concrete experience, and not merely an intellectual conception built up out of the spectator's knowledge of American history and government, his study of maps and guide books, and his messenger-boy familiarity with the names and beginnings and ends of streets. An aesthetic unity based on such elements as these has the same sort of reality as had the heaven of Jurgen's grandmother, a reality which consists in its being believed in. In real flesh-and-blood city planning that won't do. The composition must be sensible to the senses and not merely knowable to the mind. Here you stand, and there you look, and that you see—and you like it, with the help of no diagram. If the White House is to dominate the region to the northwest, the White House must be visible from Connecticut Avenue; it is not enough that the people living around Dupont Circle should know that that thoroughfare is the shortest route to Keith's Theater and that one passes the White House on the way.

L'Enfant, then, made his "President's House" the center of radiation of seven broad avenues. These avenues radiate; they also converge. Now, in general, streets are converged on a point to get two sorts of effect: there is a beauty in the view out from their intersection; there is another beauty in the vistas from the avenues in toward the building or monument which marks that intersection. The view outward produces an impression of the extent and unity of the city and gives importance to the center of the star. If the avenues are symmetrically placed and if their intersection is architecturally well expressed, the whole composition may have a decided aesthetic value, in addition to the intellectual satisfaction which comes from the perception of a convenient mechanically ordered arrangement of things. The three avenues which radiate to the south from the Piazza del Popolo in Rome make a very beautiful composition. But L'Enfant probably did not intend this view out from the center of the *étoile* to be commonly enjoyed by the public but rather to serve the pleasure of the President himself and to impress his guests. We must not overestimate the democracy of those men and those times. L'Enfant and Washington may well have thought of that part of the city as a huge formal garden, the entourage of the "President's House." Indeed, to reconstruct L'Enfant's thought, we must constantly keep in mind not alone the French formal gardens but especially the great forests, St. Germain, Fontainebleau, Chantilly, with their arrow-straight roads and many-rayed stars. And it is quite likely

that L'Enfant himself saw at Washington a closer realization of some phases of his plan than we can see now, for early accounts speak of the beauty of the newly cleared wide straight avenues with floors of grass and walls of primeval forest. Doubtless, L'Enfant hoped to preserve much of this parklike effect, since all that part of the town was intended for the better residences. The business district would be east and south of the Capitol, convenient to the river. Under these circumstances it was quite justifiable to make the President's residence a city planning feature, the center of a star of avenues. When the White House was a pioneer, the second largest of the few dozen structures in the town, and the streets of Washington were lanes cut through the forest, it was wise to play the fine building for all it was worth and to spread as far as possible its beauty and its solid promise of the urbanity to come. Today the streets are crowded with people and autos and streetcars and are lined with tall buildings, many of them very ugly. To an American these are not the ideal surroundings of a home, which, after all, the White House is, and it should be a pleasant and comfortable one. It is not easy, therefore, to protest against the growth of trees and shrubs in the White House grounds and in Lafayette, McPherson, and Farragut Squares, though that growth has hidden the White House from the four avenues radiating to the northeast and northwest.

The two avenues which radiate to the southeast and southwest (Pennsylvania and New York) are also blocked, but by buildings instead of by trees, and no discussion of the Washington plan is complete without a bit of a dash of indignation about that. Assuredly, one can only regret the failure to

Fig. 52

Fig. 53

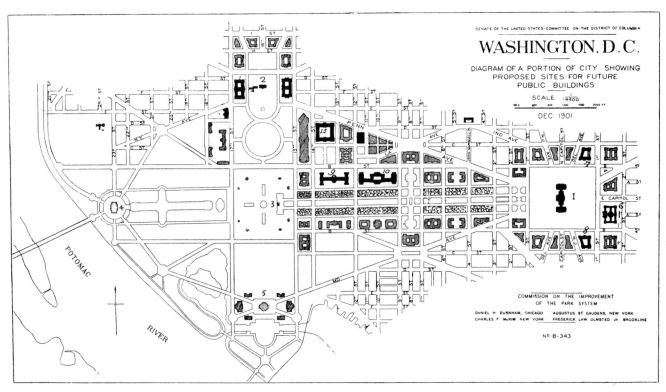

WASHINGTON. D. C.

DIAGRAM OF A PORTION OF CITY SHOWING
PROPOSED SITES FOR FUTURE
PUBLIC BUILDINGS

SCALE 1:4400

DEC 1901

COMMISSION ON THE IMPROVEMENT
OF THE PARK SYSTEM

DANIEL H. BURNHAM, CHICAGO   AUGUSTUS ST. GAUDENS, NEW YORK
CHARLES F. McKIM, NEW YORK   FREDERICK LAW OLMSTED Jr. BROOKLINE

Nº B-343

FIGURE 54. Plan for central Washington, as prepared by the Park Commission, 1901.

realize the popular conception of what ought to be the "Capitol–White House vista," but, regrettably, the popular impression that the White House now lies on the extended centerline of Pennsylvania Avenue is not in harmony with fact. In truth, the White House stands so much to one side of the course of the avenue that the north curb and tree row could be carried through without a break. An engraving of about 1820 shows the roadway thus continued across the south front of the White House. Of course, Pennsylvania Avenue is very wide, and the White House would be visible for a considerable distance up the avenue, especially from the south sidewalk, but it is erroneous to suppose that the building of the Treasury destroyed a perfect creation of civic art. If it had not been built, the avenue would indubitably now terminate in a heavy mass of trees, than which, as a street picture, the present arrangement is surely better. For the view of the Treasury from Pennsylvania Avenue is a fine one: to the left is undifferentiated foliage, but from the right juts out the robust mass of the granite building with its strong columns and cornice and mighty buttresses flanking the broad steps. Not to see the White House is a loss, a loss in sentiment and a loss, much more than sentimental, to the coherence of L'Enfant's geometrical composition, as we understand it. But that we do understand L'Enfant's intention cannot be asserted unreservedly. In his own "manuscript" plan the four northern radials and the one which is now lower New York Avenue come together pretty accurately at a single point, but Pennsylvania Avenue is deflected to the south, disquietingly like the way it was built. Since L'Enfant pretty surely thought of the President's house as a domed building, it is improbable that he intended the northern suite of avenues to concentrate on the north façade and the southern pair on the south façade. L'Enfant's plan is quite inaccurately drafted —Pennsylvania Avenue is not even shown as a straight line. But to suggest that the incorrect—at least, the unexplainable—location of the principal diagonal avenue in Washington is due to the careless ruling of a line would be absurd. Ellicott, Washington, Jefferson, and many others must have understood L'Enfant's purpose too well to permit of their being misled by a trivial error.

Fig. 54 The theory that L'Enfant intended Pennsylvania Avenue to shoot at the White House has with it the authority of the Commission of 1901, which held that the closing, by the Treasury, of a "carefully planned vista of the White House" is "inconsistent with the fundamental principles" of L'Enfant's plan.

With this expression "fundamental principles" the commission coupled an allusion to the "historic arteries representing the original states." That phrase might well have been extended to include Capitol Avenue and Sixteenth Street, which are

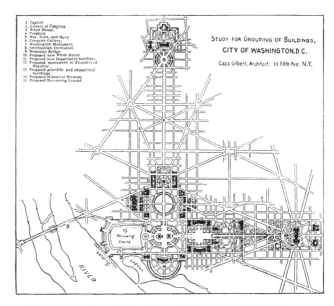

FIGURE 55. Cass Gilbert's study for a new White House on Meridian Hill. This plan antedates that of the Commission of 1901. Mr. Gilbert used the Washington Monument effectively, for it would dominate the department group to the right of it, as well as the reviewing ground. The department group forms an open plaza, the Mall being stopped to create a vast open space, a suggestion which was not taken up by the Burnham Commission. The broad reviewing ground would facilitate off-axis views in which the Monument would not interfere with the view of the Capitol dome. A minor point is that Mr. Gilbert made effective use of the Smithsonian building (at the broad end of the tapered Mall), a picturesque piece of Romanesque architecture in brown stone. The current plan calls for the destruction of this beautiful, though now unorthodox, building.

even more deeply fundamental than the radiating avenues of stately name. Sixteenth Street alone, of all the seven avenues radiating from the White House, commands a view of its objective. If only one was destined to be preserved, the Fates have been kind in their choice, for the fact that Sixteenth Street is on the axis of the White House makes it incomparably more valuable than the diagonal avenues. A diagonal street may afford a view of a building, but unless some architectural element in the building recognizes its existence, the diagonal street does not become an organic part of the design of the building, as does a street on axis. Sixteenth Street is further fortunate in being a "street" of the gridiron, thus avoiding the unbalanced openings, the distressing unordered variations in width, the unimpressive flatiron buildings, and the triangular parklets, which mar all the "avenues." The two principal diagonal avenues crossing it do so at Scott Circle, a very interestingly designed little area. L'Enfant planned two other open spaces intended to mark the importance of the street, but both were lost in execution.

The view of the White House from Sixteenth Street is across Lafayette Square. Anyone who has often enjoyed that view on pale misty mornings and bright snowy nights will read with a shock this passage from the report of the Commission of 1901: "The location of the building to contain the Executive offices is a more difficult matter; but the Commission are of the opinion that while temporary quarters may well be constructed in the grounds of the White House, a building sufficient in size to accommodate those offices may best be located in the center of Lafayette Square." This constitutes too strong a temptation to summarize the attitude of the commission relative to the seven streets which were planned to command vistas of the White House.

Two of the vistas—the central section of Pennsylvania Avenue and lower New York Avenue—are of third-rate quality because the avenues, at an angle, shoot past their supposed objective. Both are now stopped by buildings, and against this the commission strongly protests.

Four vistas—Vermont, Connecticut, and the northern sections of Pennsylvania and New York Avenues—are of second-rate quality because they strike the White House at an angle. These four vistas are now stopped by trees which could easily be removed, but regarding these lost vistas the commission says nothing.

One vista—Sixteenth Street—is of first-rate quality, on axis and practically clear. This vista the commission proposes to block with a new building.

In justice to the commission, however, it must be said that this proposal was not embodied in the published plans, which may well be construed as representing the more carefully studied judgment. If their feeling changed, it may have been out of respect for L'Enfant's axial avenue—perhaps also because Lafayette Square is of such obvious beauty and value as an open square. Real "squares" are rare in Washington. There are plenty of so-called "circles" and other open areas of various shapes at street intersections, but Lafayette is in quite another class. It is a court of honor before the White House, fortunate in its ample size and symmetrical plan, its freedom from bisecting pavements, its dignified houses reminiscent of the old-time capital, and the relative continuity of its bounding wall, for an area loses half the value of being open if wide avenues lead out from every side. It is the bounding wall which aesthetically creates the space, and well designed three-dimensional spaces are the finest fruits of the arts of architecture, city planning, and gardening.

But the bounding walls of the old square have begun a radical transformation. The Dolly Madison house, the Corcoran house, where Webster lived, the homes Richardson designed for John Hay and Henry Adams, and St. John's Church (built in 1816 by Latrobe) must soon make way, in accordance with the recommendations of the Commission of 1901, for huge departmental office buildings. The old Arlington Hotel and the home of Charles Sumner have already been destroyed. The departmental building which has taken their place overtops the "President's church" and the trees on the square. The new Lafayette Square will be crowded with automobiles and trucks, the lawns will be dotted at noon with clerks and typists, streetcar tracks may even be laid in Sixteenth Street, and the usual tatterdemalion lunchrooms and little shops will cling to the skirts of the office buildings and spread back into the residence streets to the north, producing another of those anemic business districts of which Washington already has so many.

Is it not surprising that while New York is laboriously working out a zoning law largely with the purpose of protecting established residence districts, while Boston is, at great expense, preserving the scale of Copley Square, while historical societies in many states are protecting what has survived from our great period in architecture, while all England is deeply stirred by the threatened destruction of some of the old London churches, Washington is making a business district out of Lafayette Square?

Fig. 57

Fig. 58

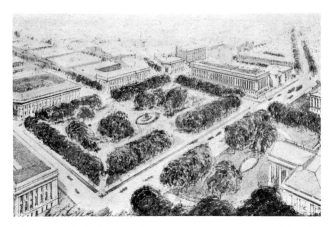

FIGURE 56. Lafayette Square as it was proposed by the Commission of 1901, surrounded by departmental buildings. A part of this plan has been carried out, but its completion is not in the present program. In this drawing the White House has been enlarged to make it dominate the group.

And for no better reason, one is bound to suspect, than that there's an idea in the wind that the President ought to be "surrounded by his official family"—in spite of the fact that, in the lump, the President probably detests the sight of his official family and the family itself would jolly well rather be near the station or up on a hill in the suburbs where Uncle Sam could afford to erect office buildings without hot and ugly interior courts.

Purely as a matter of design, it is surely to be regretted that the residence scale and atmosphere of Lafayette Square cannot be maintained to connect the White House with the residence district of the city. It seems an ideal location for those unofficial White Houses, the national headquarters of clubs and societies—all of red brick, to preserve for the White House its dominance of scale and color.

The present treatment of the central planted area

FIGURE 57. The Treasury Annex on the southeast corner of Lafayette Square. The façade design would have been carried out along the entire edge of the Square. The U. S. Chamber of Commerce on the northwest side has the same colonnade design.

FIGURE 58. The southwest corner of Lafayette Square. Old houses have been preserved, and a portion of the new U. S. Court of Claims Building rises behind.

of the square is, of course, quite impossible. Its design is as poor as the design of a dollar bill, with French-curve walks superimposed upon a florist's arboretum, plus the accumulated vagaries of a dozen gardeners, and "Mr. Clark Mills's nursery monument to the equestrian seat of Andrew Jackson"—thus Henry Adams dubbed it—as the center and gem of it all. And this exists in a country where box thrives and elms grow gloriously and there was once a fine traditional garden art whose simple materials were straight gravel walks and hedges and lawns!

These fragmentary—and quite consciously suggestive rather than conclusive—notes on the plan of Washington have been intended primarily to encourage an attitude of concreteness and reality toward L'Enfant's plan and toward the city. The plan and city form a mine of inspirational and exemplary material, but from it there is little of value to be dug by those who come with no more sturdy tools than a conviction that when L'Enfant laid down his drafting pen, his plan was perfect and complete, and a belief that the principal value of that plan is a mystical parallelism with the federal constitution, which it is unpatriotic to question. And those eyes are useless which have not the strength to search out and judge the real form which lies underneath that patina of historical association with which time covers everything, right or wrong, ugly or beautiful. What is needed now is the approach which cannot be diverted by an anecdote or a pretty bunch of trees, the unromantic attitude of the Renaissance, seemingly hard and cold but really warm with bodily life and personality, seeing clearly that beauty lies in arrangements of tangible things and not in general ideas, however grandiose.

Imperial grandiosity as an ideal—that is the great danger to Washington. Spacious monumentality may produce great beauty, but let there be a hair's breadth of deviation from good taste, and nothing remains but pompous banality. Too great an emphasis on the national scale, the impersonally monumental, is more likely to produce dullness than grandeur. Lining the Mall, Capitol Square, and Lafayette Square with monumental buildings of granite and marble may be financial and administrative daring—it may also be artistic timidity. It is much easier to follow the generally accepted idea of the "right thing to do" than it is to create the unique expression of a rich personality. Until we overcome this small sector of our deadly national idealism and realize that art is something more than liberal expenditure and good intention, students of civic art will continue to study plans of the capital of the United States—and to make pilgrimages, seeking the living touch of beautiful cities, to Paris and Rome—to Bath, Richelieu, Nancy, Ludwigslust, and Pompeii.

Part II

Critiques of Planning in Washington

5

On the Concentration and Design of Federal Buildings

The great importance to American architecture of the construction program shortly to be undertaken in Washington for the housing of the executive departments lies not merely in the number and size of the proposed buildings but also in the fact that the architectural ideas that shape them will gain thereby a prestige that will inevitably influence subsequent building in Washington and throughout the country. Unfortunately, it looks now as if that prestige will be given to conceptions of architecture and civic art no longer current and valid—as if a phalanx of turgidly formal boxes of sham masonry will be set up, a permanent monument to unlearned lessons.

The present plan of the Public Buildings Commission is based on the report of the Park Commission of 1901, which advised that future department buildings be concentrated around the White House. One group was to surround Lafayette Square. Another was to lie in the triangle between Pennsylvania Avenue and B Street, parallel with the Mall. The architectural style was fixed in general conformity with the Capitol, and a standard block plan was established, in effect, through its use in most of the buildings shown in the commission's drawings. It is the type, until recently always used for large "monumental" public buildings, in which the externally solid-seeming cube is cut to practicable room depths by the use of interior light courts.

Burnham's Commission of 1901 left a good deal of room around the proposed buildings, perhaps for the sake of the rendered plan, perhaps because it thought wide separation increased the monumental effect. The inevitable tightening of the demand for space has squeezed out these strips of lawn. The plan of the Public Buildings Commission brings most of the buildings to the sidewalk and treats as immediate or future building sites several open spaces in the older plan.

The Commission of 1901 crowded the department buildings around the White House because the Constitution divides the government into legislative, judicial, and executive branches and because the department heads constitute the President's official family. Once a week, if it isn't too warm, the President and his Cabinet sit together for an hour or two. Therefore, a hundred thousand men and women must pour in every morning from Chevy Chase, Cabin John, and Anacostia and jam themselves into twenty squares in the heart of Washington, the hottest part of the city, a business, theater, and hotel district already crowded with shoppers, tourists, job hunters, and all the rest of the varied fauna of an imperial capital. As compensation the clerks will have the pleasing thought that the President can take a visiting maharaja to his window and

FIGURE 59. A city within a city—a plan for the future development of the central part of Washington by the National Capital Park and Planning Commission, 1929.

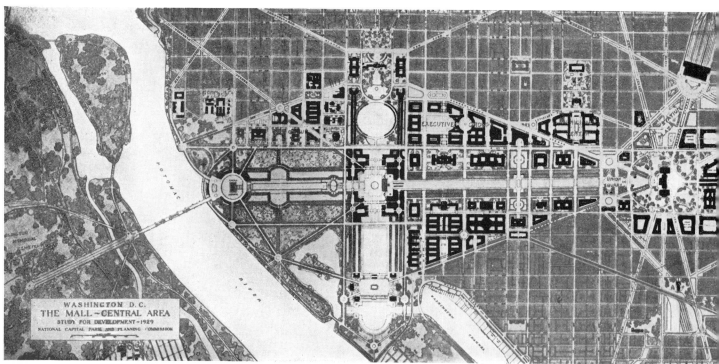

WASHINGTON D.C.
THE MALL~CENTRAL AREA
STUDY FOR DEVELOPMENT-1929
NATIONAL CAPITAL PARK AND PLANNING COMMISSION

say to him, "Servants' quarters—very convenient."

If there is one thing now plain about the planning of big cities, it is that beyond a certain intensity concentration is wasteful and that modern transportation makes such concentration unnecessary. Washington is ideally laid out for the distribution of traffic objectives and for convenient communication between them. The departments are as autonomous as so many universities. They ought to be widely spaced, even on the suburban hills, where sensible offices could be built and where the personnel could walk to work or come in their cars without producing intolerable traffic and parking congestion—where, too, an architect could make his own design, not having to follow a set of official templets.

See what the official plan is doing to Lafayette Square. In the repertory of civic art no element is fuller of aesthetic satisfaction than the plaza, an open space architecturally planned and framed. Washington has a flock of monument sites and parklets but hardly a plaza besides this open space

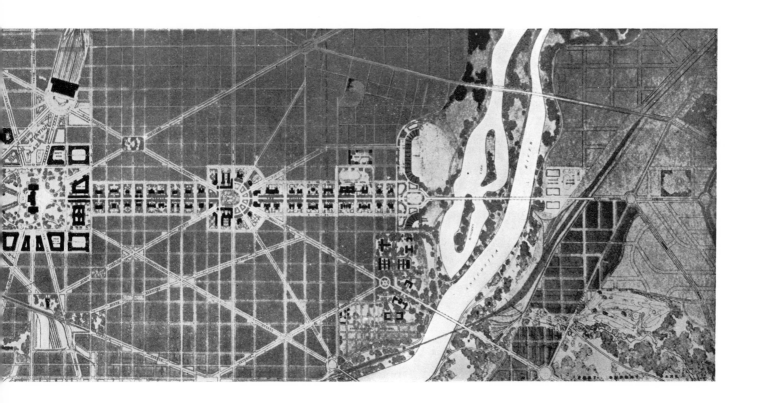

north of the White House. The Commissioners of 1901 were admirably solicitous to restore L'Enfant's mall, but for his best surviving square—or Jefferson's, for Jefferson cut its original broad area to the present proportions—they had their own ideas. One, incredibly, was to put the President's office building in the middle of it. That project died in the printing, but hardly more sympathetic was their proposal, now well toward execution, to surround the square with department offices.*

The White House is a small building depending for its impressiveness on the difficulty of comparing it with other buildings and on the sharp contrast of its white color. Both these means of distinction will be seriously weakened when Lafayette Square is lined with fourteen hundred feet of limestone façade, more than half again as high as the White House. That is wrong both in form and in feeling. The White House is a residence, and few things look more uncomfortable than a residence surrounded by nonresidence buildings. Lafayette Square ought to be a transition or point of contact between the White House and the residence district of the city. It ought to have about it the residence scale and atmosphere. The houses might be used by clubs and organization headquarters that do not induce tides of population and traffic, but they ought to be of red brick and safely under the scale of the White House.

Further, if Washington is ever to be more than a swell place for an Al Sirat convention, we must save some traces of the real men who have lived and worked there. The Stockton house and the Corcoran house, where Webster lived, at the northwest corner of Lafayette Square, were torn down to make room

* Proposed by Cass Gilbert in 1917.

for the United States Chamber of Commerce. The homes Richardson built for Henry Adams and John Hay still stand, though quite discountenanced by this great glittering neighbor. One wonders whether, when it comes to the point, Washington will allow the destruction of these stately houses and of St. John's Church, on the other corner of Sixteenth Street, built by Latrobe in 1816. There are two equal dangers—that they will be torn down and that they won't be. Brave designers they were who risked their plan on the willingness of the public to make such sacrifices. But as yet they have won. There is a lot of talk about respecting the sacred plan made by L'Enfant and Washington, but not a voice is raised when some architectural Brahmin signs a fat contract and sends a wrecking crew to make rubbish of the honest work of a father of his own guild, a building that in Avila or Bangkok would be preserved without question as a national shrine.

The other group, south of Pennsylvania Avenue, does not come into conflict with such a jewel in the Washington plan as is Lafayette Square. On the contrary, it is up against the knottiest sort of problem that the debonair L'Enfant left in his inspired sketch—the correlation of a tangential avenue with ordinate streets. The problem is a true dilemma: a large building on an avenue either must be queer-shaped or must stand at an angle with the avenue. The Public Buildings Commission has hit on a statesmanlike solution. Between Fifteenth and Fourth Streets, along Pennsylvania Avenue, will be six public buildings. Three will stand parallel with the avenue and three at an angle of twenty degrees! This enormous group—for there will be fifteen large public buildings in the triangle south of Pennsylvania Avenue—might make the Imperial Fora, the palace of Diocletian, the Louvre-Tuileries, and the Escorial look like Boy Scout stuff. But it won't. The Buildings Commission does not group its buildings; it parks them. The plan thumbs its nose at the concept of axiality, the soul of architectural grouping. It has never heard of the connections between buildings, the modulations of height and interval that give charm to the group at Nancy—and to Mount Vernon. As for fine courts and plazas, I suspect that they were disdained as un-American. The one opening that resembles an architectural square bears the apologizing label, "Site for Future Building." The plan has the aesthetic tone of a baker's window—neat rows of nicely frosted cakes.

Lest this seem the emotional reaction of an erratic taste in window dressing, let me give reasons. A group of buildings uniform in height and material, neatly laid down between gridiron streets, shows a certain primitive sense of order. More advanced peoples, for instance, the ancient Mayas and the modern Swedes, are not content with so naïve a design. They see that the streets chop the group into self-sufficient cubes, that there is really no unity in the place. So they cut and shape these chunks of clay until there appears a single unified organism with front and back, ends and middle. Almost invariably there is at the center of the group a large open space, capable of mastering the buildings and secondary spaces around it. The furnishings of this great room and the form and color of its walls make of it a unique and living work of art.

That there is nothing unique or alive about the present official plan is due to two general causes. First, the men who made the basic sketch thought too much in terms of general monumental atmosphere and too little about specific architectural organizations, a tendency favored by the absence of a definite program. Second, members of the Cabinet like buildings all their own, and it is easier to get appropriations, make plans, and let contracts for separate structures. These last ideas are the more difficult to dislodge because they have their cranial seats in the very men who will make the final decisions. But they are almost wholly mental bunkers which a good swing with the psychic brassie would easily overcome. The loss of the moated castle could be made only partial by clever designing and would be more than compensated for by participation in a real architectural knockout. The planning would mean only a little more careful work and forethought. Practically, it would be an advantage to use connected buildings housing several departments. Each department or large bureau should have its separate entrance and permanent nucleus of administrative offices, but where the space of one department ends and another begins is no Balkan boundary to be fought over. Every few years the construction of a new group or wing would make it possible to take up without waste the normal variations of space requirement. A single construction and maintenance bureau should operate the whole group, just as if it were a private office building in which the departments rented space.

As architecture the present plan is an anachronism, a travesty on the most brilliant national group of architects in the world—unless, to be modest, we except the Finns. There is no recognition in it of the California fairs of 1915, of the new M.I.T. buildings, of Harvard Medical School, or of the extension plans for the Universities of Illinois and Minnesota, or of other splendid groups of buildings in every part of the country. A comparison of the plans submitted in the Wisconsin Capitol competition with those entered in the Nebraska competition should prove the folly of building now on a block plan sketched in 1901 and rendered still further out of date by incompetent revisions.

Simple Christian charity and elementary civic engineering condemn the concentration of these buildings. But if it must be done, it should be done in a way that will win the beauty that may come from concentration. How can we bring our architectural capacity to bear on the problem? Perhaps there is a hint in the German institution, the *Ideen-Wettbewerb,* often limited to general plans, economically rendered. In our competitions a heavy overlay of mosaic and snappy shadows obscures the general ideas, if any. These scandalously perfect rendered drawings are not made for architects: to them a quick soft-pencil sketch would often be as clear. They are made to influence the committee and to set the public agog. They have the same relation to architecture that an attorney's address to the jury has to justice. If a competition is held, the program ought to be very liberal, for it is precisely in the drafting of the program that imagination and freedom from bureau tradition are most needed.

Competitions are a nuisance, but it is a crime to ruin this group of buildings just because of a timid desire to pass around the plums. Personality expressed in the aesthetic vitality of the finished work is the thing that counts, not the bold signature on the rendered plan. The masterly plan of the San Francisco fair somehow got itself made, though its authorship must be distributed among a dozen architects of very different predilections, not to mention Wren and Bernini and various forgotten builders of Spain, Italy, and India. It is pleasant to avoid dissension and to be quite fair and to have everybody happy, but the really important thing is to get a good design.

6

On the Plans for Washington

Evening, on the Mall, Washington. I walk on the grass, on axis. Flocks of swift starlings sweep toward the Triangle and the city. Soon the lights will come on at the Capitol. I turn to look at the soaring Monument and then back at the dome of the Capitol, rising above broad horizontals. Reciprocal forms, would that be the word? I walk, thinking inevitably of Versailles and St. Peter's and then of the things I am to write here. Are the old arts of space and form dying, as some say? How stands civic art after so many centuries of striving? What is being done and with what intention? Under the influence of what models and ideas, with what popular response? Forming what augury for the future?

Here is the Mall, surely tonight the most beautiful place man has yet made in America. At last the Monument does not stand beyond a woods from the Capitol; with the flow of space between them, they now join in formal relation. The verticality of the Monument has at last the appearance of rising from a horizontal plane. And the Capitol is for the first time quite beautiful: it must have been for this view that Thomas U. Walter designed the dome. Here is begun, as if Michelangelo had roughed a block of marble into the promise of a figure and finished part of it, a work of plastic art potentially more majestic than any other that man has created. I am sure of that, and sure that in this serene light the body of that beauty is already felt. Yet, here at its heart, on the axis of perfection, our architects have made no place for people to walk; the Mall is deserted, while in the city whose rumble comes to me from beyond the Roman palaces of the Triangle, thousands of people are watching movies, listening to radios, playing fashionable in furniture of chromium and red leather, looking at improvisations in paint, talking about art, and sincerely studying the appreciation of art. It is evident that domes, monuments, and malls are not for us the deep and stirring personal experience that they have the power to be.

One would like to know what the people of 1791 thought about L'Enfant's plan. Apparently the plan was accepted on sight, with minor criticisms, by Washington and Jefferson. I have not happened on any evidence of astonishment as concerns the type of planning. Oddly enough, the plan seems to incite expressions of surprise more frequently now than it did then. The point may be that a planned variation from a simple gridiron appears more remarkable to us than to the men of 1790 just because such a mass of gridiron plans has grown up since then. The language of American city planning, then as now, was based on the gridiron plan—based but not debased, for in the eighteenth century the gridiron was still plastic, still fundamentally an art style, as the architects of the Renaissance made it. Plans of Philadelphia, Reading, Savannah, and Williamsburg can be printed alongside plans of Charleroi, the towns of Versailles, Bloomsbury, and Edinburgh. The average statesman or the average architect of 1790 was better prepared by education and experience to find meaning in L'Enfant's plan than was the average statesman or architect of 1890—not to cite a later date. The Renaissance still lived in the cultural air. The language of Renaissance planning still retained some of its inflections; soon all was to be lost in America save its broadest grammatical principle—of course, not at all exclusive to it—the straight street. My point is that the straight street is a deep blood bond between Versailles and Omaha,

that the American gridiron is not ineligible to the cult of Renaissance planning. L'Enfant's plan stems from France and Rome, but the form language in which it was cast was the lingua franca of old and new Europe in the eighteenth century. George Washington needed no interpreter to help him understand it.

But the sentimental feeling art that liquefied like a lovely mold the rigid form arts of the winter-and-spring century crept early over the genteel fringes of land planning in the post-Puritan America. Gardening melted first. The Washington Mall became a potential landscape garden before Andrew Jackson Downing was born to lay it out, and the Washington Monument was placed on a hill overlooking the Potomac, a typical landscape location, three hundred feet from the point marked by Thomas Jefferson's stone pier. And so it went. Buildings were placed where they would make a handsome appearance. Trees were planted in every open space to make the city look as little like a city as it might. L'Enfant's vistas were veiled with foliage. East of the Capitol, where our most spectacular piece of Roman architecture demanded an imperial forum to complete its formal life, a pretty arboretum was laid out in the mode in which Currier and Ives prints depict the lawns of neo-Gothic mansions overlooking the Hudson.

Around 1900 came the L'Enfant revival. For a moment it seemed as if the totality—the interwoven completeness—of L'Enfant's plan would be rediscovered. But the art of gardens was too English and romantic, architecture too dazzled by the Chicago Fair. Neither could see the beautiful *city* that was L'Enfant's vision. The Mall, L'Enfant's Grand Avenue, was at last to be carried out—but as an

FIGURE 60. Looking southward down the Eighth Street axis, which is blocked by the Archives Building.

Fig. 60 "undulating lawn"! Its median cross axis, Eighth Street, commanding a vista of the lovely Parthenon front of the Patent Office, was to be plugged up. And the plan of the Commission of 1901 proposed a monumental area where the buildings housing the government of a nation newly conscious of its high place in the world could exist forever in impeccable monumentality. Around the Capitol, along the Mall, in the Triangle, around Lafayette Square, was to rise a city-within-the-city, aloof from the rest of Washington just as the Court of Honor at Chicago in 1893 was unaware of the vulgar Midway. Much of this has come to pass, but of it I count the clearing of the Mall, imperfect though the work is, as the only part of all this prodigious labor that reveals the beauty of L'Enfant's plan and the glorious power of civic art.

The recent works of public architecture in Washington are so well known that it is no longer necessary to repeat the facts concerning their cost, cubage, and authorship. They have not had, it must be said, the delighted acclaim of critics and other thoughtful persons. On what might be called moral grounds, the attack has been particularly sharp. Blatant grandiloquence, pompous grandeur, criminal squandering—these phrases have been repeated. When a fire in the windowless rooms in back of the cornice of the new post office building burned on for hours while firemen chopped holes in the floor above, leftist architects read the item with broad smiles. Increasing congestion and the growth of government departments faster than buildings could be erected have aroused even within official planning groups much opposition to the policies of concentration and monumental design. My own criticisms of the new work do not need to go much beyond its bearing on the L'Enfant plan.

The inventory can well begin with the Supreme Court Building. L'Enfant, presumably with Washington's approval, intended it to stand in Judiciary Square, a site somewhat aside from the principal elements of the plan but well connected with it. The Commission of 1901 inexplicably assigned it the site across East Capitol Street from the Library of Congress, where it now stands. For the Court, the site is meaningless, but it would have made a good place for the Library Annex. One feels here the good old American principle that a good site is one within a certain zone of elegance. The Judiciary Square site was available, but it would have been impossible there to eliminate all vulgarity from the adjacent streets. What effect such a conception would have had upon the planning of Rome or Paris can be imagined. A planner who wishes to unify a whole city cannot afford to be snobbish. After the place indicated by L'Enfant, I should have

FIGURE 61. Further south on the Eighth Street axis, again looking south right at the center of the Federal Warehouse.

FIGURE 62. Looking at the Washington Monument (*arrow*) along Louisiana Avenue, now blocked by the Justice Building.

chosen a site on the hill east of the Anacostia River, on the extended line of East Capitol Street.

L'Enfant's median cross axis, Eighth Street, one of the important and highly developed lines of the plan, has been blocked by two new buildings. The Archives and the Federal Warehouse (closing, north and south, the so-called "Mall transepts") cut off the Mall from the rest of the city plan. Though so planned by Burnham and McKim, the ruling conception here probably springs from the principle of landscape gardening that a park must be isolated from the surrounding town. The designers of the Triangle went further than the Commission of 1901 and wiped out the section of (old) Louisiana Avenue running from Pennsylvania Avenue toward—though not straight at—the Washington Monument. This, the only vista of the Monument from the historic avenue, might have been trued up and made into one of the finest views in Washington. Instead it is stupidly blocked by the Justice Building.

Constitution Avenue is the most destructive of all the crimes yet committed against the L'Enfant plan. The heart of that plan was a triangle of which Pennsylvania Avenue and the Mall were two sides. Constitution Avenue has now been made stronger in some ways than either of those lines. It is wide and grossly insistent, parallel to the Mall and cutting across Pennsylvania Avenue. Essentially a service street, without axial function and weakly terminated, it is overloaded for a short distance with the spectacular walls and pediments of the Triangle buildings, which, however, have on this front no architectural organization. As civic art, the street is a piece of sumptuous stupidity. Its effect on L'Enfant's plan can be expressed crudely by some such analogy as this: If on a broad parade ground some beautiful military ceremony was taking place, say in honor of a national hero, and if at the highest moment a company of visiting firemen marched across the field, with band playing and helmets shining, that would be like the effect of Constitution Avenue on L'Enfant's delicately adjusted city plan.

FIGURE 63. Constitution Avenue (*left*) intersecting Pennsylvania Avenue (*right*)—looking westward.

When you are covering some two dozen city blocks with monumental buildings, you have to lay hands on everything you can get, and especially on buildings that do not have those absurd office windows stuck all over them. So the National Archives are in the Triangle, although elementary sense would suggest, in these days of air bombardments, that they be housed in low buildings, spread out on some suburban hill. Mr. Pope's building is a rousing fanfare; if the stone weathers contrastingly, the building will shortly be touching the popular heart.

Poor old Pennsylvania Avenue, to which our historical memories used to cling, apparently hasn't a friend on the Art Commission. Nearly all the quaint buildings that one used to recognize in old prints of the Lincoln and Grant inaugurals are gone. A vast open space, largely to remain open, weakens its eastern end; Constitution Avenue crashes across it; the plaza at Eighth Street is maimed; vast walls of stone weigh down one side of the Avenue, while parking lots cut gaps in the other, making the north

FIGURE 64. Constitution Avenue crashing across Pennsylvania Avenue.

side even uglier than the south side was claimed to be in early Triangle propaganda; finally, the plaza between Thirteenth and Fourteenth Streets has been ruined by an open space yawning wide toward the west.

The old Patent Office has suffered further indig-

FIGURE 65. The Old Patent Office, with its grand front staircase missing.

Fig. 65

nities. One Sunday morning I attended the unveiling of a monument, over his grave in the Congressional Cemetery, to the memory of Robert Mills, the architect of the Washington Monument and of the Patent Office, a building that is acquiring standing as one of the finest of the fine old structures of Washington. Robert Mills was praised, and the Patent Office was praised. On the way home, I drove through E Street. The granite walls and steps (marred by modern pipe handrails) that led up to the Parthenon portico of the south front had been torn away. Now the lovely columns stand on a rusticated wall with three crude dark openings. The side view is especially gauche: the wall is ill-proportioned, its top is not sufficiently emphasized, and an absurd window stares at you. The old steps expressed, in the side view, the existence of the Eighth Street axis, and in the south view they took the ris-

ing flow of Eighth Street and carried it up to the portico. I regret, particularly, that it will no longer be possible to go up, at night, and have that dramatic view of brightly lit F Street, framed by the ponderous yet graceful columns, with the Treasury colonnade in the distance.

Of the Triangle, specifically, little need be noted. *Fig. 66* It is planned in the eighteenth-century French mode and closely resembles a plan submitted in the competition that resulted in the formation of the Place de la Concorde. It was influenced also by the San Francisco Fair of 1915 but falls far short of that plan's fine outline and masterly subdivision. It is the type of plan that needs spirited detailing, with enough verticality to vivify the horizontals and enough dark narrowness to give light to the open areas. The theatrical pediments that are tacked to the Constitution Avenue front in order to flatter Mr. Mellon's hypothetical art gallery would have been used by an Inigo Jones or a Contant d'Ivry to give *Fig. 67* a voice to the big plaza of the Triangle.

Around Lafayette Square no public construction has been done for some years, and it is evident that the 1901 plan has here met a disastrous defeat, leaving the Square definitely less attractive as a setting for the White House than it was when the Burnham group was named. This part of the commission's plan forms the clearest proof of its brutally destructive all-or-nothing attitude. With incredible assurance Burnham, McKim, and Olmsted—in this part of their work Burnham probably took the lead —said flatly that the procedure used in designing the Court of Honor at Chicago, the establishment of a standard "ordonnance" and material, was the only way to create the setting for a public building and that everything in the areas they marked out

FIGURE 66. The Federal Triangle.

for this treatment was bad and must be torn down, wiped out. If, in war, the forces of an enemy nation had bombed and destroyed the buildings that stood around Lafayette Square in 1901—the Dolly Madison house, Webster's home, the Hay and Adams houses that Richardson built, the Decatur house, which thousands of people pay to enter when it is opened once a year, that exquisite white and buff mansion across from the State, War and Navy Building, and above all the fine old St. John's Church, one of the beloved buildings of Washington, with its picturesque old wall and centenarian sycamores— if all these had been destroyed by an enemy, the whole nation would have been stirred with grief and anger. But when three of our leading architects proposed the destruction in order that they might set

up a copy of a vainglorious World's Columbian Exposition as the setting for the modest mansion of the President, we acclaimed the plan and conferred high honors upon its authors. The destruction began, but the intolerability of the program had its inevitable effect. The Treasury Annex may be extended, but there is no likelihood that the whole plan will be carried out. The present state of the enframement of the Square is, to put it plainly, a mess, and it will get worse before it gets better. If in 1901 a more modest plan had been adopted, one based on the preservation of what was good among the existing buildings, plus new public architecture harmonizing with the old work, the beauty of the Square could have been maintained even during reconstruction. The plan, if necessary, could have been adapted to

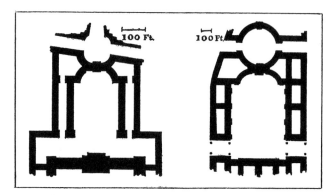

FIGURE 67. The Triangle designers followed the French eighteenth-century style of planning. Part of Contant d'Ivry's project for a city hall for Paris and the two plazas of the Triangle plan.

FIGURE 68. The Interior Building.

changing conditions and would not have been ruined by abandonment after fractional execution.

The new Interior Building stands in an area shown as park in the plan of 1901. It is too close to the Pan-American, D.A.R., and Red Cross buildings and will bring upon them the curse of auto parking. *Fig. 68* It projects so close to the line of Virginia Avenue as to make impossible the realignment of that street, as formerly proposed by the National Capital Park and Planning Commission, to bring the Washington Monument on its axis. This was, I believe, the *Fig. 69* last possibility of creating a perfect vista of this unequaled avenue objective.

Fig. 70 The planting around the Lincoln Memorial has been extended in recent years so that it now hides almost all of the architecturally important line where the earth comes against the great stone retaining wall. As the enormous box bushes of the initial planting grow larger, they still further reduce the scale of the Memorial. A very interesting chapter could be written in analysis of this gorgeously beautiful and thoroughly inappropriate planting. In a formal French park stands a Greek temple, so we plant it in an American stylized mode derived from English sentimental landscape gardening, partly by direct descent and partly by way of Puvis de Chavannes and other illustrators of Tempe and the dales of Arcady.

The striking thing about this roster of the efforts toward beauty and impressiveness of architecture and civic art in Washington is the consistency with which L'Enfant's plan is ignored—not to say flouted. The Triangle wipes out a large patch of the L'Enfant plan, substituting not merely a different plan but a different type of planning so that, whatever may be said in its favor, it destroys the stylistic unity of the Washington design. At the same time the national officials and planners effect a gorgeous exhibition of self-deception—for I think they are quite sincere about it—by interminably lauding L'Enfant. The mental mechanics of the situation might seem to permit only one explanation, that the planners have never looked at L'Enfant's plan. The self-de-

FIGURE 69. Looking eastward at the Washington Monument, which appears almost on an axis with Virginia Avenue.

FIGURE 70. The Lincoln Memorial, shrubbery at the base having reduced its original scale.

ception theory, however, is more plausible, for we Americans have to an extraordinary degree the power to entertain in our minds diametrically opposed ideas. A trained capacity for dutiful self-deception sustains our religion, our politics, and our patriotism. Why should it not also enter into our art, particularly here at Washington, the busiest market for this kind of thought, in all its branches?

Thus it is wise, in accounting for current Capitoline civic art, to disassociate it from the L'Enfant plan, and to seek outside of L'Enfant's purposes for the ideas that have engendered the Washington we see so often in the rotogravures.

Fig. 71

The Triangle is not, in its roots, identical with municipal civic centers, but it is the fruit of similar purposes and values. American city planning derives its power from two kinds of ideas—those prevailing in the chamber of commerce and those of the social settlement house. To the energy of the chamber of commerce, city planning is a tool for the creation and preservation of land values. Planning, control of traffic, cutting new streets, zoning, fine parks and pleasure boulevards, impressive civic centers—these exist because individuals forming energetic groups believe that they pay in greater population, more business, and higher land values. The other source of impulse in city planning is the benevolent social people, lay and professional, who, through psychological circumstances which real estate dealers look on as abnormal, advocate better housing, broader education, and playgrounds in the slums. The Federal Triangle, plainly, is the product of the land-value type of human energy. It is the highest flower of that motive, expanded by patriotism, etherealized into a symbol and a justification of a way of life. It is our national conspicuous waste, our display of superfluous power.

Fig. 72

In its practical aspects, there is no question that

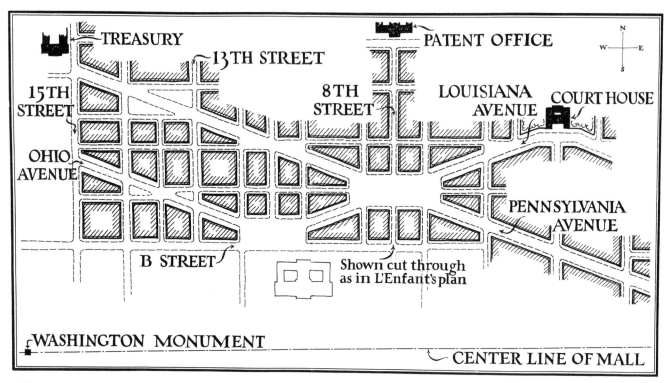

FIGURE 71. Plan of the Federal Triangle area carried out according to L'Enfant's principles.

the concentration of office buildings has been overdone. It would appear to be axiomatic that a building group that is certain to grow should be planned so that it can expand centrifugally, and that such a group ought not to be planned—as has been done in the Triangle—within rigid external boundaries. A department office building has in its use character more affinity with a school or hospital than it has with an exposition hall or a Roman palace, and it ought to be placed and planned in harmony with that character. The perfectly suc-

cessful operation of the Bureau of Standards in a suburb of Washington has been cited by the National Capital Park and Planning Commission as evidence that concentration is not an unquestioned necessity, while the Department of Agriculture's new Beltsville experiment center, some ten miles from Washington, may be the first evidence of a broader centrifugal movement from the crowded city.

The thing that finally wrecks the heart of a city planner who knows and loves Washington is pictur-

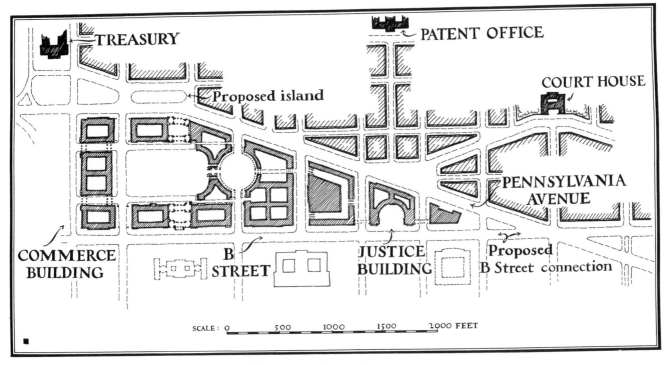

FIGURE 72. The Federal Triangle in one of its stages of conception.

ing to himself what that money could have done if it had been spread less thickly and more wisely. Let us say, and the figure is not impossible, that a hundred million dollars could have been saved since 1901, in land and construction costs, if the government offices had been built neatly of brick in a number of groups, out of the high-value zone. That amount of money, carefully administered and supplemented by taxing, zoning, and encroachment laws, could have influenced the architectural design of new buildings throughout the city, could have

secured changes in existing buildings, and could have preserved old buildings. It could have brought about the rehabilitation of depressed areas and could have controlled the blight of parking lots which threatens important streets. It might have made the Triangle an attractive residence district and might have preserved the colonial atmosphere of Lafayette Square.

Efforts of this kind would have tended toward a harmoniously developed Washington. L'Enfant designed a whole city. He designed in terms of signifi-

Fig. 73

cant points, lines, and long vistas, thus organizing
large areas and forming a space composition having
an effect of totality. The present procedure follows
very different ideals. This concentration of monuments, memorials, museums, and endless department office buildings in the central area of the city
is destroying the city, as a work of art and as a
social entity, in the process of glorifying the capital
—or perhaps more accurately the government.
People who have no sense of the beauty of large
spatial organizations, people who do not love the
life of a city and who do not see that snobbishness—
even though it be official snobbishness—is fatal to
civic art, people who cannot distinguish between
art and splurge, obviously cannot see how far we are
getting from L'Enfant's conception. For he dreamed,
not of a beautiful court of honor, but of a beautiful
city.

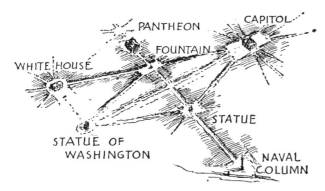

FIGURE 73. The aesthetic structure of the central portion of
L'Enfant's plan.

7

On the Mutilations of L'Enfant's Plan

Washington's Center Market must go, and friendly obituaries of the old building are being published. They recall its mellow middle period, but they all overlook an important point—the dubious legitimacy of its birth. For Center Market was erected in defiance of the hallowed L'Enfant plan on which the artistic renown of the capital depends.

In fact, the market obstructs a fundamental line in that design. Eighth Street, just halfway between the Capitol and the White House, was one of the key lines of the geometrical scheme that makes Washington unique among the cities of the world. L'Enfant made it the most highly enriched secondary axis of his plan. Two squares, in one of which the city library now stands, lie on the northern part of the line, but it is the southern stretch that was to be of greatest importance. The break occurs at a break in topography—on the high point where the Patent Office now stands.

L'Enfant intended to erect there a great pantheon, looking south. Eighth Street was to be the monumental approach to this national temple. Its first enlargement is a square where the mid-point of Pennsylvania Avenue is marked by a "grand fountain." From this square radiate eight vistas, in L'Enfant's plan, including views of the Capitol, the President's house, and the memorial statue of Washington. The axis continues south between two market houses—or possibly open market places—across the canal and Mall, though another square, and down to a naval memorial column at the Potomac shore. By means of such streets as this L'Enfant produced the sweeping breadth that is his plan's most precious quality.

Fig. 74

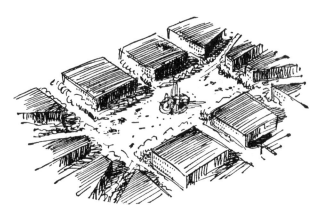

FIGURE 74. The intended square at Eighth Street along Pennsylvania Avenue.

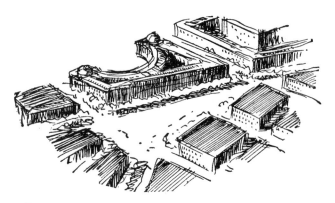

FIGURE 75. An early version of the design for the Department of Justice Building, blocking Eighth Street and destroying the shape of L'Enfant's would-be plaza. The Archives Building was built here instead, blocking the Eighth Street axial vista but not jutting into the space.

Fig. 75 But the mad Frenchman's successors had never seen Versailles and could not rise to his largeness of view. So, for one thing, they built Center Market, blocking the vista southward from the Pantheon. Now the old building is to be torn down. Is the reader waiting for me to say that this is being done as the first step in the restoration of L'Enfant's fine conception? Well, it is not. A huge office building for the Department of Justice will replace the market and all the fine old elms that stand in front of it and nearly half of L'Enfant's square to boot. With the help of another building it will obliterate the only vista—though an imperfect one—of the Washington Monument from Pennsylvania Avenue.

In other words, the government architects are annihilating an important part of L'Enfant's plan. Yet, oddly enough, they profess to adore the plan. President Taft once remarked that "the ablest architects now, more than a hundred years after the plan was drawn, have confessed themselves unable to improve" upon L'Enfant's design. This confession must be ascribed to the architects' charming modesty—in public. In the privacy of their drafting rooms there is nothing they so much enjoy as cutting a leg off M. L'Enfant's trousers.

This is illustrated by the accompanying before-and-after plans of the Center Market square. The supposed compensation is called the Mall transept, a transverse axis—developed by the use of water and other garden features and terminating in the recessed front of the Justice Building. The garden treatment would doubtless please L'Enfant, but he might remark that the Mall was not an independent formal garden but a detail in the plan of a large city. The Mall was, in L'Enfant's conception, a kind of promenade from which the superb size and unity of the city could be observed. For this purpose deep and impressive vistas into the city are essential. *Fig. 76*

Of all the tragic passages in the Capitoline architectural drama the wrong location of the Washington Monument is the most dolorous. It stands some four hundred feet from the intended point. So we have here the most glorious vista objective in the world without a single street shooting straight at it —and, to make the pathos complete, this happens in a city especially designed to take multiple advantage of every such objective, a city world-famous for precisely that quality. One vista will indeed be realized when the Mall is cut through in accordance with the present plans. But it was the essence of L'Enfant's conception that architectural high points of this sort should dominate symmetrical street vistas running deep into the city in many directions. That was his way of cashing in on the monumental effect of his show pieces—his way also of knitting the city into a vast but constantly felt unity. He counted on bowling the visitor over by repeated surprise blows of stunning beauty.

FIGURE 76. Evolution of the intersection of Pennsylvania Avenue and Eighth Street, on the median axis between the White House and the Capitol. In L'Enfant's plan, at the left, there is a market between the intersection square, which contains a large fountain, and the Mall, the center being open to permit reciprocal views along the axis. This also illustrates L'Enfant's way of grouping commercial and monumental elements. In the middle of the plan, by the Commission of 1901, the axis is blocked. In the present Triangle plan the square is destroyed, and a diagonal avenue, which by a slight change could have been aimed straight at the Washington obelisk, is obliterated. (The final plan failed to leave Louisiana Avenue open, but the Archives Building, astride the Eighth Street axis, "squares up" the plaza.)

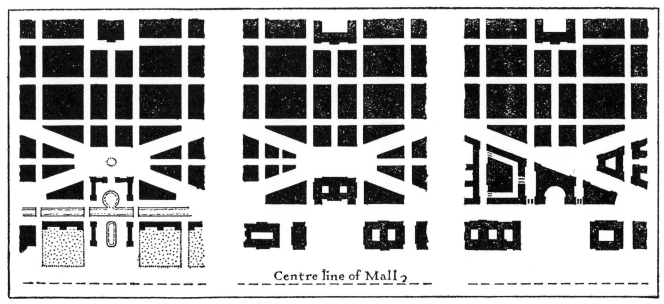

Centre line of Mall

FIGURE 77. The vista to the Washington Monument, looking westward on Louisiana Avenue, had it been kept open. Compare this with Figure 62.

FIGURE 78. Louisiana Avenue blocked, as envisioned by Elbert Peets in the faulty plan formulated in 1930. See Figure 62 for this view as it is today.

The intersection of Pennsylvania Avenue and Eighth Street, accordingly, a vital nucleus formed by the meeting of his principal diagonal and his halfway cross axis, L'Enfant made into a kind of clearing house for his vistas. From no other point in the city were all the essential objects of his great composition visible. And they were not to be casually visible to the eye. They were to be tied to this place by impressive receding perspectives, each forming a monumental setting or frame for its ter-

Fig. 77

minal accent. The lower section of Louisiana Avenue, even though it does not shoot at the monument, at least opens up a picturesque view of the mighty obelisk. Now that the government controls the entire area south of Pennsylvania Avenue, it seems a pity that the architects could find no way

Fig. 78

to relocate the diagonal in the direction of the monument, thereby realizing L'Enfant's intention and producing one of the most stunning street vistas in the world.

It may be argued, in defense of the proposed location of the Justice Building, that the distance from the Mall to the F Street hill, where L'Enfant intended his Pantheon to rise, is too great. The effect

of the new plan is to cut the length of the vista by more than half, reducing it from 2,800 feet down to 1,200. It is true that the most satisfactory views of buildings are from reasonably close standpoints.

Fig. 79

But it is also true that there is a pleasant sense of mystery in a long street view. The distant building exerts a pull in that direction, and whether we re-

Fig. 80

spond to the pull or not, it gives us a lively sense of the great area brought into aesthetic control. In most cities we can't see the woods for the trees. L'Enfant had no intention of letting the houses of Washington hide the city.

Perhaps it is not unquestionable praise to call Washington the city of magnificent distances, but by

Fig. 81

architectural skill it is possible to make great distances truly magnificent. Paris is, of course, the classic example, and several Parisian vistas, com-

Fig. 82

parable to the vista from the Mall to the F Street hill, are longer. The Avenue de l'Opera, for instance, is 3,300 feet long, as against 2,800 in the Washington dimension with which comparison is

Fig. 84

being made. The distance from the Chamber of

Fig. 85

Deputies to the Madeleine is about 3,000 feet.

Fig. 86

FIGURE 79. The view southward down the Eighth Street axis as L'Enfant would have had it.

FIGURE 80. The same view, blocked by the slanted early version of the Department of Justice Building. See Figure 60 for this same view as it is today, blocked by the Archives Building.

From the Avenue des Champs Elysées to the dome of the Invalides, one of the finest street views in Europe, it is more than 4,500 feet.

Fig. 83   In Rome the Porta del Popolo is about 6,000 feet from the Piazza di Venezia. The beautiful vista up the narrow Via Condotti from the Corso to the church on the hill is only 1,500 feet, but more distant views are also fine. By the test of these universally admired European examples it can hardly be proved that L'Enfant erred in this passage of his plan, particularly when you remember that he intended a strong intermediate accent, the fountain in Pennsylvania Avenue, to break the distance from the Mall Avenue to the Pantheon.

Another phase of the new plan is its unfortunate effect from the air. Washington is hardly beyond infancy. The city's middle and elder years will be lived in the Age of the Air. It is utter stupidity to put up buildings in Washington without considering their beauty as seen from above. What have the government architects done? With the help of pro-

fessional committees, the approval of Cabinet members, and the blessings of the Art Commission, they have chopped the tail of their triangle into three lopsided chunks. The conspicuous lack of symmetry and block-plan beauty in these buildings will make them forever a blemish in the air view of Washington. And isn't it tactless, to say the least, to give the Department of Justice a crooked plan?   *Fig. 76*

A few years ago an excellent critic, Kingsley Porter, used the phrase "paper architecture," a graphic condemnation of the current building art. By it he meant the tendency to design in terms of flat façades rather than in three-dimensional solids. Since then the American skyscraper, with its setbacks and towers, has showed us the value of the controlled plastic mass. As we become used to seeing buildings from the air, this attitude will strengthen, and beauty in the flat façade will be more and more

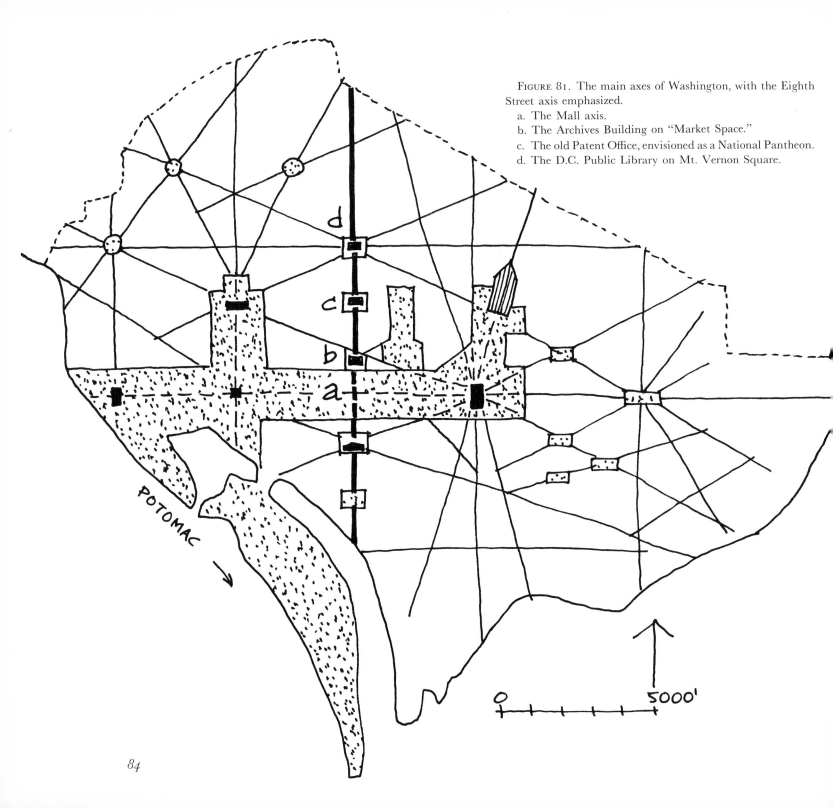

FIGURE 81. The main axes of Washington, with the Eighth Street axis emphasized.
a. The Mall axis.
b. The Archives Building on "Market Space."
c. The old Patent Office, envisioned as a National Pantheon.
d. The D.C. Public Library on Mt. Vernon Square.

POTOMAC

0   5000'

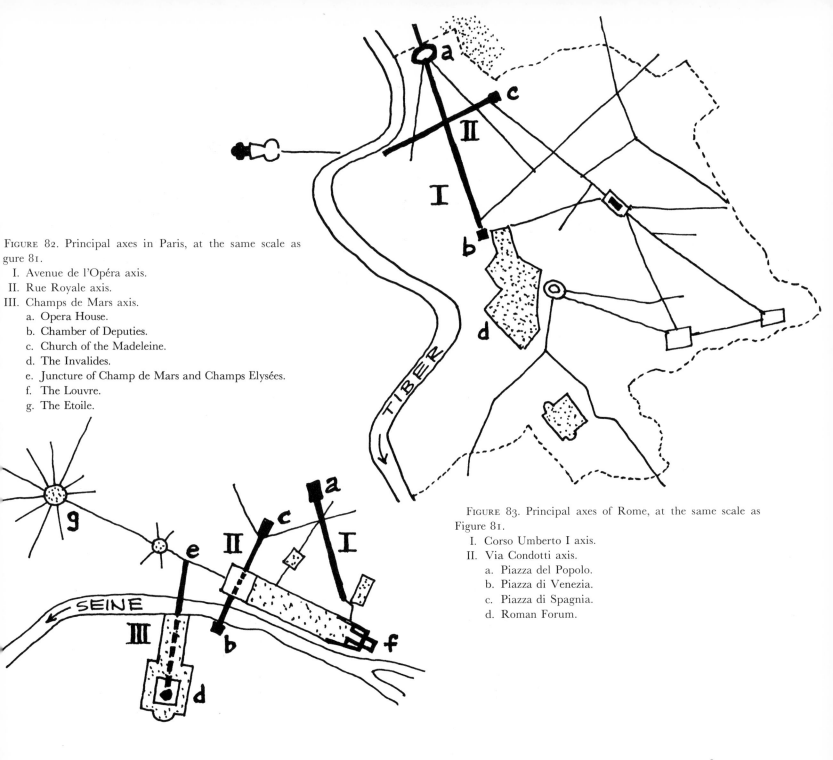

FIGURE 82. Principal axes in Paris, at the same scale as
gure 81.

  I. Avenue de l'Opéra axis.
 II. Rue Royale axis.
III. Champs de Mars axis.
    a. Opera House.
    b. Chamber of Deputies.
    c. Church of the Madeleine.
    d. The Invalides.
    e. Juncture of Champ de Mars and Champs Elysées.
    f. The Louvre.
    g. The Etoile.

FIGURE 83. Principal axes of Rome, at the same scale as
Figure 81.

  I. Corso Umberto I axis.
 II. Via Condotti axis.
    a. Piazza del Popolo.
    b. Piazza di Venezia.
    c. Piazza di Spagnia.
    d. Roman Forum.

FIGURE 84. Looking up the Avenue de l'Opera in Paris, a vista 3,300 feet long but seemingly much grander than its actual dimension suggests.

FIGURE 85. Looking from the portico of the Madeleine toward the Chamber of Deputies, a 3,000-foot vista.

supplemented by a bold sculpturing of the whole body of the building. No longer will it be possible to pretend that a building is a solid cube when it is punctured by miserly interior light courts and wells. But the government architects are conservative. Apparently they think that by crossing their fingers and collecting a dozen impressive signatures they can preserve forever the good old long-skirt days when a building could be internally lopsided and knock-kneed and nobody would be so impolite as to discover it. The Justice Building they have planned will make a brave show of symmetry on the side toward the Mall, but in the air view the eye will be wholly distracted by the contorted and dissimilar interior courts.

Actually, of course, there is no reason for calling L'Enfant's plan sacred. It was far from perfect when it left his hand, and its defects multiplied in execution. But it was a plan for the whole city, conceived with unique largeness of view. Though he worked so hurriedly that the details suffered, L'Enfant attained, by his "reciprocities of sight," the grand expansiveness and command of great areas that are the characteristic qualities of French park and city planning. He anticipated precisely the qualities that harmonize with the modern American spirit.

The Triangle Plan is the greatest blow Eighth Street has suffered but not the first. The important function of this tie rod in L'Enfant's structure was never understood, and its weakening began with the first working drawings. The emotional significance of a pantheon can hardly, even in Yankeeland, radiate from a patent office, though in justice it must be added that the south portico of the building is a full-sized copy of the Pantheon front and that it affords, in spite of Eighth Street's relative want of dignity, one of the very few good architectural vistas in Washington. Throughout its length Eighth Street

Fig. 34
Fig. 60
Fig. 65

Figure 86. Looking at the Madeleine from 1,000 feet away.

has suffered, but the mistakes of the past have not been so vital as to justify those of the present. It is clearly wiser to retain an imperfect detailing of a fine general plan than to introduce a change that renders the general conception forever unattainable. We are dealing with the centuries here. The right tactic is to keep L'Enfant's big lines open so that the future can gradually realize his magnificent plan.

It is almost fantastic that President Hoover is urging the correction of a solecism committed long since in the proverbial dark age of our national taste, while at the same moment he is building into enduring stone the much more vital mistakes inherited on paper from the administration immediately preceding his. To scrap the mansard roof of the State, War and Navy Building and to wreck its many-storied porticos will be a heartbreaking and costly job. The President must often wish that the change could be made—as in his engineering work

he has effected so many changes—by incinerating a few blueprints. A generation or two from now, if L'Enfant's art chances to be more perfectly understood, the then President will be urged by his advisory architects to cut a hole through that confounded old Justice Building so that a view of the Pantheon portico—behind which a noble pantheon may by then be built—can be had from the Mall. In some such way as that the Fates will surely have their laugh at the chaotic, changing, and spotty state of our contemporary architectural thought.

The L'Enfant association, I believe, is petitioning Congress for some $200,000 with which to erect a memorial. I suggest that the statue be set up in the remaining corner of the square that marks the midpoint of Pennsylvania Avenue. Let the sainted hero of American civic art be shown facing toward the Department of Justice Building, violently tearing out his hair.

8

On the Rebuilding of the Mall in the 1930's

They are laying out the Mall avenue in Washington. After 144 years the main axis of L'Enfant's New Versailles is being cut through a forest planted long after his time, through soil that has been dug and moved without thought of his plan, opening up vistas of a dome he never saw and a mighty obelisk that never came to his dreams.

There is a sweet sense of rightness about this long-postponed victory of an idea, a satisfaction that should divert us from the sorrow of seeing the old trees felled and the pretty lawns plowed. The future will thank us. Yet I am not sure that the future—even the immediate future—will accept, either as beautiful or as practical, all the details of the form in which L'Enfant's simple diagram is being worked out. I'll tell you what I mean—but first let us pay our respects to that fine old institution, the historical background.

Two sacred scripts guide and solace the city planners of Washington. They are L'Enfant's plan (with its voluminous legend and explanatory letters) and the report of the Commission of 1901. We must examine these regarding the detailing of the Mall.

L'Enfant's general intention is clear. He knew that this premier line in his thoroughly integrated scheme must have a physical form that would give it a role in the life of the city as clearly dominant as its place in the drafted plan. So he made it a "Grand Avenue, 400 feet in breadth." Without question he had in mind a wide central roadway paralleled by rows of trees, after the manner of the avenue of the Champs Elysées in Paris.

Fig. 87

Quite likely, too, he was influenced by Patte's famous book of plazas,* containing a fine engraving of Gabriel's plan for the Place de la Concorde. There are several points of likeness between that plan and L'Enfant's—the big equestrian statue at the intersection of two axes, for example, and the broad central avenue of the Champs Élysées flanked by balanced spreading lines to which Pennsylvania and Maryland Avenues correspond exactly. Another parallel, not appearing in Patte's engraving, is that a number of fine houses in the Rue du Faubourg Saint-Honoré had deep gardens running down to the boundary of the Champs Elysées, precisely as L'Enfant intended for the Mall.

As for the lengthwise profile of his avenue, L'Enfant must have meant it to be cut through level at a grade slightly above the elevation of the quays along the river and canal. This would harmonize with a remark he makes about slopes up from the gardens to the houses. To give the avenue this straight profile would have meant a large grading operation. For this reason, and because it opened up no business frontage, the Mall avenue was postponed—postponed until now. The land stood wild and brush-grown until the Smithsonian grounds were laid out by Downing and Vaux, around 1850, as a pretty landscaped park, the first of its kind in this country. In time the park treatment spread all the way from the botanical garden under Capitol Hill down to the Washington Monument.

All this, of course, ignored completely the L'Enfant plan. Even the Monument—which, as an equestrian statue, was to have been the western objective of the Grand Avenue and the pin that tied

* Pierre Patte, *Monuments Érigés en France à la gloire de Louis XV* (Paris, 1765).

together the Capitol and White House axes—was casually set on a rise of ground nearly four hundred feet southeast of the true intersection. This haphazard placing of the great obelisk just escaped compelling a radical change from the L'Enfant conception of the Mall. By good luck, however, the error was mainly from the White House axis—the offset from the Capitol axis being only 120 feet. Thus, by a deflection of only one degree, the Mall could be aligned with the Monument.

The recognition of this fact was a first fruit of the L'Enfant renaissance that began with the approach of the city's centennial. The Columbia Historical Society, in 1899, printed the letters in which L'Enfant described his plan. Colonel Bingham, officer in charge of public buildings and grounds, studied the plan itself and had a copy made of the Mall area. Late in 1900 the American Institute of Architects held a symposium in Washington. Some of the speakers favored the retention of the true Mall line, letting the Monument stand south of it; others, including Glenn Brown and Cass Gilbert, advocated the deflected axis. All spoke with enthusiasm of the L'Enfant plan.

Enter now the Commission of 1901, the trio of architects—for the sculptor Saint-Gaudens was hardly active—who were brought to Washington to plan some such beauty as they had helped to create in the Chicago Fair of 1893. It was they who sowed the seed that bore the Union Station and that now is fruiting in the Triangle, the Capitol group, and the new Mall.

After taking a bird's-eye view of the ground, Burnham, McKim, and Olmsted, with Charles Moore as secretary, very sensibly went over to Europe to study in its native haunts the style of

FIGURE 87. French influence on L'Enfant's designs.

Avenue des Champs Élysées, Paris, in the 18ᵗʰ Century

Conjectural section through L'Enfant's "Grand Avenue"

civic and garden design that L'Enfant worked in. They measured and photographed avenues and fountains and buildings in formal parks, seeking precedents and motifs that might shed light on the right planning of the Mall, the Monument Gardens, and the Lincoln Memorial. To Versailles they went, of course, and to Vaux-le-Vicomte, down near Melun, to Hampton Court, to the Pincian gardens in Rome, to Schoenbrunn in Vienna, and to many other famous formal gardens. And when they got home, they prepared a very beautiful and broadly conceived design.

It is only their version of the Mall, however, that is under the microscope now. Inevitably, of course,

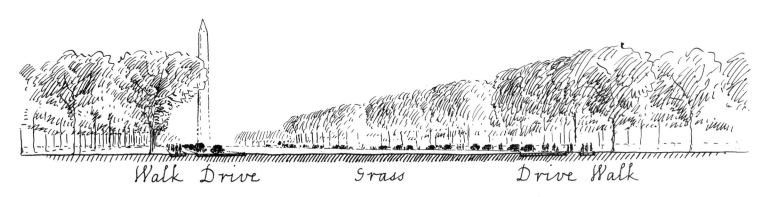

Walk   Drive   Grass   Drive   Walk

The 1901 plan for the Mall, as now being carried out
Section, with view from south walk

Grass   Walk   Grass

Probable future arrangement of the Mall

the L'Enfant plan had to be modified. But one radical change was made that was not inevitable. On the axis line, where L'Enfant had his carriage drive, they put a wide strip of grass flanked by narrow roadways. That is to say, they took as their model not the Avenue des Champs Elysées but the tapis vert at Versailles, the charming carpet of grass, with walks along its sides, that graces the slope from the Parterre of Latona to the Basin of Apollo. In those old days, you know, grass was a luxury, and bits of lawn were used as part of the garden pattern, contrasting with the gravel, which was the normal ground surface. Farther out on the main axis—without gravel walks or drives, since they would reduce the scale and the atmospheric effect of distance—tree-framed avenues of meadow were often used to pull the perspective out from the garden to the blue horizon, so that the king might have from the windows of his apartment that vista into infinity that was the ultimate value of Renaissance art.

For this change the commission's reason was, in substance, that grass is more beautiful than pavement, at least in the intended proportions. And this reason was valid to the commission because they thought of the Mall as a park.

Now it is the American custom to make an antithesis between park and city—a park is a place of quiet, far from the madding crowd, and all that sort of thing. But L'Enfant, the good Frenchman, was untouched by this romantic corruption. The Champs Elysées doubtless seemed most delightful to him when the avenue and the Cours de la Reine were crowded with cavaliers and carriages. In the Washington plan he wove together business streets, canals, markets, monumental vistas, elegant residences, and public gardens, as if his whole purpose were to make them all equally animated. Certainly this Grand Avenue, the heart of his city plan, he would have wished to see alive with citizens and guests of the city.

But the members of the Commission of 1901 were, as I have said, definitely garden-minded. So we have this all-too-human situation: L'Enfant, when the site of Washington was a forest, dreamed of the Mall as a fashionable Parisian avenue, while the Commission of 1901, with a big city spreading all about them, dreamed of the Mall as a quiet sanctuary from the city's noise and bustle.

Yes, precisely that. Reading the Mall section of the commission's thoroughgoing and interesting re-

FIGURE 88. The northern "sidewalk" along the Mall, the Capitol Dome obscured by trees.

port, I am absolutely shocked to discover how rustic—I cannot think of a better word—their conceptions were. They cited as a precedent the grass-planted avenue at Old Hadley, in Massachusetts, and verily one might say that the Washington of 1900 had greater affinity to Old Hadley, in the manner of its life, than it then had to the city it was to become a generation later. Heavens! That was eight years before the first Model T Ford was built!

The word "automobile" does not occur in the commission's report. The nearest I can find is "spirited horse." In speaking of the streets that cross the Mall, the report remarks that the passing of "street cars and teams will give needed life to the Mall." (In the present plan three of these streets are buried in tunnels so as to give the Mall a little peace and quiet.) The report's charming illustrations (by Jules Guerin) showing the intended appearance of the Mall in, let us say, the remote year

FIGURE 89. The southern "sidewalk," with much the same effect—looking eastward.

FIGURE 90. The central axis view of the Mall in winter. [Consider Mr. Peets's 1935 premonition about the Mall becoming a parking lot.]

1935, are as sweetly rural in tone as if they were views of an avenue of stone pines in the Roman campagna. Through the trees, at a great distance, one has glimpses of white marble buildings.

And the Mall, incredibly, seems to conform to the rolling ground surface of the old naturalistic park. Two full-page pictures show very clearly the billowing of the ground, the rise and fall of the stunning rows of trees. And this was not a romantic whimsey of the artist. In cool type the text tells us: "The axis of the Capitol and Monument is clearly defined by an expanse of undulating green a mile and a half long and three hundred feet broad, walled on either side by elms, planted in formal procession four abreast. Bordering this green carpet, roads, parklike in character, stretch between Capitol and Monument, while beneath the elms one may walk or drive, protected from the sun." Why should this surprise us? It was written in the year that Queen

Victoria passed from the undulating green of England to the undulating green of the Anglo-Saxon heaven.

Yes, these pictures in the 1901 report, showing the Mall as it was intended to appear in 1940 or 1950, are worth study. Let us consider the view of the Mall at Fourteenth Street. Lawns undulate, the parklike drives look at least twenty feet wide, and the Monument floats in the background. And then, giving "needed life" to the charming scene, we discover:

    1 horse, pulling a dogcart
    1 man, driving same
    1 shepherd
    1 flock of sheep!

This world, in 1901, lived still in the age of the horse, and American landscape architecture still wistfully remembered the grazing flocks of the eighteenth century. Little did 1901 dream what fate and the internal-combustion engine had in store.

I can see what happened. Our tourist-architects, doing their work thoroughly, did not restrict their explorations of the European château parks to the neatly kept regions around the palaces, as most visitors do. At Hampton Court they walked under the lindens of the *patte-d'oie* and through Bushy Park. At Versailles they probably took a boat and rowed to the end of the canal and discovered that the Etoile Royale was a daisy-starred meadow. In Italy they were smitten by the avenues of pines one sees from the train between Pisa and Rome, and in Vienna they climbed to the top of the "Gloriette" and discovered that much of Schoenbrunn is as easy and informal—in spite of the straight lines—as an old pasture. This rusticity of detail, associated with a magnificent formality in the general organization, must have charmed them as it surprises and charms every garden lover who goes to Europe with the preconception that formal gardens are all white marble, neat flower beds, and swept gravel. To Mr. Olmsted, in particular, with his large vested interest in naturalistic landscape gardening, this informal formality must have seemed a happy reconciliation of American garden tradition with the L'Enfant architectural framework.

But the charming genre he discovered is not as easy as it looks—it requires a natural gift, some lucky accidents, a century of slow growth, perhaps another of graceful decay. It would never have fitted our palace-lined Mall, where the upkeep will have to be meticulous and the crowds will every year be larger. Mr. Olmsted, in guiding the execution of the plan he helped to make so long ago, has been very wise to make the Mall a perfectly flat plane and to give up the parklike character of the roads. But is he wise in adhering to the general plan—in main, making the Mall a tapis vert paralleled by narrow drives? I think not. I feel that the absolutely radical change in conditions since 1901 ought to have been recognized in a radical revision of the plan.

Crudely expressed, this is the question: Is the Mall country, or is it city? Now if the Washington Monument—this doesn't hold true of the Capitol!—stood in some deserted place, visited only by an occasional pilgrim, it would be glorious to approach it along a grassy opening between dark and ancient trees and to find it standing alone in a broad meadow. But the Monument is not a hermit.

One day last fall from a hill near Washington I saw it in the distance, and with it, so surprisingly far to the left, the Capitol dome. There was a quickening heartbeat as I said "The city!" I felt somehow the presence of all those human beings filling the city with life. I felt with new intensity the significance of those majestic buildings, how the great city lying there in the dark valley was a prodigious work of human art formed about these two sacred structures. It moved me to know that the dome and the obelisk were not accidental and separate but that they together created a line upon which the whole city was organized, so that they and the space between them formed the heart of the city.

As you see, my own answer to my question is that the Mall's fullest significance derives from its civic role—it is neither country nor countrylike garden. So far from being a place of escape from the city, it is precisely in the Mall that we must find the ark and epitome of L'Enfant's heroic composition. There, along that line between the Capitol and the Washington Monument, we have the strongest im-

FIGURE 91. Looking westward on Constitution Avenue, at about Twentieth Street. There is no vista termination; it simply dissipates.

FIGURE 92. Looking eastward on Constitution Avenue; again no vista termination.

pression of geometric order, topographic rightness, and architectural beauty—the strongest impression also of being in a capital, the capital of a great nation that honors its great men. No open space in America is so charged with human value—and this space we are planting with meadow grass and permitting ourselves normally only a slantwise view of *Fig. 88* it from narrow drives and niggardly walks beneath *Fig. 89* the trees.

In L'Enfant's time it was right to make of the Mall a Grand Avenue, a paved way for carriages. But carriages are one thing; automobiles are another. Today it would be wrong to make it a vehicular thoroughfare. With true grief I say it: our enclosed cars are fatal to all but the crudest perception of that Titanic space modeling which is civic

art. Only now are we beginning to appreciate this and to see that there are places to which we cannot open the floodgates of traffic. Where there is aesthetic reward for walking, people walk, as to an exceptional extent they do in Washington.

And so I say that as the commission secured the withdrawal of the railroads from the Mall, so ought we to ban the auto; few architectural groups are less adapted to be seen from inside a modern turtle-shaped car. Just think of it concretely—the driver bending over his wheel trying to see the point of the Washington Monument; mother, with guidebook in hand, searching through the rear porthole for Miss Armed Liberty atop the Capitol, and Willie saying, "Look, daddy, there's an Arkansas car!" Oh ye traditional gods and little fishes! What an insult

FIGURE 93. The Mall as a whole, as most visitors see it, from the Capitol Terrace looking westward.

those cars will be to the blue sky that vaults that giant corridor of space! And an insult no less to the sweet level ground that your feet must feel if you want to sense keenly the rugged piling up of the Capitol and the prodigious verticality of that miraculously balanced obelisk.

Think, too, how this renunciation of motorcars would simplify the Mall as a psychological experience, stilling the distracting battle of traffic and saving these calm, soaring, white buildings from this impious twinkling foreground. Under the present plans persons who have the good taste to enter the Mall on foot will have to look diagonally across a channel of motor traffic to see the Capitol or the Monument. That is preposterous. Suppose that on a rainy day they invited all the baby buggies in Central Park into the Metropolitan Museum—what good would Rembrandt do you?

Actually, the narrow walks now planned will be only thirteen feet away from the lateral tree rows that form the 300-foot opening. Do they think that people are frightened agoraphobic rats that want to run always with one shoulder touching the wall? Are multitudes of people being herded along the sidelines and kept from fully experiencing our grandest work of outdoor art merely to flatter the idyllic reveries of some anachronous sect of grass worshipers or to compose a pretty set picture seen only from an imaginary royal window? The beauty of symmetry is not an abstraction—it is an ocular and muscular phenomenon that occurs with greatest emotional effect only on the axis line. I expect to see a little bootleg path straight down the middle of that green carpet, made there by hardy souls who like to inhale their beauty with both lungs.

Yes, and if I could, I surely would take out the grassy carpet, the two one-way drives and their narrow sidewalks, and would put in, *on the axis*, one whopping wide walk, with seats along the sides and lots of new-style lamps, with poles flying the flags *Fig. 90* of every state and nation. It would be the most thrilling place in the world on a midsummer night. And the turtles would be well provided for, at that. For serious traffic there are Constitution Avenue and B Street SW. For access to the museums and to the Department of Agriculture there are also the two proposed outer Mall drives.

Up to this point we have just been having a chummy chat about this business. Now I want to lay before you a real argument. It is parades. City planning is art, engineering, and social morals, but it must also be showmanship. In planning a city, we plan the movements of people. In ancient times streets were built to honor religious processions and military triumphs. An Egyptian king, leaving his river barge, approached the temple through an avenue of sphinxes or obelisks; the march of his soldiers and priests became part of the architecture, as the architecture was part of the land. At that moment the natural Egypt, the built Egypt, and the living Egypt were one. And here in America, what of the architectural heart of our own land—will the Mall form a noble stage where our national pageants may derive added dignity and beauty from a wholly satisfying setting?

Don't be absurd: parades would spoil the grass! Our official planners have decreed that parades shall pursue Constitution Avenue. One of these gentlemen, in a phrase I'd be happy to forget, in writing of the new avenue, referred to "the processions that will wend their way along the length of its course." "Wend" is the *mot juste*. They will wend their way over the hill at one end of the street and down to the river at the other, slashing slantwise across fine old Pennsylvania Avenue on the way. Constitution Avenue may be the rear front side of the Triangle and may have cost a hundred million dollars, but it is the back alley of the Mall and never will be anything else to an eye whose partner knows the difference between a cocotte and a queen.

Fig. 91
Fig. 92

L'Enfant would never have condoned this effort to push B Street ahead of Pennsylvania Avenue and his avenue mall, the two master lines of his geometric framework. We can suppose that in laying out a Via Triumphalis he would reveal the French flair for combining the festive and the dignified. He thought of such things: he rode in the first inaugural parade and designed floats for a patriotic pageant in New York. Excepting perhaps the inaugurals and other formal movements between the White House and Capitol, I am sure that L'Enfant intended the Mall to be the route of state parades. Certainly under the conditions that exist today it seems unthinkable that this magnificent theater for pageants should go unused.

The weak element in most parades, from the standpoint of the stage producer, is that they come from nowhere and go nowhere. In Paris, when a procession marches from the Place de la Concorde up the Avenue des Champs Elysées and under the Arc de Triomphe, its movement takes on a rationality that makes the event impressive. And as every architect knows, buildings never look larger, distances are never more clearly sensed, and the emotional associations of a historical place are never more poignant than when large crowds are gathered; and when a parade is sweeping along an axis line, the formal logic of the composition is felt with heightened meaning.

So I would make the pavement of the Mall walk good and strong, with no curbs at the street crossings, and with a little slope in the lawn at each side —but why go on? It will be long, alas, ere we hear the fife and drum and see the gay flags of peace borne down L'Enfant's "grand and majestic avenue." Those sheep have gone, but their aesthetic preferences still prevail.

Well, we who love beautiful cities must be patient—didn't it take some two thousand years to evolve the finest plaza in Rome? Suppose we let them go ahead now and plant their funny grass and lay their nine-foot walks. In ninety years or so, when the trees are nicely grown, we'll call out the CCC boys and build a noble promenade. Then we can sit on the clouds for a jolly eternity, enjoying the air view—and the last laugh!

Fig. 93

Part III

Monuments in Washington

9

The Interior of the Lincoln Memorial

The sun of a Washington morning is behind me as I walk toward a great rank of marble columns glowing like sunlit snow. In front, above the last flight of steps, three intercolumnar spaces are dark —the entrance openings in the cella wall of the Lincoln Memorial. Back of the middle opening floats a gray, mottled, ghostlike form. As I come nearer, the ghost becomes a huge seated figure, the statue of Lincoln. It has no pedestal—that is, below the horizon line of the topmost step of the approach. This horizon rises as I walk forward, and Lincoln sinks behind it to the knees, to the chest. Finally, at the bottom of the first of the two long flights of steps near the building, he disappears entirely. I feel a chill of horror, for it is a tragedy, this grotesque first sight into the heart of a really noble temple.

The interior of the Lincoln Memorial is an ob-long hall divided into three parts by two transverse colonnades. The middle hall is a little larger than the others. At its west wall is the statue of Lincoln; at its east side are the three great openings forming the only entrance to the Memorial. The interior walls and the transverse colonnades are of gray stone. The floor is of neutral pink marble, the ceiling of bronze beams and translucent marble slabs. The statue's broad pedestal of gray-pink marble stands about twice a man's height. The seated figure, in white or grayish marble, rises another fifteen feet or more.

The central room might be called the statue hall, and the flanking rooms the inscription halls, for the walls opposite the transverse colonnades, the north and south walls of the Memorial, carry long inscriptions. One is the Second Inaugural, in three great

FIGURE 94. The statue of Abraham Lincoln by the American sculptor Daniel Chester French.

panels; the other is the Gettysburg Address, in a single panel. Above each of the speeches is a subdued and broadly composed mural painting.

This all sounds very reasonable—a statue to give you the man, the speeches to give you his work, each separately enshrined. It is a studied, symbolic scheme. But the Memorial, one supposes, was built for people to visit and enjoy visiting, and so that symbolic scheme was intended to unfold itself movingly to every visitor. For myself, I feel that these intentions have not been realized, that the interior of the Memorial is neither a fine creation of form nor a clearly expressive vehicle for the memorial symbolism that is the fundamental purpose of the building.

It was only after coming into the statue hall that I felt the great size of the room and of the Lincoln. But still I could not easily read the statue or feel the disposition of masses and the relative position of planes and projections, the things that are the materials of sculptural design. The principal source of light was back of me. I thus lost all but the fringes of shadow, and I lost also the concentration of light which you get when you have a tangential view of an illuminated surface.

The remedy plainly was to find a sidewise view of the statue. The two flanking halls seem intended expressly to create viewpoints from which the statue can be seen at an angle, framed by the columns of the interior colonnades. If I had been alone in the building, I should have gone into one room and then the other, trying out views of the Lincoln at various angles and distances. But I was not alone, for a sightseeing busload of people had come in.

They looked at Lincoln when they entered the hall, but he did not hold them long. In that unfavorable light the statue could not compete with the attraction of the dark rooms behind the colonnades. Before they had been in the hall twenty seconds, most of the crowd had turned and discovered one of the inscriptions. And the moment they saw it, they moved toward the columns and took their stance where they could see the first panel. I could sense the relief with which they turned away from the statue, not very expressive at best and quite meaningless to them, and began to read the familiar words of the inscriptions. Few of them walked out into the inscription halls. The lettering runs so high on the wall that it cannot be read comfortably from nearer than the colonnades. Many people read it from well out in the central hall. The result is that half a minute after a group of people enter the Memorial, they are all standing with their backs or shoulders toward Lincoln—which is as if at the king's coronation everyone ran to the windows to watch the fire engines go by.

So I waited until the crowd reading the Gettysburg speech had thinned out before I ventured into the southern inscription hall in search of better views of the statue. One or two bold spirits followed. I felt that if there were a seat along the base of the wall, or even a few wooden curia chairs scattered through the inscription halls and faced toward the Lincoln, the stiff ritual of the speech reading could have been broken up.

A more radical remedy would be to remove the long inscriptions. There is no good reason for mixing up architecture with literature. The Gettysburg speech is beautifully phrased, but that does not make it architecture. People read it and get their heads all muddled up with recollections of school readers and Decoration Day blaze-of-glories. The

realities of architecture and sculpture mean nothing to senses floating away on the dear, familiar clouds of sentimental memory.

But the inscriptions are not the fundamental difficulty. It is plain that the interior plan was controlled by the most important function of the building, its place at the west end of the Mall. That function required that the broad side of the building face toward the Washington Monument, that the approach and entrance be from that side, and that the statue be on the axis of the Mall. The unclassical side entrance killed the interior, because you can't get a true impression of an oblong space if you have to turn one way and then the other to see it. As an attempt to dodge this difficulty, a hall of longitudinal proportion for the statue was created by the device of the transverse colonnades. Result: the statue stands in a hall fifty by eighty instead of in one that is eighty by a hundred and fifty. And people still look to right and left rather than at the statue. The interior of the Memorial, all three rooms together, has almost exactly the dimensions of the interior of the new Bowery Bank in New York. For effective spaciousness there is no comparison between them.

These faults in the placing and lighting of the statue are intensified by the choice of the material from which it is carved. It is obviously the kernel of the Memorial, the generating idea that built the vast temple. It cannot function simply through our intellectual perception that it is a likeness of Lincoln. Its form and material must give it the power to speak, though we furnish words. Materials vary in the strength of their emotional spark. I think of this sometimes as a difference of internal tension. The heart of a design must be the place of greatest tension, the fullest of life. When we open a casket of brass, we do not expect to find objects of brass, but gold and precious stones.

The statue of Athena in the Parthenon was of gold and ivory. Why not make the statue of Lincoln of pure, solid gold? That would be a jewel precious enough to justify that magnificent casket—and it would give the pastoral pilgrim a real emotion, a thing he needs much more than he needs a demonstration of aesthetic chastity. Whether the statue was a work of art or not, it would be sensuously lovely, for gold is a gorgeously beautiful material. Of course, it couldn't be done, because in our corrupt symbolism gold means filthy lucre. We are so afraid of idols that we dare not make anything beautiful enough to worship. And to soothe our consciences we call gold barbaric.

A gold statue would be clearly distinguished in color and feeling from the stone around it. To some extent the same thing could be done by covering with gold leaf the panel back of the statue. Indeed, there is something to be said for covering most of the interior of the building with dark gold. Gold leaf does not excite our cupidity as does solid gold. Beside being in welcome contrast with the statue, the gold would more strongly distinguish the interior of the building from the exterior. And the right feeling, on entering a temple, is that one is entering a sacred treasury. When one thinks of the interior of St. Mark's at Venice, one rebels against the deadly poverty to which our asceticism compels us.

We Americans are very loath to answer the sensory appeal of architecture. We will say of a building that it is honest, homelike, or convenient, that it expresses its use or construction, that it is a pure example of that charming colonial style, or that it's the highest building west of New York. We do not say that its façade is like a dance of fairies or gnomes, that it lifts us flying into the air, or that it seems a sacrilege to let any but beautiful and beautifully clothed men and women enter it. We dislike the sort of feeling these attempts at statement suggest. Ideas are so much safer than feelings and are more convenient to talk and print. Print and pictures have hurt architecture by giving us too great wealth and weight of precedent, but even more by facilitating the substitution of the mental attitude for specific sensory responses. The tactile and equilibratory sensations, so fundamental to the perception of architecture, do not respond to pictures. The superficies of a style can be photographed, but plastic arrangements of solids and space cannot be represented to our feelings any more than a picture will serve a frightened child in place of its mother's arms. One of the little tragedies of our civilization is the hundreds of architects who live between their files and their drafting boards and find it no conscious loss that they have never in their own bodies felt the coherence of a column, the tension of an arch, or the squadron sweep of a château and formal garden.

The interior of the Lincoln Memorial is like a play written by a preacher. It was shaped by ideas, but its essential dramatic symbolism has not been fused with its architectural form. It is a series of speeches rather than a beautiful dance that has the power to draw crowds of men into its overpowering rhythm.

10

The Jefferson Memorial and Blocked Vistas

The Memorial to Jefferson is often defended by citing authorities. They tell you Mr. Pope* can't be wrong because he is famous. They point out that the proposed memorial accords with the McMillan Commission plan, which in turn has the solid backing of the Commission of Fine Arts. Finally, they utter the magic name of L'Enfant.

As for Mr. Pope, he would never have become famous if he took a skeptical attitude toward three-million-dollar memorials. It is a safe assumption that he was retained by the committee to plan a temple to be located at a designated point and that he did what he was employed to do.

A few years ago, on an order from the Theodore Roosevelt memorial group, Mr. Pope designed, for the Tidal Basin site, a round pool, two curved col-

* John Russell Pope.

onnades, and an enormous spout of water. It is probable that then, as now, he left the details of appropriateness and even of civic art to the cultivated gentlemen who were paying the bill.

Certainly, concerning the relation of buildings to the city plan, Mr. Pope's name is not a sure cachet of superior quality. The Archives Building blocks the vista along the median cross axis (halfway between the Capitol and the White House) by which L'Enfant tied his Mall avenue into the city plan. As for the Scottish Rite temple, its placement is the most banal in Washington. It stands at a street corner like a filling station, and its steps encroach upon the breadth of the avenue with which L'Enfant did honor to his "President's Palace."

In the Archives Building vandalism Mr. Pope was betrayed by the McMillan Commission, the

FIGURE 95. View of the Jefferson Memorial.

principal guide and comforter of the pro-temple Jeffersonians. The sacrosanct Commission of 1901 bowed down and worshiped L'Enfant—then quietly cut his coattails off. They destroyed L'Enfant's cross axis, Eighth Street, one of the most beautifully developed street plans ever made. They devised Constitution Avenue smashing across Pennsylvania Avenue, and doing its best to outshine the Mall.

If anyone thinks he has a good idea, I advise him not to say that the McMillan Commission favored it. Nor are supporters wise in mentioning L'Enfant and his plan. In that plan the terminal point falls well out in the Potomac. Neither in this nor in the other avenues running south from the Mall did he make any effort to terminate a vista with a large building. He knew that the principal façade of a large monument must not face north. And it was absolutely not a principle of French formal planning to terminate every vista with a solid object.

You will remember that Spengler discusses the "vista into space" as the ultimate value of Renaissance art. Unquestionably, L'Enfant left his west and south axes open purposely, not accidentally. It is as idiotic to talk about the Jefferson temple "completing" the L'Enfant plan as it would be to say that Versailles is not complete because there is no palace at the west end of the canal.

Finally, we are told not to worry—the Commission of Fine Arts will never let a mistake be made. When people tell me that, I invite them to go for a walk. If Mr. Pope's production department should draw a Corinthian column with an Ionic base or submit a bas-relief that projects one millimeter beyond the legal limit, the members of the commission will be there with their microscopes to defend the interest of the nation. When they put their OK on a tub of butter, you can be sure it's the very best butter. But it will still be butter.

II

The Golden Horses and Civic Art

The title of this essay refers to the four sculptured groups set up in 1951 near the Lincoln Memorial in Washington. I shall also discuss the Arlington Memorial Bridge and, in general, the meeting of the Mall with the Potomac River—the Mall being the great creation of civic art that stretches from the Capitol to the Potomac. First I want to consider what kind of art it is that works with golden horses.

Naïvely defined, civic art is community action to make the cities more agreeable places to be out-doors in. It is a drama in which structures and open spaces are both stage and theater, the people are both actors and audience.

I once studied the people who came to visit the Lincoln Memorial, noting how they approached the entrance, the expressions on their faces, where they stood, what interested them. This was part of civic art, a drama played unconsciously.

For full participation in this drama the audience-actors need guideposts, measuring points, indicators of level and vertical direction and relative size. For novelty and variety of tactile perception they want to see objects having characteristic mass and material unlike the feel of ordinary buildings. These functions are traditionally fulfilled by vegetation, water, simple stone structures, and sculpture.

Sculpture has lived its life in civic art. It is the ideal medium for commemorating civic and national heroes, for symbolizing patriotic emotions. Of its forms, the equestrian statue is the most forcefully monumental. A man plus a horse is more noble than a man alone. And the horse has the attribute of giving to this partnership a heightened effect of movement along a specific line. This quality is best (though lightly) explained by a simplified description: A horse's sides are relatively neutral compared to its ends, and its ends are so strongly differentiated that the horse is effectively directional. It seems to be headed somewhere.

Strongly expressed movement and positive frontality make equestrian sculptures very touchy factors in civic design—one must be sure they are set in the right place and headed in the right direction.

Take, for example, our four golden horses. They stand in two pairs, five hundred feet west of the Lincoln Memorial, toward which they look. (Let me make it clear that this is the rear of the Memorial, which has no opening in it.) One pair flanks the east end of the Arlington Memorial Bridge; the other pair guards the entrance—from the circular drive around the Memorial—to the Rock Creek Drive, which from this point curves north along the Potomac. The sculpture is more than twice life size; the groups—for human figures accompany the horses—stand on granite pedestals about twenty feet high.

Figs. 96–98

Figs. 99–100

The models were made by the sculptors Leo Friedlander and James Earle Fraser, in the late 1920's, for execution in granite. Carving was delayed, however, and at the end of World War II the Italian government, as an act of friendship, made bronze castings from the plaster models and gilded them. This change in materials—violating a primary principle of design—accounts for the very compact grouping of the figures and their ponderous membering. They have no such vibrant silhouettes as Ivan Meštrović gave his Indians and horses in Chicago.

The two teams of horses are linked by a great arc

FIGURE 96. Looking northeastward toward the Lincoln Memorial and the pair of equestrian sculptures flanking the east end of Memorial Bridge.

FIGURE 99. Looking southeastward at the Lincoln Memorial and the pair of sculptures at the entrance to Rock Creek Park.

FIGURE 97. Close-up of the two sculptures. On the left is *Sacrifice*, on the right *Valor*. Both are from the designs of Leo Friedlander.

FIGURE 98. The equestrian pair seen from the Lincoln Memorial, looking southwestward.

FIGURE 100. Close-up of the two sculptures. On the left is *Music and Harvest*, on the right *Aspiration and Literature*. Both are from designs of James L. Fraser.

FIGURE 101. The pair of sculptures seen from the Lincoln Memorial, looking northwestward.

of granite steps leading to the river and known as the Watergate. Although the teams are placed symmetrically and although each team is closely matched, the two pairs are quite unlike. Friedlander's horses, standing at the entrance to the bridge, are ordinary earthbound steeds, quite smoothly modeled. Fraser's pair are descendants of Pegasus, almost immersed in feathery wings; the handling of surfaces is more broken, more reminiscent of the wet clay. Because of the different modeling and because the gilding of this group is Roman gold and the other more yellow, they are weathering quite differently. I must add that even the romantic names—War, Music, and so on—given to the groups by the sculptors, to the great delight of the professional guides, do nothing to unify the two teams.

This disparity, I think, exceeds the limits of individuality customary in balanced sculpture. One could pass over the difference in color and surface. But an earth horse and a sky horse make such different pulls on one's muscular system and on one's imagination!

Let me move on now from the horses as sculpture to the role they play in the design of our study area —from the Lincoln Memorial to the Potomac. This part of the Mall plan has a considerable history. The Commission of 1901, which inaugurated the modern monumental development of Washington, made the fundamental decision—that the proposed bridge should lie on a radial from the Memorial, not on the Mall axis. This was sound; the diagonal location gives you picturesque views of the Capitol, Washington Monument, and Lincoln Memorial— views in which their relative positions and sizes can be perceived. If, as some architects proposed, the bridge had been built as a direct extension of the Mall axis, a person approaching from the west could see only the blind side of the Memorial with the Monument looming above it.

The Commission made no detailed plan for our area. It is responsible, however, for the great practical fault of placing the Memorial inside, instead of outside and to the east of, the traffic circle. It also committed the solecism of "balancing" the entrance to the curving Rock Creek Drive with the entrance to the Arlington Memorial Bridge.

The details of the present arrangement derive mainly from the plans made, around 1924, for the bridge and for the land at each end of it. The bridge itself is an impressively beautiful structure, worthy of the Potomac. Certain features of the bridgeheads, however, are questionable. Before we consider them, please allow me a few sentimental words about bridges and rivers.

A bridge and a river make together a very poignant human experience, in which the approaches to the bridge play a good part. It has been traditionally the duty of the pontifex to mark well that dramatic moment when we leave the land to begin our crossing of the water and equally the moment when we arrive safely at the other side. Identical sculpture, towers, even arches, have been used to emphasize this experience of coming to the bridge and crossing it—and to strengthen the construction.

Let us also note the aesthetic rights of rivers, those close friends of cities. We should respect their continuity, and not meddle needlessly with the lines of their banks. Rivers prefer also that bridges be laid squarely across the stream, be at about the same level, not too close together, and of similar construction. To these criteria we should at least aspire.

Let us return now to the Arlington Memorial Bridge. Its designers did not follow the custom of building identical pylons at each end. At the east bank they provided places for two equestrian statues. At the west end they built two thirty-five foot pylons surmounted by eight-foot granite eagles. Well, it is quite a long bridge, and in the fauna of symbolism a brace of eagles and a span of horses are not too remotely related. But there are two pairs of equestrian statues—as you already know—and two pairs of tall pylons. The point is that a pair—one pair—of heavy pylons, at a bridgehead, has practical and dramatic significance to an approaching traveler. It tells him that at the point so importantly marked he can cross the river by a well-built and handsome bridge. But who will be impressed by what the bridge pylons say if two other pylons, at some distance away, say the same thing? Briefly, the planners created an axis parallel to the river, whereas the most exciting event taking place is the bridge across the river.

At the east bank our golden horses are caught in another confusion of axes. There are three radiating lines—the axis of the bridge horses (which is the axis of the bridge), the Watergate axis (the Mall axis extended), and the axis of the Rock Creek Drive horses (which is the axis of a few feet of the Drive).

A symmetrical threesome of radiating vistas is a *patte-d'oie;* the classical example is a fine group of three streets in Rome. But this poor goose's foot at the Lincoln Memorial is sadly maimed. Its middle toe is largely theoretical, and the northerly one is curvilinear, an awkward quality in a vista.

So we have a trumped-up axis endowing the Rock Creek Drive with a pair of horses although it is only one of five streets that come into the traffic circle surrounding the Memorial. The horses that mark it really mark nothing but themselves—they alone constitute the axis. The pair that "balance" marks a granite arched bridge around two thousand feet long. One is a travesty on the other.

A few moments ago I said that the planners of our study area were hypnotized by an imaginary axis. They were also influenced by the idea that the Memorial should be surrounded wherever possible by circular lines struck from the center of the building. A rectangle within a circle is one of the least pleasing geometric patterns; it is kept in use, probably, by some feeling that there is virtue in contrasting forms. Hence, we have the vast steps of the Watergate bulging outward against the Potomac. A concave front toward the water would be more courteous to the river and to the anticipated boatmen. The concave form would improve most ground views of the steps and would suit much better their present use for summer concerts.

This story of the golden horses and their very axial pasture by the river's bank should prove, I think, that simplicity, sincerity, and a broad view are as necessary in civic art as in other affairs of life. So much contriving was done to relate, as the phrase is, the Lincoln Memorial to the Potomac River—which the Memorial needs about as much as Bear Mountain needs an axial relation to the Hudson.

Therefore, you are, no doubt, asking what I'd have done differently. If there must be four equestrian statues, my formula would be: At each end of the bridge there would be two horses, facing each other, the pedestals being perpendicular to the balustrades. This would afford patrons of the bridge lateral (instead of dorsal) views of the horses and would give the bridge stronger ties with the banks. The Rock Creek Drive would be brought into the area informally, without hint of axiality. To supplant the Watergate, there would be a wall following the river bank.

If you seek a cause for the things that have been done less than perfectly, I ascribe it to excessive dependence on an accepted style and, in general, the practice—too characteristic of our culture—of following accepted ideas rather than observed conditions. Our friends who made an axis where none was needed had certain rules in their minds and followed them to the bitter end. Yet this does not mean that the style they followed is without value. Symmetry is often a useful simplification, and perspectives are based on our way of seeing. In terms of human feeling, the difference between formal and informal is largely a matter of detail.

The contemporary manner of architecture—a fundamentally sound one, as most of us will agree —seeks, I believe, to keep clear of both classic and romantic dogmas. Thus purified, it is entering the field of civic art. Will it find a place for golden horses? Probably not, if they are romantically symbolical; probably it will, if George Washington is in the saddle. In any case, I hope that the civic art of the future will not neglect the people's need for emotions and for stimulating optical experiences, that its planners will not be too deeply indoctrinated in any style, and that their plans will come from the site as well as from the things people do and feel.

The case we have studied certainly revealed a few mistakes, but we examined only a small and difficult corner of civic art in the capital. Taken all together, the Mall is glorious. So are the Lincoln Memorial and the Arlington Memorial Bridge. If you haven't done so, you should experience the crowds that come from all over the world to see these things. Last Saturday morning I took some friends to the Lincoln Memorial; the place was like Times Square. These crowds are not necessarily evidence of high quality in the designing, but I believe that they do prove that civic art is worth studying —and worth doing.

Part IV

*Other Times, Other Plans,
and Other Planners*

12

Plans for Rebuilding London in 1666

Because John Evelyn's plans for the rebuilding of London after the Great Fire are relatively little known, I shall consider them first, before the more important work of Wren; after these, two minor figures are to be noted.

Briefly, Evelyn was a wealthy gentleman of character and intelligence, member of the Royal Society, writer on forest trees and architecture. He had a talent for drawing, was interested in the arts, visited the finest buildings and gardens of Holland, Belgium, France, and Italy. At Paris, his diary tells us, he admired the Tuileries Gardens, the Luxembourg, the Cours-la-Reine, the botanical garden, and the neighboring estates of St.-Germain, St.-Cloud, Rueil, and Fontainebleau. This was in 1644, but he went frequently to France and must have followed the development of garden art and Le Nôtre's glorification of the old garden motifs. Evelyn visited also the new town of Richelieu. In Genoa he marveled at the smooth-paved Strada Nuova and in Florence was charmed by the Boboli gardens. At Leghorn he wrote: "The piazza is very fair and commodious, and, with the church . . . gave the first hint to the building of the church and piazza in Covent Garden with us, though very imperfectly pursued." At Rome Evelyn stopped seven months. He was impressed by the straight streets of the eastern part of the city, an enthusiasm that lasted long. "We had the entire view of the Via Pia down to the two horses before the Monte Cavallo, one of the most glorious sights for state and magnificence that any city can show a traveller. . . . Thence to the Via Felix, a straight and noble street, . . . till we came to the four fountains of Lepidus, built at the

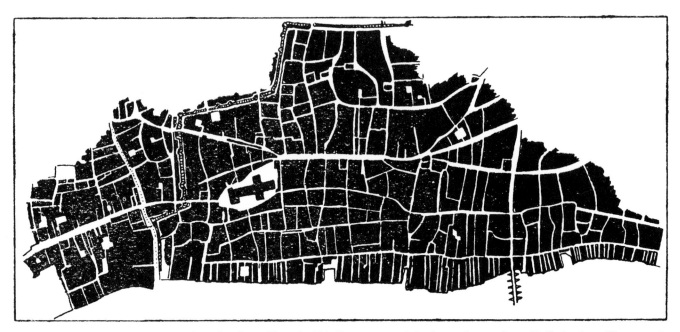

FIGURE 102. Plan of London before the Great Fire of 1666. Street map of the burned area, from Hollar's plan. The central part of the old city had an approximately rectangular layout, a fact which influenced all the plans for rebuilding the city.

abutments of four stately ways. . . ." He saw the great gardens—Borghese, d'Este, Aldobrandini, Caprarola. Apparently he did not visit Turin and thus never saw a large chessboard town.

After the Restoration, Evelyn became an unofficial adviser and aide to the King, serving on many commissions. He published a pamphlet, "Fumifugium"; in it the London smoke problem was "dissolved." Of particular interest to town planners is this entry in his diary:

14 May, 1662. To London [he lived south of the Thames, near Deptford], being chosen one of the Commissioners for reforming the buildings, ways, streets, and incumbrances, and regulating the hackney coaches in the city of London, taking my oath before my Lord Chancellor, and then went to his Majesty's Surveyor's office in Scotland Yard, about naming and establishing officers, adjourning till the 16th, when I went to view how St. Martin's lane might be made more passable *Fig. 102* into the Strand. There were divers gentlemen of quality on this commission.

Evelyn pursued his many interests, writing, collecting books and prints, publishing a history of engraving, helping a friend to "contrive his garden after the modern," noting (June 9, 1662) that the park at Hampton Court was "now planted with *Fig. 103* sweet rows of lime trees," and setting trees at Sayes Court "the same year that the elms were planted in

Greenwich Park." In 1684 (Diary, June 12) he advised regarding the location of streets in the vicinity of Berkeley Square.

Evelyn's first plan, presented to the King just after the Fire, attained a high degree of schematic regularity. In the Fleet area an eight-rayed star is developed; east of St. Paul's is a kite-shaped layout. The larger of the two triangles forming the kite has twice the altitude of the smaller. The flanking streets of the St. Paul *patte-d'oie* thus diverge 22½ degrees from the axis, while the diagonals from St. Dunstan's diverge 45 degrees. Tied in with these triangles are several rectangularly disposed streets. The minor subdividing streets are not shown. Most of the intersections of the diagonals with the ordinate streets are fitted up with plazas, round or square, two or three hundred feet across. At the intersection of the axes is a square of 400 feet.

Fig. 104

Seeking antecedents, I am inclined to ascribe the western spiderweb passage to an ideal town plan in Speckle's *Architektura von Festungen,* Strasbourg, 1608,

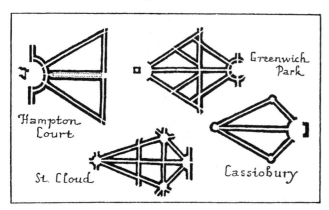

though Evelyn has much simplified the pattern. In his study for this plan—see the Society of Antiquaries engraving—he tried out the idea of stopping two of his radials at two buildings facing each other across the plaza. In Speckle's plan four intermediate radials are similarly stopped. The dominant feature of the plan, the kite-shaped figure, had better be ascribed to the general spirit of French park and town planning. Certain lines, indeed, from the Petit Parc at Versailles, where walks forming a diamond are tied into a frame of rectangles, might have furnished the immediate suggestion. One place where the Petit Parc could hardly help Evelyn was the cutting of a right-angled street intersection by a diagonal, and in the study sketch there is fumbling at such points. Memories of Rome may have influenced the radials from St. Paul's, the angle being a trifle less than that of the Campo Marzo streets, instead of spreading to 30 degrees as in the Versailles entrance drives and at Hampton Court. But the kite shape was almost a stereotype in France and was not unknown in England. This first plan of Evelyn's is full of buildings in pairs, facing each other. He may have remembered the balanced palaces of the Strada Nuova, the effect of which is

Fig. 105
top

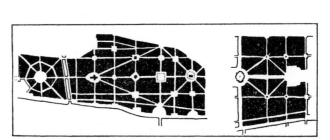

FIGURE 104. Evelyn's first plan, in its finished form, and part of the Petit Parc at Versailles, omitting minor walks and features; from Sylvestre's engraving, published about 1662.

FIGURE 103. Diagrams of park plans, none of them accurate, that of Greenwich being a hazarded reconstruction. All, except possibly St. Cloud, antedate Evelyn's plan.

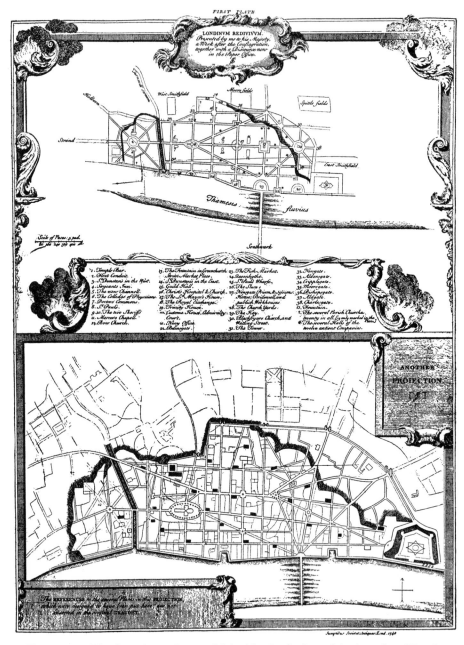

FIGURE 105. The first of two plates published by the Society of Antiquaries of London, dated 1748, showing John Evelyn's first and second studies for rebuilding London in 1666. The upper plan was inspired by the plans of the parks at Hampton Court and Greenwich.

FIGURE 106. The second of two plates published by the Society of Antiquaries of London, dated 1748, showing John Evelyn's third plan for rebuilding London in 1666 and Wren's plan.

so fine that oppositeness has become a sort of folk art motif in modern Genoa. The other type of twin location, with parallel axes, as exemplified in the churches facing the Piazza del Popolo, is also found in the plan. Only one of those churches—begun in 1662—then existed, but Carlo Rainaldi's balanced scheme was doubtless well known. Covent Garden, also, and St. James's Square, had taught Londoners the beauty of a street mouth marked by symmetrical buildings.

This elegant geometrical plan was defeated, along with its rivals, by the intolerable difficulty of executing a wholly new layout. In particular it was objected that the churches ought not to be moved. Evelyn threw aside his first scheme and drew a second project regularizing not the whole city but each important street, separately. He straightened Cheapside, extended it to Cornhill, and gave it a little plaza at its intersection with an extended, widened, and straightened Bow Lane. He gathered up Watling Street, Cannon Street, Great Eastcheap, and Tower Street and made a straight thoroughfare from St. Paul's to the Tower. Only to distribute the bridge traffic does he find new streets necessary. A strong executive body, one must feel, could have done much with this approach to the problem, for this technique would have preserved the economic membering of the city, the quality and repute— even the local names—of each neighborhood.

In a third study Evelyn gave himself greater freedom. Over an approximately rectangular plan developed from the old street layout he drew diagonals connecting the traffic centers of the city. It is a rough draft, crying for restudy. Several bridges across Fleet Ditch are omitted, one being essential to the most interesting provision of this sketch, the

Fig. 105 bottom

Fig. 106 top

continuation of the Thames quay along the river, presumably to Westminster. A street from Blackfriars to St. Paul's and through the city anticipates the modern tributary of the Embankment, Queen Victoria Street. The ground given to plazas is drastically cut. An oval 450 by 800 feet for St. Paul's, five small circuses, and a square of 250 feet in front of St. Mary Woolnoth—precisely at the present hub of the city—are all that survive of the dozen open places of his first plan. It is on the whole a utilitarian conception. Eight or ten streets, however, command vistas of St. Paul's, and the new Cheapside is impressive. Physicians' College stands just within the gate at its west end, a busy circus is at the midpoint of its half-mile length, and a large square and a church mark its east end.

We all know Sir Christopher Wren, famous architect of a cathedral and fifty churches, builder for five sovereigns, living ninety-one years, interred in St. Paul's—but what precisely was Wren when he made the only design by which we can judge him as a town planner? He was a highly gifted and well-connected young man of thirty-four, esteemed as a mathematician and astronomer, noticed and favored by the King, assistant in His Majesty's Office of Works. He had built a chapel in Cambridge in 1663, had designed a university theater, and was studying the repairs necessary in old St. Paul's. His only foreign travel had been a stay of seven months in Paris in 1665, when he met Bernini and Mansart. The principal books on architecture were, of course, known to him, as were the great buildings of Europe through prints and drawings. When a talented young architect with this kind of background makes a first city plan, we may expect it to reflect his peculiar genius, but we can count on it also to contain evidence of the teachers from whom he has learned.

Fig. 106 bottom

Wren's plan needs no description. It comprises two types of street pattern, suggesting that its designer had looked in upon two schools of planning. The middle section, a plastic gridiron, is developed from the old plan of this part of London, modified in the light of the Campo Marzo in Rome. The region of

Fig. 107 top

St. Peter's also may have influenced Wren's thought. It would be impossible, certainly, for an architect of the time to study the plan and setting of a large church without thinking of St. Peter's. And the set-

Fig. 107 center

ting of St. Paul's, in Wren's plan, has some likeness —in the lines spreading to embrace the church—to the setting of the great progenitor of all Renaissance domed churches. True, Bernini quite certainly did not intend to clear the buildings between the lanes which converge toward the Tiber, but such a clearing suggests itself the moment an architect looks at the plan—the convergence of the *piazza retta* and the convergence of the *borghi* form too conspicuous a coincidence to be ignored. At least, surely, Wren found in Bernini's parvis plaza the assurance that convergence of the sides of a forecourt may be an

Fig. 107 bottom

aesthetic asset. The sides of the Piazza del Popolo, also, in his time, formed a wedge shape like Wren's plaza. In each case a city gate stood at the narrow end of the wedge. Wren, of course, showed a single dome where there were two in the Roman plan, but he strengthened his hold on the receding streets by introducing a pair of flanking churches. The resem-

Fig. 108

blance of the Campo Marzo street layout to the central section of Wren's plan is clear.

Wren's design is studded with churches terminating street vistas. This is too primary a motif to imply specific genesis, but one cannot help thinking again of the Campo Marzo, for the vista of Trinità de'

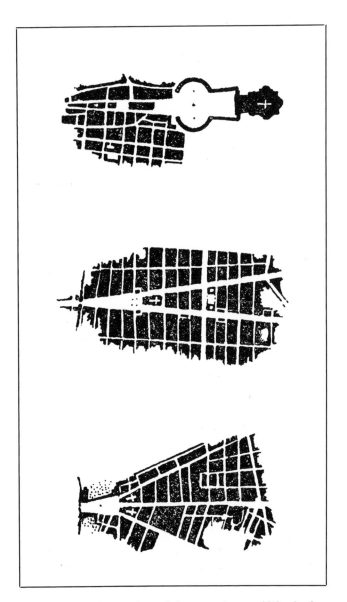

FIGURE 107. Comparison of the central part of Wren's plan with the approach to St. Peter's and the Rione Campo Marzo, Rome.

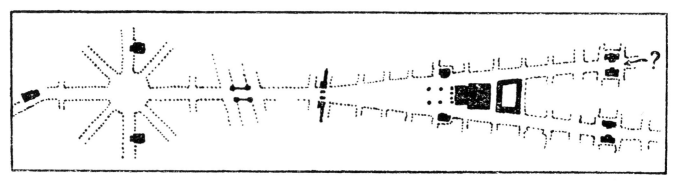

FIGURE 108. Wren's St. Paul group. The pair of churches marked with an interrogation point appear in Gwynn's engraving of the plan, not in the original.

Monti from the Via Condotti must have been, even without the Spanish Steps, one of the finest street views in the world. In London there was the short piece of Russell Street, with St. Paul's Covent Garden on axis, but in all Paris there was hardly what an American surveyor would call a straight street. The formally terminated vista was known in both countries chiefly as a garden feature. But every town was rich in picturesque street vistas. In London the view of St. Dunstan's in the West from the curving Fleet must have been fine, and St. Michael's was strikingly set at the end of Cheapside. Sharp bifurcations, such as those Wren used, were of course common, and a church often stood at the point of the included block.

In its eastern part the tempo of the plan quickens —the reposeful rectangularity of the cathedral region gives way to a dynamic bustle of radials and tangents. This was a difficult part because there was no precedent in town planning to help Wren manage the awkward areas produced by intersecting radials. Arachne modestly spun from a single center, and the military architects who, for two

hundred years, had been making radial plans had all followed her example. In French hunting forests, to be sure, there were groups of stars, but the shapes created thereby were of little moment. Speckle, I think, was Wren's immediate teacher in radial planning. He also helped in the arrangement of the commercial group, though Wren, as always, chose and rejected to suit his needs. Speckle's octagonal plaza becomes two lunettes with the square Exchange between them.

Fig. 109

The best evidence that Wren learned something from the *maestri delle strade* who shaped the Rione Campo Marzo is that Wren grasped the golden aesthetic value of the Piazza del Popolo—the emotional power of those long balanced vistas deep into the crowded city. That spatial pathos has given an unforgettable moment to every sensitive Roman pilgrim. Wren must have heard many descriptions of this unique work of art and of the twin churches with which Rainaldi planned to give it still greater plastic tension. So anxious was Wren to secure this contrast of advancing masonry against receding space that he risked the unfavorable ground levels

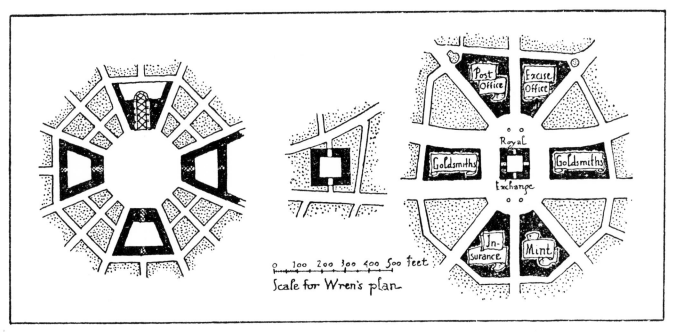

FIGURE 109. Wren's commercial center and the central part of Speckle's radial town plan, with a sketch showing the old location of the Exchange, from Hollar's plan.

and all but reduced St. Paul's to the size of a parish church in order to do it. His genius told him that he must keep the two rays quite close together if they were to count as a unity. For this and other reasons he kept the angle down to 12 degrees, as against $23\frac{1}{2}$ at Rome. This gave him a cramped site, but there may be no aesthetic objection to setting the cathedral back to a wider plot, although that would involve the regrading of Ludgate Hill.

The flanking churches were, doubtless, intended by Wren to increase the size of his composition, to tie the street vistas into it, and to anchor St. Paul's firmly in its place at the top of the hill. In a sense— if we may presume that steepled churches were intended—Wren dismembered the St. Paul's he was

actually to build and set his two towers 300 feet apart, with streets passing between them and the façade of the cathedral. A minor contribution to this unique conception may have come from Inigo Jones's Covent Garden triptych, where the church is flanked by balanced buildings separated from it by some 60 feet. Wren gives his cathedral still another pair of outriders, two churches equidistant from the Fleet plaza. These steeples would have played an interesting part in the views from St. Paul's, and their relation to the cathedral might have been apparent in distant views of the group. Behind St. Paul's, on his street toward Tower Hill, Wren shows a pair of churches, and Gwynn's engraving adds another pair at the corresponding point on the northern branch.* If these are called canonical and if St. Dunstan's are counted in—Wren shows it exactly on the axis of the Fleet—then we have a cathedral, nine churches, a bridge, a triumphal arch, and sundry monuments, joined in a single grand architectural organism. Further, the streets connecting these accents were to be lined with uniform façades. The inferior size of the St. Paul site in Wren's plan, certainly, does not prove that he saw things *in petto*.

West of Fleet Ditch, Wren joins Evelyn in using an eight-rayed star. But the differences between the two stars show Wren's professional hand. He bends the circumferential street between the rays, not at them, and the rays themselves are divided into two groups. The principal cross street is attained by violently displacing Hatton Street, but possibly Wren's map was at fault. He connects the Temple Gardens with Smithfield, as Evelyn does in two studies. Is there a special reason, or was it done to give a vista of the trees?†

Few other works of Wren can be classed as town planning. The speculative association of his name with Williamsburg, Virginia, is hardly justified by the quality of the plan.‡ He designed a plaza to surround St. Paul's and proposed a portico 2,000 feet long, overlooking the Thames, to connect Whitehall and Westminster. His church steeples were definitely thought of as civic ornaments, and few cities ever owed as much of their beauty to one man as London owed to Wren at the time of his death.

After the Fire, several maps showing the extent of it were printed. Two Dutch engravings, by Door- *Fig. 110* nick of Vygendam, and Craalinge of Amsterdam, contained identical little chessboard plans titled "Nieuw modell om de afgebrande Stadt London te herbouwen." Tradition ascribes this plan to Robert Hooke, the physicist and mathematician. At least one good authority has questioned this ascription, but I am loath to give it up. Hooke, an unkempt, petulant Merlin, had a genius for ingenuity. He moved nervously from one phase of nature to another, making surprising discoveries, sketching inspired theories, producing profound simplifications both intellectual and mechanical. He was lecturer in astronomy at Gresham College, London, and in some ways paralleled Wren's early career. Practicing on occasion as architect and surveyor, he designed several buildings and was employed after the fire to locate property lines.§ It is known that Hooke "constructed a model" for the rebuilding, and it appears to me quite probable that this gridiron of the Dutch engravings is a version of his plan. It is based on an incorrect map of the site, but the integration with the surrounding features is studied with more ra-

---

* It is not with entire confidence that I follow Gwynn in his wishful thinking. The twin churches on the street toward Tower Hill fall precisely on the rise of ground where Queen Victoria Street now crosses Cannon Street. It is not impossible that Wren set the churches here to afford a sort of optical compensation for the lower level of this street—about 10 feet lower here than the north branch—as well as to obscure the bump in the longitudinal profile at this point.

† Wren used an incorrect survey of the city, and it is not possible, in laying his plan upon an ordnance survey, to preserve all the elements of the design. W. G. Bell, in his book on the Fire, finds it necessary to give up the axial position of St. Dunstan's—the new line of Fleet Street lying north of the church—and he does not bring the new Exchange into coincidence with the old one, as Wren intended. If St. Dunstan's and old Ludgate are taken as fixed points, the new Fleet aligns with the street to the Exchange instead of with the axis of St. Paul's.

‡ See *Town Planning Review*, July 1928, p. 40.

§ For an account of Hooke, as architect, see E. B. Chancellor's *Lives of the British Architects from William of Wykeham to William Chambers* (New York: Charles Scribner's, 1909).

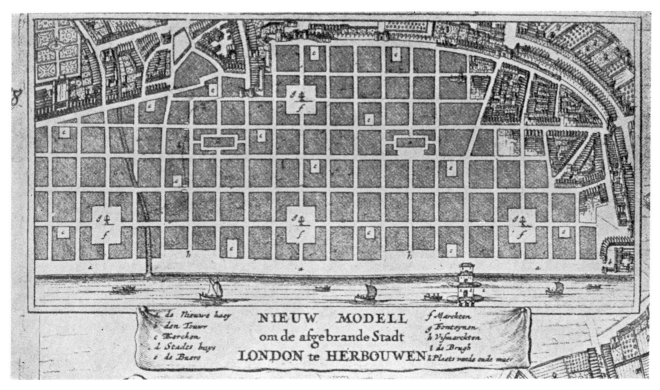

FIGURE 110. Plans traditionally ascribed to Hooke. From *A View of the Fire* by Doornick.

tionality than one expects of a hack draftsman. The plan is not a uniform chessboard, as a man would be fairly sure to make it if he were merely filling out the corner of a drawing. The east-west streets, for example, are farther apart toward the river, probably to accommodate the larger market places near the quay. The churches lie on the east-west streets, as is predominantly the case in the Wren and Evelyn plans, many of the London churches being entered from the side instead of from the west end, the standard Continental practice. Surprisingly, there seems to be no St. Paul's, but that is an error so stupid as to be impossible, considering how conspicuously St. Paul's appears in the map and view of the Fire. A thoughtless designer would be more likely to overemphasize the cathedral than to omit it. I suspect that St. Paul's was intended to stand where the largest church is shown —it is precisely the size of the St. Paul's in Wren's plan—on the quay. The block it occupies stands 200

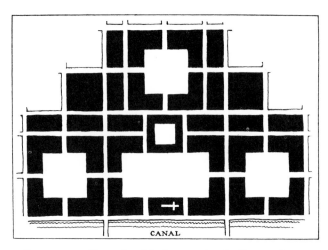

FIGURE 111. Part of an ideal town plan by Scamozzi.

Fig. 111

feet from the river, at the end of a stretch of 750 feet in which this broad quay is widened an additional 70 feet. Could there be a finer site for London's chief church? One thinks of the Salute, but Palladio's San Giorgio Maggiore is more like Hooke's arrangement, in plan. The design appears to owe its four plazas to the model town plan in Scamozzi's *Idea dell' Architettura Universale*, Venice, 1615.

This is precisely the sort of plan to expect from a geometrician of the time. Instead of being unworthy of Hooke's intelligence, the plan strikes me as a demonstration of it. It is said that the Aldermen preferred Hooke's plan to Wren's—isn't that almost conclusive proof that Hooke's was a chessboard? And their preference was not absurd. The thing London needed most was wider and longer streets. The absolute distances were not great, and the dis-

tance advantage of diagonals is commonly over-rated. The saving of Wren's plan over Hooke's in the distance from Ludgate to London Bridge is only 500 feet, about 12 per cent, a two-minute walk. From Cripplegate to the bridge the linear saving would be greater, if you cared to go through the heavy traffic around the Exchange. By anticipating the destruction of the London wall, Hooke avoids several "bottlenecks" at which traffic would lose more time than the diagonal streets would save. Besides being easy to plot and stake, Hooke's plan has the psychological advantage that all the streets appear to have the same importance. That would have rendered less difficult the allocation of building sites.

The aesthetic value of the plan—beyond the solid merit of all rectangular plans—lies in its broad quay and the four plazas, three of them 375 by 460 feet. These, if they existed today, would be the jewels of the City, its equivalent of the "squares of London" that give the metropolis its characteristic town planning flavor.

There are extant a few copies of a broadside issued about a week after the Fire by one Valentine Knight, a captain in His Majesty's service. Knight's approach was social and economic. He entered the replanning lists, not with a pretty pattern, but with a description of his conception, giving details as to the widths of the streets and the manner of building, a calculation of rental values and a financing scheme. (Do the historians of sociological town planning render him due honor? His was a first uncertain arrow, let fly before the enemy's range was known.) A crude engraving was added later, a naïve variation on the gridiron, with the longitudinal streets in long sweeping curves. These are twenty-

Fig. 112

four in number, two of them 60 feet wide, the rest 30. The twelve cross streets are 30 and 50 feet. In addition to these widths, all the streets have "piazzas," 5 or 10 feet wide.* Including the arcades, the average block is about 70 by 500 feet. Knight makes his houses two rooms deep, only 25 feet including the footway. He does not give the lot depth, but it figures about 30 feet, without the walk. The front rooms would look on a space of 30 feet clear, the rear rooms on 20 feet. Just half the acre would be built on. If one counts the covered walks, the public ways cover 40 per cent of the area. The houses, if they were 20 feet wide, would stand about forty to the gross acre. Knight obviously did not design a garden village, but it is doubtful if there was a more sanitary way to replace the 13,200 burned houses.† This plan is the only one of the group that would have done away with the old maze of dark alleys and passageways. Few of Wren's blocks are narrower than 150 feet; Hooke's are more than twice that.

* Knight endowed his London with some fifty miles of covered footways. Wren and Evelyn, and probably Hooke, each had in some degree the same intention. Inigo Jones had charmed them all with the "piazzas"—as by a popular transfer the arcades were called—which he had brought to Covent Garden from Livorno. In that preumbrella day of foot traffic, of splashed mud and shouldering for the wall, these protected walks must have seemed the height of civility. In view of the antirachitic value of sunlight, however, there is no reason to regret that this additional instrument of darkness was not visited upon the city.

† Knight did not invent the narrow block. There were many in London, and Hollar's plan shows, north and east of Moorfields, numerous straight and parallel streets—he exaggerates their regularity—about 100 feet apart, center to center. Some of them survive—there is a district of very narrow blocks east of Charterhouse. This was, perhaps, a low-cost suburban land subdivision in competition with the new streets of Holborn and Westminster. Knight adopted the shallow lot as a means of avoiding the notorious narrow passageways. His building depth limit doubtless could not have been enforced permanently, but the large proportion of the city devoted to streets formed an irreducible reserve of open space.

The total length of Wren's streets is about half of Knight's total.

The captain's *pièce de résistance* was a canal running back from Billingsgate and swinging around to join the Fleet canal near Holborn, further proof that he saw the city clearly as a place of commercial activity. One phase of this canal was counted on to win the royal favor; instead, it got the designer into jail, a form of discouragement the modern town planner is usually spared. The soldier-sociologist had argued that by the levy of fines and tolls the canal would bring revenue to the King, whose benevolence, or political acumen, he underestimated.

Critical discussion of these plans must be illustrative and provocative rather than conclusive. Anything in the manner of a qualitative comparison is impossible because the program was not a fixed one and because the plans differ so much in the skill with which the general conceptions are detailed. In order to make a fair competition, a skilled architect would have to draft the plans at the same scale, discounting Wren's advantage by inventing appropriate detail for the optimum realization of each conception. And it seems necessary to set aside as impossible of measurement the practical merits of the schemes. What standard will you set up—convenience to the modern city? But some of the plans would have created a city so unlike the existing one that the present traffic situation would have no relation to it. All the plans show a broad quay breaking the contact between water and warehouse. That feature would have revolutionized the plan of London, as Knight's canal would have done. Regarding convenience of street plan, it would be easy to make a case for the proposition that the best plan was simply the one that gave the largest proportion of the area to streets.* On that basis the crown would go to the man who was jailed for his pains, because Knight gives over a third of the city to roadways and walks. My critical comments will, therefore, center on such points as tend to show to what extent this group of designers recognized and used the treasury of ideals in civic beauty which the art of Europe had accumulated, and on such points of contact as there are between these plans and the subsequent development of town planning.

Evelyn, like most amateurs—and not only amateurs!—did not realize clearly that beauty does not lie in general concepts but in specific objects. The schematic pattern of his first plan implies familiarity with certain real Renaissance values, but he lacked the technique to carry the general conception over into reality. At certain vital points the order of the design is of the plan only and would hardly be felt on the ground in the way that the spatial composition of a good formal park is felt. He provides, to be sure, six fine vistas of St. Paul's, against Wren's one. But the streets spreading east from St. Paul's, which seem in the plan to form an admirable *patte-d'oie*, have the fatal fault that you cannot stand at the confluence of the three ways and therefore cannot penetrate visually thrice at once into the city, as at

Rome you can. Evelyn, surprisingly, did not understand the true delicate value of the *patte-d'oie*, an art form alive with the very soul of the Renaissance. The plazas ask less of his novice hand, yet the two perfect examples in the first plan have awkward neighbors, and the street intersections of the second and third are hopelessly bad. His gift was practical —when his first pretty plan was rejected, he went over to the hackney coaches. Yet he never forgot Fontana's Rome. His one eternal value was the long straight street.

If one takes a general view of Wren's plan, the first thing to be said is that there is light in it. The town is not hidden by the houses. It is opened up by the straightness and length of the streets and still further by the numerous points at which vistas are grouped. The general effect of these radiating views is excellent, but of only a few can it be said specifically that they are of the highest quality. The **V** of streets from Ludgate, which I have praised, is indeed fine in plan, but the profiles of the diverging streets would be convexed by the high ground around St. Paul's, and the receding street planes could not be seen from any point on the ground. This would not be fatal to picturesque effect, but it would destroy that absolute perfection of perspective without which such compositions cannot have soul-stirring spatial pathos. The **V** from London Bridge falls on more favorable ground. In the two axial street groups radiating from the Exchange the angle of divergence is 40 degrees, which, in a *patte-d'oie*, is ten or fifteen degrees too much.

The Exchange plaza has been praised too highly. There are actually two small plazas whose relation would be felt intellectually but hardly aesthetically. The buildings facing on the lunettes would have

* No accurate comparison of the street widths of the various plans can be made. Knight alone states his widths clearly—40, 70, and 80 feet, including the covered walks. As to Hooke's, we know nothing: they scale 50 feet, but the engravings are small and may not be true to his design, nor is it known whether he intended arcaded walks. In Evelyn's first plan the streets scale narrower than he has allowed in his description, in which the widest is 100 feet. In his third plan they vary from 30 to 60 feet. As for Wren's plan, the street widths are given in the "Parentalia" as 30, 60, and 90 feet, but the wider streets scale, in the accurate second draft, no more than 50 and 80 feet. Ralph (1730) says that Wren "proposed to build all the houses uniform and supported on piazzas." If that is true, the walks are probably to be added to the widths scaled from the plan.

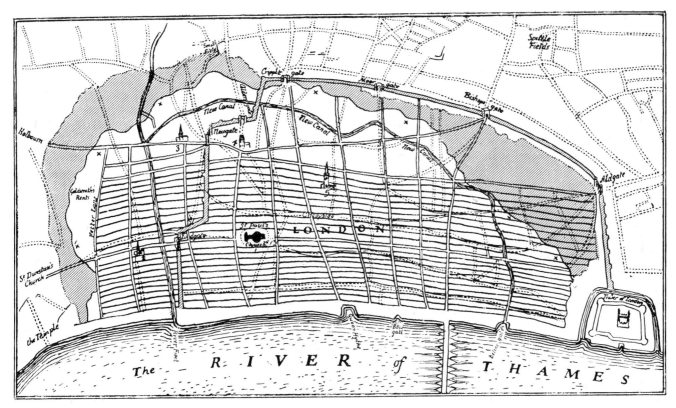

FIGURE 112. Valentine Knight's plan.

narrow fronts and awkward block plans. The accessibility of the Exchange, one of the cited virtues of the plan, might have proved a fault. A financial district may well lie adjacent to through traffic routes but is less wisely placed directly over their intersection. The treatment of his open spaces shows that Wren's veins were not yet full of the blood of the Renaissance. His plan does not contain a square of the type already becoming typical of London—more justly, of suburban London—nor a true civic plaza of the French and Italian tradition. All the

openings are furrowed by traffic routes. The first answer lies in the cost of land, of which Wren was taking as much as he dared for streets. But further than that, he clearly did not have the strong taste for the plaza genre which he would have had if he had been an Italian or had lived a century later in England.

Yet Wren's city is a pleasant one to imagine living in. It is full of a sense of design. Particularly do the many street vistas of church spires and domes give you a sense of human art, of intelligent life running through the town. There is something orderly about the streets, definitely of three different widths; the few widest streets form a simple framework that makes the layout of the town easy to grasp. There are lights and darks, unstereotyped variations that fill the city with areas of local flavor. Wren was more sensitive to medieval architecture than were most of his contemporaries—there seems even to have been an anticipatory touch of Sitte in him. At any rate, there are passages in his plan that are far from absolute; there are even a few cynical hints that accident may produce greater beauty than can be made by taking thought. An older architect might have looked askance at some of those accidents of street plan and building site. The bold young Wren depended on his ingenuity to sustain his whim. A gentleman, after all, does not need to study etiquette. Taken as a whole the plan is lucid, imaginative, charming. But it must be added that there is no place in it where one's breath is stopped by the vision of large perfection, where one says "Some god has done this."

Wren's design and the other Fire plans form exceptionally rich material for tracing the veins of town planning thought. There were echoes in them of the past and prophecies of the future. From the past we see a corner of the vast shadow of Rome, we see once more the eternal plan of squares, we trace some rays of Le Nôtre's light, we sense acquaintance with the fine intellectual experiments of the Renaissance architect authors. We may note, too, some hints that the "square," that gift of Italy, France, and Inigo Jones, was already becoming precious to London. Does this list sound archaic? One could hardly better sketch the knowledge a young designer of today ought to command.

The Fire summoned to London much of the thought of the past; it also made an opening into the future. In a sense, the Fire created a town planning problem resembling the problem presented by the rapid growth of a modern city. The questions to be answered were not remote and abstract—the burdens of large population, of heavy internal traffic, and of correlation with a regional plan were present and crying for immediate resolution. Before that time, and long after, almost all town planning thought was concerned with small colony towns, neat walled bastides, and elegantly patterned copperplate cities. The programs and the values to be attained were wholly unlike those with which Wren and Evelyn found themselves involved. The expansion of Rome under the Renaissance popes was the nearest parallel and accordingly furnished the most useful teachings.

Wren and Evelyn quite unconsciously forecast the great distinctive element in modern civic form, the dominance of the street over the building—of, one might say, the dynamic over the static. The great population of London, the traffic, and the newly invented hackney coach were seen by these practical men to demand straight, wide, and long streets. Of these dimensions, those which make for street dominance are perhaps breadth and continuity—not necessarily straightness. Modern streets have many continuous elements—curbs, poles, tram tracks, fast traffic—which make of the street such a powerful psychological experience that the buildings become almost casual factors. Only when we look at an old painting by van der Meer or Canaletto can we realize that a town was once a group of solids in which the street was the open space in front of a house, kept clean by the family servant.

All the old predesigners of towns, it is true, made their streets straight, but the power of them was diminished by their narrowness, by the frequent use of terminal features, and of course by the slower tempo of movement in the streets. The older and the Renaissance designers—to risk an epigram—sought a balance between solids and voids; the Baroque artists set space and stone in a dance together; and as for the modern engineers, they ask the buildings to stand aside while the streets rush madly by. Wren and Evelyn, confronted with a modern problem born before its time, made plans more modern than the proposals elicited by the competition of 1748 that resulted in the Place de la Concorde. Not until L'Enfant planned Washington, not until the "reformation" of Paris and the piercings and diagonal-style suburbs of all the fast-growing European cities, can we collect a body of plans to fill up the portfolio opened by Wren and Evelyn.

The then-existing corpus of architectural and town planning knowledge was sufficient to make possible a better and particularly a more rigorously ground-fitted plan than any of those drawn up. This criticism does not imply merely that Wren's fine plan was, after all, an extempore and first effort—it is based also on the fact that the techniques of land measuring, plan drafting, and organizing for action were not sufficiently developed and not strong enough in the current civic ideology to make possible the fruitful application of the best existing architectural knowledge. The very want of a good plat of the city, until several months after the Fire, rendered impossible an accurately correlated solution. Wren went far beyond his predecessors in freeing himself from dogmatic patterns, but he felt it

necessary to consider as *tabula rasa* an area which, psychologically at any rate, was anything but that. He put upon his white paper numerous, though secondary, passages of picturesque design, without relation to any existing construction. Blondel, in his plan for the improvement of Strasbourg, a century later, took existing picturesque constructions and drew them into the formal organization of his design. This difference is illuminating. Wren, in the London plan, was an individual genius, an experimenter, without long allegiance to any school, without seasoned knowledge of any style. Blondel had established convictions and methods, was the facile instrument of a generally esteemed and well-digested manner of civic architecture. It is perhaps a corollary to this distinction that the group of plans we have been considering reveals the lacuna I have just mentioned—a design which, though following with some closeness the old plan of the city, would yet be a beautiful and convenient architectural creation. Evelyn sensed the value of that direction, but he did not have the imagination or the knowledge necessary for following it profitably. Wren was better equipped, yet he did not—under the circumstances, could not—have at his command such a fluent vocabulary of civic art as that with which the French architects of the following century met gracefully their varied problems. Wren, therefore, could not see the rich possibilities of the detailed approach and felt that nothing of high value could be done without calling the slate a clean one.

Civic art is perhaps essentially Baroque. Only the Baroque fantasia, at least, has been worthily equipped to exploit this art of solid and space. Wren was not at all fully a Baroque designer. Neither by cultural environment nor by training was he favorably conditioned to become an unquestioning communicant at the Baroque inner shrine, its esoteric civic art. Yet I cannot say that Wren did not, even in 1666, feel some intimation that the exaltation of architecture is in forming beautiful civic spaces. His setting of St. Paul's is proof of an incipient understanding. If through a long period he had guided the detailed reconstruction of London, he would surely have developed into a great civic architect.

Thus Wren, Evelyn, Hooke, and Knight dreamed their various dreams. By the way of envoy some notes on the actual rebuilding ought to be added. An Act of Parliament, early in 1667, set up a Fire Judges' Court; another fixed the manner of rebuilding. The judges had power to use their wisdom practically without reference to existing laws or contracts. Since the leases relieved tenants from replacing buildings destroyed by act of the enemy, the Fire was declared an act of war, and an unlucky Frenchman was hanged. The judges investigated the financial means of the parties to the innumerable suits brought before them and fixed accordingly between owner and tenant the cost of rebuilding. If neither would undertake it within three years, the Lord Mayor and Aldermen had the right to sell the land to a builder, giving the proceeds to those entitled to them; but this power was used only as a threat.

The Rebuilding Act defined the few changes of plan that were thought essential. A 40-foot quay was reserved, a measure which proved impracticable; part of Thames Street was widened; King and Queen Streets were opened south from Guildhall; and a budget of short streets, Poultry for instance, were widened.* The cost of these improvements, as of other public works, came from a tax on coals. The act also fixed four house types of two, three, and four stories—including the ground floor but not cellar and garret—and defined the story heights and fixed the thickness of the walls. The Lord Mayor and Aldermen were enjoined to draw up a corresponding classification of the streets, but in practice they made only two classes, designating six streets as suitable for four-story buildings and assigning all other streets and passages to the three-story class. Noisome and perilous trades were kept from the city. Since outside labor was indispensable, the guilds gave up their ancient monopoly of the crafts. Very complicated negotiations had to be undertaken between the City, the Church, and the King—and it is said by historians that Charles II was wise and active in his help. The term of the Fire Judges had to be extended twice, but eventually their onerous task was honorably done. Their portraits can be seen on the walls of Guildhall. As individuals, declining the King's suggestion of a Lord-Surveyor, the merchants of the City accomplished the vast work by dividing it. By no financial agency then existing could a pooling of the work have been carried through. That, more than anything else, was the reason why London was rebuilt on the old plan.

* The need for new streets—direct north-south routes especially—was well recognized. A month or two after the Fire a committee was studying the feasibility of new streets to the Thames from Aldersgate, Cripplegate, and the Exchange, but only the street from the Guildhall to the river was realized. We can be sure that there was a great deal of talk about town planning while the city was in ruins and many a bitter "if" and "I told you so" for long years after.

13

Haussmann and the Rebuilding of Paris

This is one of those symbol names with which we generalize events and ideas and so modify their content, to suit our own purposes, that we really make of them common nouns, so little remains of the man and so much of our idea. In city plan reports the words Baron Haussmann stand for the "transformation of Paris" and usually for all the beauty and convenience of modern Paris. And since Haussmann has been given an ample Olympian niche, his name sanctifies any operation for which it can be cited as precedent. It is, therefore, much used.

Yet a very real man he was who bore the name. Persigny, Napoleon III's minister, who made Haussmann prefect of the Seine, found him real enough at their first meeting. "He was big, fat, strong, forceful and yet subtle. As he spread himself before me with brutal cynicism I saw that he was just the man

to set against the savage financiers and lawyers. Where the most able and magnanimous nobleman would surely meet disaster this thick-necked athlete, meeting craft with craft, would come safely through. I enjoyed in advance the vision of that huge beast of prey let loose among the wolves and foxes that were barking against every noble effort of the Empire." There is a portrait of him in his memoirs that tells more about him than all three volumes of text. A head like that needed to raze and rebuild cities.

Haussmann was born in the Faubourg St. Honoré, in that fruitful year 1809, and was baptized Georges Eugène, in the Oratory near the Louvre, for the family was Alsatian Huguenot. His father and grandfather had held important positions in Napoleon's commissary; his mother's father served under

Lafayette in America. He went to Collège Henri VI, studied law, entered the civil service, became prefect of Bordeaux, and in 1853 was called to the prefecture of the Seine to carry out Napoleon III's colossal program of street cutting.

The field Haussmann came to plow was marked by many an old furrow, for every ruler of France has in some way affected the plan of Paris. The new Paris, Marcel Poëte says, dates from the Revolution. But the city on which the Revolution broke was a city studded with gems of civic art. There were the grand boulevards (from the Madeleine to the Bastille), Henry IV's brick and stone Place des Vosges and Place Dauphine, Place Vendôme with its big statue of Louis XIV, the little round Place des Victoires, the broad Place de la Concorde (then Place de Louis XV), the gardens of the Tuileries, Luxembourg, and Palais Royal, the Invalides with its broad esplanade to the river, the Ecole Militaire and the Champ de Mars, the Cours-la-Reine, the Champs Elysées, the triumphal gates of St. Martin and St. Denis, the twin columns out at the Barrière de la Trône, and innumerable courtyards and formal gardens built as parts of the enormous wealth of fine buildings—royal, private, scholastic, and ecclesiastic—that crowd with unbelievable richness the old maps of Paris.

After the Revolution an advisory Comité des Artistes was formed. It probably did not draw up a general plan of any sort. By holding a competition and by itself formulating suggestions, it made up a budget of schemes covering the subdivision of the confiscated church lands and a number of changes in the old city. Many of these recommendations merely recorded proposals long current. Napoleon I said that the idea of cutting a straight street from the Bastille to the east front of the Louvre was "as old as Paris." Napoleon carried out some of the Committee's recommendations: the Rue de Rivoli (as far as the Place du Carrousel), the Avenue de l'Observatoire, the Place St. Sulpice, and extensions of the short streets on the axis of the Place Vendôme. He also did much engineering work, built bridges and quays, the Madeleine, the column in the Place Vendôme, the Arc du Carrousel, and began the Arc de Triomphe. After 1814 work went more slowly. Napoleon's projects were completed, and the Boulevard Malsherbes was begun. In the 1830's the obelisk and fountains were set up in the Place de la Concorde.

Louis Napoleon must have dreamed of the transformation of Paris, while, as a prisoner at Ham, he worked on his history of artillery. Made president, he started in 1849, with an agreement between city and state, to extend the Rue de Rivoli and to cut a number of new streets. When Haussmann came to Paris, Napoleon had completed the Boulevard de Strasbourg, had built the Rue des Ecoles, and had made progress with the new section of the Rue de Rivoli.

Napoleon explained his plans to Haussmann, and the new prefect went to work. The first thing he wanted was an absolutely correct map: high scaffolding towers were built, and the whole city was triangulated. Engineers and architects drew plans. Money came from the octroi, from city bonds, from the nation. Land and houses were condemned. Huge contracts were let for razing old houses and building new streets complete with houses, pavements, lighting, water, and sewer. Municipal and national buildings sprang up, a dozen caserns, a dozen churches. Year after year the work went on.

When the end came in 1870, for servant as for master, many projects were unfinished, but with peace new hands took hold, and when France invited the world to the Exposition of 1878, it was to a new Paris.

And what a worldly success that transformed Paris has had! The style of planning marked by cannon-shot boulevards and open traffic plazas ruled unquestioned throughout Europe until, late in the century, the counterinfection of Sitte and his friends wilted the Haussmann tradition in the Teutonic marches. France has for the most part remained loyal. American cities, still tied to their gridirons, though an occasional suburb has sought surcease in romantic landscape curves, yearn for the relief of slashing diagonals. Chicago has her Haussmannizing planned, and the next generation is being prepared for it. From *Wacker's Manual of the Plan of Chicago** the schoolboy learns that

Haussmann, who lives in history as the greatest city builder of all time . . . opened up all the old city of Paris to light and air. He cut new streets here, widened old ones there, tore down hundreds of old structures that beautiful buildings could be brought to view. He created new diagonal thoroughfares to shorten distances in the city. The people supported the men advancing the improvements because they believed that an improved city meant greater wealth for its people. This theory has been proved correct, as people from all parts of the world visit Paris in great numbers each year, and there spend large sums among the merchants and tradespeople.

Subtle minds may detect a certain flavor of *ad hoc* in this argument, and with reason, for it ignores various unpleasant facts and a sheaf of discordant opinions.

The gestation of Haussmann's Paris began in 1848, and simplicity is not in anything born of that year. The republican government promised work for everyone in the national workshops. But the shops could not be kept going. The east section of Paris felt hunger and donned the red cap as it had done so often before. There were riots, barricades, regiments besieged in their own caserns. President Bonaparte, sure of the peasants of France, saw his only enemy in the *peuple* of Paris. They must be given work. That tangle of streets, the Bastille of the people, must be broken down. What could be simpler? Hire the fellows to cut artillery shooting galleries through their maze of streets to build new caserns, churches, and new streets in the *faubourgs*. The nation would pay part of the cost of thus protecting its capital; the octroi would do the rest, thriftily taking out of Pierre's pocket the wherewithal to pay his wages. The razing and rebuilding would scatter the people and start rows of honest vegetables among the red-flowered weeds. The savage fighting of December 1852 confirmed the need and baptized in blood the transformation of Paris.

Motives are always mixed. Napoleon wanted to reign in a convenient, healthful, and beautiful capital—but first of all he wanted to reign. His basic motive in cutting new streets was military. The plan he drew with his own hand, long before Haussmann was called to Paris, had two main provisions, both of obvious tactical value. One was the eastward extension of the Rue de Rivoli, which separated the "belly of Paris" from the Louvre and the Hôtel de

* *Wacker's Manual of the Plan of Chicago,* by Walter D. Moody (Chicago, 1911).

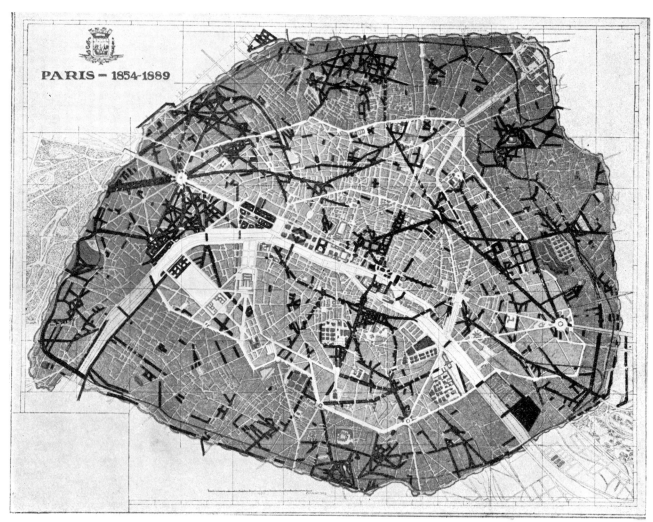

PARIS – 1854-1889

FIGURE 113. Paris. Plan showing the extent of Haussmann's transformations between 1854 and 1889.

Ville and completed a direct route from the Tuileries to Vincennes. The other was the Place de la République and three streets spreading from it. On the Place itself was built a large casern. One of the three streets, Boulevard Magenta, gives access to the Gares du Nord and de l'Est; the Boulevard Voltaire connects by the Place de la Nation with the large military depot at Vincennes; the Rue de Turbigo slashes through the reddest patch in Paris. When Napoleon first conceived the Avenue de l'Opéra, he intended extending it by a straight street from the Boulevard des Capucines to the Gare St. Lazare. There would thus be a direct route from the Tuileries to the station, a route which, with the railway tracks, would form a dead line separating the "impressionable" parts of Paris from the impressed part and from the Tuileries.

Haussmann wrote his memoirs about 1890. In many passages he tries to establish other than strategic motives for the street cuttings, defending his emperor against the Parisians *"qui se sont montrés toujours si peu reconnaissants de sa solicitude et de ses bienfaits."* On another page he lapses into realities and tells how he suggested to Napoleon that the Canal St. Martin be depressed and covered over. The Emperor was enthusiastic at the thought of establishing "a clear shot from one end to the other of the controlling line whence one might, at need, take in the rear the whole Faubourg St. Antoine. Better yet, the boulevard would substitute for the means of defense which the canal offered to rioters, a new way of access to the accustomed center of their manifestations." And, *détail curieux*, the workingmen liked the idea!

Haussmann was conversant with financial strategy, too. A few sentences from Ollivier's *L'Empire Liberal* will indicate the general texture of his methods.

A halt seemed necessary: not for a moment did he think of it. Out of an authorized loan of a hundred and fifty million francs he got one hundred and seventy; out of the treasury of public works he took a hundred and fifty million instead of the hundred million authorized. Finally he hit on a pleasing formula for raising the money to meet the needs of the land-condemning jury. He agreed with certain rich contractors to cede them definite areas of partly built-up land. They were to take the land in the city's name, cut streets, sell the scrap material, build houses on the abutting land or sell it, and turn the streets over to the city, which agreed to make payment in six or eight annuities. But the city had to pay for the expropriated land. The contractors were therefore required to deposit the needed sum. Incidentally, this gave the city cash with which to meet current obligations. . . . [And regarding certain "veiled loans"] In order to incline the contractors to take up the loans Haussmann baited them with the right to issue "bons de delegation." These bonds, drawn on the city, accepted and endorsed by the city, were cashed by the contractors as they needed money. The Crédit-Foncier discounted most of them. This was contrary to the law which required legislative approval of such loans. But time pressed . . . and the Emperor approved.

Such was some of the popular support to which the Chicago manual refers. One can imagine that the contractors and bankers were enthusiastic.

It is impossible to deny, obviously, that the broad streets Napoleon and Haussmann built are a great boon to the traffic of Paris. Taxicab strategy, after all, is not without similarities to artillery strategy. But, as physical and social sanitation, their work was not in advance of the crude standards of the time. The water service was mainly by yard hydrants. The land was crowded with high tenements, and in spite of the broad streets the proportion of area built on was increased. As to the light and air they let in, there was not enough of it, at least, to prevent the writing of a red page in the history of Paris, during a certain year when Baron Haussmann found it wise to be traveling abroad.

Haussmann himself is fairly explicit in disclaiming general credit for all the work supposed to have been carried out by him, though he takes pride in being the author of certain details. The general scheme of all the streets outside the Etoile section was almost certainly devised by Napoleon, who thought of himself as a gifted strategist. The prefect's duty, as he states it, was to penetrate the Emperor's intention as embodied in his general plan, to determine the changes made necessary by more accurate surveys, to point out the important gaps, and to foresee all the intricacies of accommodating the new streets to the old. The Boulevard St. Germain is an instance of an important change in the Emperor's plan. He had intended placing the circuit street on that side of the river a little further south, using the Rue des Ecoles. But when the matter was studied under Haussmann's direction, it was seen that the Rue des Ecoles was too high on the slope of Ste. Geneviève, and a lower, shorter, and wider route was worked out.

Heading the large office needed to carry out the Emperor's huge commission was the architect and engineer Deschamps, an old employee. He apparently had charge of the details of the cross sections and profiles of the streets and the planning of the many traffic plazas. Haussmann gives liberal credit to Deschamps: *"Le Plan de Paris, c'était M. Deschamps!"* And he adds that "if it is not well known that he laid out all the magistral thoroughfares of which the breadth and fine alignment are now so much admired, his modesty is doubtless to blame." But this seems to refer to detailing rather than to the inception of general plans, though Deschamps may have determined some street locations in the later stages of the work, after the most pressing military needs had been met. For the Etoile, Haussmann claims credit for himself and Deschamps, since Napoleon's plan had only a *croisée* where there is now a twelve-rayed star. For the crisscross of streets around the Opera, too, the Emperor cannot be blamed. Garnier, architect of the Opera, says heatedly that its setting is the very worst known to architectural history, ancient or modern. When he protested to the Emperor in Haussmann's presence, the Emperor agreed and sketched on the plan a setting of rectangular plazas. But he was a busy man, and Haussmann built his "fichus," as the Emperor had called them, just the same. Haussmann's admirers usually praise this setting of the Opera as his masterpiece. In his memoirs (they were written after Garnier's book appeared) he hardly mentions it.

The parks—Boulogne, Vincennes, Monceau, Buttes Chaumont, and the gardens of the Champs Elysées—which Haussmann considered the crowning glory of his *"édilité,"* are usually credited to Alphand. When Haussmann came to Paris, the Emperor took him out to see the work beginning in the Bois de Boulogne. The old gardener in charge was digging a river. Haussmann saw difficulties and had profiles made and showed that instead of a river there would have to be two lakes. The Emperor was impressed and let Haussmann send for a member of his staff at Bordeaux, Alphand, an engineer in the "Ponts et Chaussées." Now this Alphand, thanks to the opportunities thus opened to him, became a famous *architecte paysagiste,* entered the service of the republic, and was made grand officer of the Legion of Honor after the Exposition of 1889, quite in contrast to the loyal Deschamps, who died in a small position found for him by his old chief. One senses a consequent difference of feeling, perhaps, in Haussmann's remark that Alphand was chosen because there were so many roads to be built in the parks. And he goes on to say that Alphand showed marvelous facility in adopting the ideas of the "administration," however they might vary from his own, and that he carried them out with conscientious fidelity and irreproachable zeal. In these little encounters it is pleasant to have the last word. Alphand was elected to Haussmann's chair in the Academy of Fine Arts, and delivered the conventional eulogy. "His astonishing faculty for assimilation," he said, "enabled him to understand and retain everything, to such a point that he often took for his own, with entire good faith, ideas he had adopted."

As for the gardening in the parks, that was done by Barillet-Deschamps, *horticulteur.* In 1873, Haussmann was in Constantinople. Being shown a viceroy's park, he felt *"comme en pays de connaissance"*—the familiar concave lawns, the familiar curving paths. Barillet had been there.

It is easier to say why and by whom Paris was transformed than it is to solve the much more important problem of the aesthetic quality of the transformation. That quality is not questioned, naturally, in official France, and English architects almost always look on Paris with mingled love and envy. Yet, while he was still at work, Haussmann was very sharply attacked because of the many fine old houses he was pulling down (his own birthplace was one of them) and on the ground that his new streets were too long and too uniform. Garnier, in his bitterness, said that the law should forbid setting two houses in line. There were letters to the papers. Politicians made charges; ministers answered them.

The criticisms touched, and Haussmann's memoirs stress the artistic side of his accomplishment—the section of the Boulevard St. Michel axial to the Sainte-Chapelle, the Boulevard Henry IV commanding vistas of the Colonne de Juli and the dome of the Panthéon, the dome of the Tribunal de Commerce set in line with the Boulevard de Sébastopol, and especially the Etoile. He hits back at the good people who regret, in their libraries, the destruction of *le vieux Paris*—and tells how he started the Carnavalet Museum.

During the last two or three decades, though the traffic convenience of the *percements* has yearly grown more striking, the negative pan of the scales of aesthetic criticism has gained counters, and the positive has lost. After all, are straightness and breadth of themselves very beautiful? Ask the Renaissance men who were masters of straightness and breadth, and take as their answer such streets as the axial street of Karlsruhe, the old Lower Regent Street, and the Avenue de l'Observatoire. These are not merely straight and convenient thoroughfares. They are definitely mastered, rhythmically articulated aesthetic compositions. When you come into the street, you feel its organic entity, usually as part of a dominant building. But come into the Boulevard Strasbourg-Sébastopol from the Gare de l'Est. You see, generally, a long vista lost in blue haze. Descending, you make out a smallish dome on axis;

still further, and you come into one corner of the Place du Châtelet and discover that your street has no actual connection with the domed building, which faces in another direction. The Avenue de l'Opéra is better. But the buildings near the Opera are too high, and its façade is not especially effective as a vista objective, the end pavilions and not the central entrance being emphasized. Thus the Opera does not seem to dominate the avenue or to integrate with it. Look the other way, and you see what appears to be a domed building. Go nearer, and you find that the Avenue bumps against the cut-off corner of an ordinary hotel. The dome, square on plan and seen at an angle, is five hundred feet beyond, in the new Louvre, and is finally wiped out by the perspective. Haussmann and Deschamps may have done the best they could, but it takes more than good intention to produce great art. These casual stagy effects are not the stuff of good civic design.

The Etoile was Haussmann's pride. Certainly the plaza photographs well from the air, and the radiating streets make the fullest use of Napoleon's arch. The star, as a street-plan motif, is very old—perhaps first used in hunting forests to facilitate watching game. The essentials of a good star plaza (not considering now the views in from the rays) are that you should be able to stand at or near the center and that corresponding rays should be or seem to be at the same ground level and of the same length. In the Etoile the twelve rays vary in length from three hundred meters to infinity and slope away from the plaza at sharply varying gradients. Good plazas are generally level and enclosed by a definite wall of buildings. The wall of houses around the Place de l'Etoile is so broken that one hardly feels

it as circular, and the floor is so convex that autos encircling the arch disappear behind the central hill. However convenient a traffic center it may be, and however effective may be each of the dozen shots in toward the arch, the Etoile surely has no right to be called a *place* in the sense of the word established by the French architects of the seventeenth and eighteenth centuries.

These criticisms would have meant little to Deschamps and nothing to Haussmann, for the period had lost the feeling for plaza design which was so strong a century before. And it is not quite fair to say that their work is without aesthetic value simply because it is not perfect architecture and because Blondel, in the time of Louis XV, could have done better. Napoleon did not ask for great works of art—beyond his practical requirements he asked only for grandiose sparkle. A period that thought of opera as the queen of arts naturally thought that wide, straight avenues laced with rows of trees would make Paris the queen of cities. An inspired pamphlet, defending Haussmann, which appeared in 1868, quoted him as aiming at *"un aspect général plein de grandeur."* And that is exactly what, to the average man, he got. A trained artist, thinking specifically, finds the Place de l'Opéra an odious sham and dreams of the Campidoglio at Rome. But the bank president and the *midinette,* feeling only general effects, are struck by the silk-hat slickness of everything. They like it, just as they like to be among prosperous people, modishly dressed. They like the wide streets shooting in every direction, revealing the bigness and wealth of the city. They are not critically sensitive to specific aesthetic relations, but there is a sort of grandeur which is quite within their grasp. And some elements in this effect lie

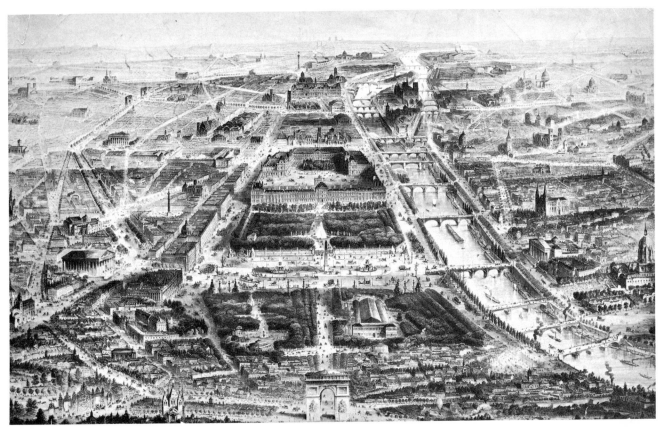

FIGURE 114. A popularized view of Paris, probably about 1866. Note the boulevards cutting through the ancient urban fabric. Dimensions are distorted considerably.

within the hazy borderlands of art. Along with the banality can be found many passages of real beauty —the harmony of dappled plane trees and shadow-spotted gray stone, arrow-straight cornice lines disappearing into an evening mist, rows of street lamps reflected on wet asphalt. And the general spaciousness, though crudely formed and not making the most of its fine aesthetic possibilities, has a certain

value, something like the value of cut building stones before they are laid in the wall.

The uncritical visitor makes somewhat the same reaction to Haussmann's Paris as he does to the gardens of Versailles. The trained critic sees Versailles as a perfectly co-ordinated space composition, and Haussmann's boulevards as spacial raw material, from which Le Nôtre and Mansard could have fashioned a Paris infinitely more beautiful than the one we know.

What the transformation of Paris cost us in architectural beauty destroyed must not be counted in judging the work of Haussmann and Napoleon as it stands, but such damages can justly be assessed against them as artists and as the heroes and models of city planning. The indictment is not a brief one. The spoiling of the little Place des Victoires and of the circular street round the old Halle au Blé, some changes in the Place Dauphine, clipping a corner off the gardens of the Luxembourg and moving the Medici Fountain, building the Palais d'Industrie in one of the large open "Elysian Fields" and filling the other with inane gardening, the destruction of beautiful old courtyards, buildings, and "bits" uncountable—these are some of the sins of vandalism civic art must hold against Emperor and prefect. And we must debit most of Haussmann's "fifty-eight old buildings restored, isolated, etc." The restorations were generally in bad taste, and the policy of *dégagement* is now quite discredited. In particular, clearing, irrelevant planting, and inappropriate building have harmed both near and distant views of Notre Dame.

That Haussmann was not one of those sensitive souls (as the Austrian Sitte was, for instance) to whom one could trust a conflict between "practicality" and a precious heritage of civic art is shown clearly enough by a story he tells in his memoirs. Traveling in Italy, in 1871, he was invited by a group of big businessmen to take the presidency of a company for which they were seeking a contract for the transformation of Rome, *"à l'instar de Paris."* He declined but offered to make a plan showing the necessary *percements* through the Eternal City's "tangle of crooked streets and uneven topography." The seven hills have not been leveled, but it is possible that to Haussmann we owe the gash in the north end of the Piazza Navona. He tells the story as evidence of his honesty and professional standing, apparently unconscious of the light it sheds on the motives that may lie at the back of zeal for city planning undertakings.

Whether Haussmann was the "greatest city builder of all time" depends on what you mean by city building. In any case it is certain that what is most genuinely beautiful in Paris was built long before Haussmann's time, that Napoleon III and the architect Deschamps had more to do than Haussmann with the planning of the work he carried out, that the motives at the back of the work were not exclusively humanitarian, and that its aesthetic quality is not the highest. But such *banderillas* make no mortal wounds. Haussmann was not an artist and had no need to be: he was the apotheosis of a steam shovel. He was the perfect symbol of the ideals of his time, an honest, tireless, successful worker. He had a right to be proud of his work and to tell his peers in the senate of France that he would leave his post of duty with head high and heart firm—*"la tête haute et la coeur ferme!"*

14

Camillo Sitte

The fine flower time of architectural city planning was the second half of the eighteenth century. That was the time of the Nancy plazas, the French squares in honor of Louis XV, Karlsruhe, the New Town in Edinburgh, and L'Enfant's Washington. But in the corners of these very plans appear the signs of the coming decay. Many passages in the plan of Washington are touched by it, or more than touched. With the eighteen-hundreds, streets and plazas begin to lose their architectural organization and fall apart into blocks of houses and traffic routes. Straight roads slash across each other at awkward angles and come together in irregular stars which are labeled plazas and decorated with bunches of foliage and dotted with fancy lamp posts. The "transformation of Paris" in the 1850's and 1860's gave a final blessing to this brutal style,

and it flourished in the suburbs of all the rapidly growing cities of Europe, just as an equally brutal application of the gridiron shaped most American cities, though Savannah and La Roche-sur-Yon had shown that the gridiron was capable of imaginative application. In America public buildings were set in the middle of squares, surrounded by trees, and in Europe many an old church was disengaged from the little buildings clustered about it.

In spite of the taste for the picturesque and archaic which dominated architecture, painting, and the applied arts, especially in Germany and England, during the middle decades of the century, there were surprisingly few picturesque street layouts—only a scattering of sinuous-wayed suburbs in England and the United States, inspired by the fashionable landscape style of gardening. Perhaps the engineers and surveyors were protected against the ideas current in art and literature, but the flood was rising and was sure some time to break into the field of city planning. It did, in 1889, with the publication of Camillo Sitte's *Der Städtebau.*

Sitte was as clearly the fruit of his time as was William Morris, and they were much alike—lovers of old towns, workers in many crafts, attacking the art of their time and restating it more perfectly in the spirit of the time. They were a little alike physically. At least Sitte, like Morris, was broadshouldered and stocky and had a big head, but the face is one of the types we think of as German, amply rounded and bearded below, rounded and bald above, with cheerful little nose and spectacled eyes between.

He was born in 1843, son of a Viennese architect. He began to draw as a boy at the Piaristengymnasium. At the technical high school and the university he studied the history of art and art anatomy, and both subjects became permanent interests. He was a very accomplished musician, an ardent friend and supporter of Wagner, whom he served as architect. He was made director of the state school of applied arts at Salzburg in 1876. (In charity let us try not to think of *our* applied art in *our* year 1876!) In 1883 he was promoted to the corresponding institution in Vienna and remained its head until his death in 1903. During these years he practiced architecture, painting, and even sculpture, building churches and decorating them with his own mural paintings. His summer journeys took him to Germany, France, Near Asia, and especially to Italy. He made a number of plans for the extension of Austrian towns, and that was the direction of his principal interest after the success of his book.

German architects might have been waiting for the book, so prompt was their response. In six weeks a second edition had to be printed. In the preface to the third edition, ten years later, Sitte could truly say that the book had given city planning a new orientation, but he said too that the movement must have been in the air, ready to take substance when the right word was spoken. A French version of the book, considerably modified especially as to the illustrative material, was made by the architect Camille Martin, of Geneva, in 1902, and a second edition, in 1918, was ascribed to the need of guidance in reconstruction—and contained no reference to Sitte's nationality. No English edition has been printed, but Sitte's work is well known to English town planners, and the plans of his followers, though less so his own designs and writings, are familiar to city planners in this country.*

The purpose of Sitte's book, as he states it, was to induce city planners to go to school to nature and our forefathers—*"zur Natur und den Alten."* About half the book is given to the citation of innumerable examples of medieval plazas and church settings, showing that the old plazas were kept open in the center, that they were tightly closed in visually by the surrounding buildings, that churches very rarely stood free, that the old plazas were very irregular but that this irregularity was often not apparent, and that plazas were consciously grouped. He passes to modern work, condemning its poverty of invention, its mania for long wide streets, its sprawling open "plazas," its disregard for the *genius*

* *Editor's note:* For the authoritative works see Camillo Sitte, *City Planning According to Artistic Principles,* translated by George R. and Christiane C. Collins (New York: Random House, 1965) and George R. and Christiane C. Collins, *Camillo Sitte and the Birth of Modern City Planning* (New York: Random House, 1965).

loci, alleging every possible fault in the gridiron plan, from inconvenience to traffic to unsuitability for use as stage settings. But later, having described what is best in modern work, he gives examples, his own designs based on standard Baroque plans, of good building groups fitted into rectangular street plans. The gridiron he thinks of as a necessary evil; whenever possible, though not without practical or aesthetic considerations, curves, breaks, offsets, and closed vistas should be used to produce a refreshing picturesqueness—and to stop dust-raising winds. The book closes with a discussion of the Vienna Ring, with proposals for its redesign according to Sitte's principles.

There arose at once a school of city planning which adhered to Sitte's gospel. Official city plans prepared for future growth were hastily revised in the new-old mode. The new style won all the competitions. The Germans showed their prodigious (and dangerous) willingness to learn; the tricks of the style were seized on by all the architects and municipal plan bureaus in middle and northern Europe. The English were sympathetic and accepted certain ideas, but they did not give up the architectural tradition of orderliness which they feel so strongly. America, content with the gridiron plan and its antipode, the curves of landscape gardening, gave little heed, though spots of Sitte feeling have appeared on plans since the first years of the century. Forest Hills Gardens and Roland Park are amalgams of Sitte and the landscape style, by no means unfriendly elements. In Brussels, Burgomaster Buls used Sitte's authority in his fight against the "freeing" of old buildings. The French are slow to learn of foreign, most of all German, movements, and perhaps in this case they felt that conscious

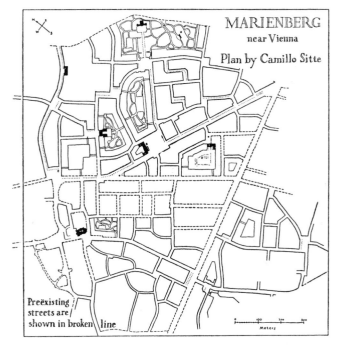

FIGURE 115. A town plan made by Sitte in his developed style, about 1900. The terrain is fairly level. The upper part of the plan is for row houses, and the curved streets in the lower part are for detached houses.

picturesqueness was not among their gifts. But after the war the reconstruction of old towns was too strong a temptation. Almost pathetically, plans for rebuilding villages destroyed by the Germans have been made by French architects in a style which the Germans invented thirty years ago and which they have now abandoned, under the influence of the fine French designing of the eighteenth century.

The *Sittesche Stil* had the fine asset of being, at least superficially, easy to learn and to use, somewhat in the way the "informal" manner of house planning is easy. You start your house with a front door or a living room and tack on halls and dens and dining rooms as fancy or fancied convenience suggests. If you walk through a door and bump against a porch post, well, that is a touch of picturesqueness. Upstairs, if you need a little more room, you make a loggia below to support it; if you have too much, you make a balcony. It will all be charming if it's built of expensive materials. When the house is finished, you plant a few poplars to take the place of the cypresses the architect had in his rendered sketch—and you are ready for the photographer. It is easy to laugh at such work, but it is often done with loving sincerity, and to Sitte and his followers there was a sacred joy in imitating the really beautiful old towns their fathers had built in the dear *Meistersinger* days before French hardness and straightness had seduced them.

Sitte took most of his illustrative material from irregular Gothic plans, but he acknowledged the fine quality of the Baroque work. In practice, however, the designers of the Sitte school ignored the Baroque and developed a version of medieval growth planning, though it is a very marked stylistic version that cannot for a moment be mistaken for its prototype. The streets are nearly straight (no pretzel curves such as the landscape architects use in American suburbs), but they are not entirely straight either. They have slight bends which occur at fairly close intervals. They are curved or bent to produce a concave façade or to close a vista. Two streets rarely cross each other, and where they come together, there is typically a little offset widening of one, or a little corner plaza, room for a tree or a fountain. The larger squares are not very large and are always irregular, with perhaps a church enclosing one corner and a statue in another, with a few small trees around it. At every opportunity there are steps, archways, terraces, low retaining walls, little rows of trees. The houses are quaintly, the public buildings austerely, picturesque, and always very roofy. It is unsafe to make extensions of supposed national tastes—still, one sometimes hears these German roofs spoken of as fat.

In 1903 Sitte and Theodore Goecke, of Berlin, started a monthly journal, *Der Städtebau*, devoted to the social and economic as well as to the artistic aspects of city planning. Sitte died just before the first number came out, but articles and designs by him were published in the magazine, and it was accepted as the organ of the Sitte school. His name as cofounder is still on the title page, but *Der Städtebau* of these days publishes many plans which would have seemed out of place in the first volume. For symmetry and formality have gradually worked their way back into the German plans. At first there were casual passages in generally picturesque layouts—a straight street, perhaps, with a building truly on axis, not merely in vista, or a plaza actually regular. The new German architectural movement, though at first it welcomed the picturesque style of civic art, found that it needed the cooling effect of symmetry and straightness. The steadying influence of English town planning, which had not surrendered to informality, was felt. The historians and critics found that every period had its formal work: the magazine which had begun by teaching that modern cities must copy the artistic informality of Rothenburg a dozen years later was printing articles to prove that the medieval colonist settlement towns were charming little checkerboards.

And so it comes about that when you go out from the city of Mannheim, that pleasant old rectangular town which Sitte cursed as the mother of evil, you may pass through a pre-Sitte belt of wide uniform streets in the French diagonal system, then through a typical net of gently bending "Sittesque" streets, then into a mildly formal straight-and-circular garden suburb in the English manner, and, finally, if the newest plans are being carried out, you may come to a new rigidly formal gridiron, as strictly right-angled as old Mannheim, and yet rhythmic and imaginative, a true Baroque design.

The Sitte style of city planning ran its course in three decades but (supposing it could have got started) would have covered three centuries in the happy days of slow communication. The brief story of the growth and decline of the Sitte style would be all there is to say about Sitte except that in some corners of the world (the new plan of Moscow proves it) the picturesque style is still viewed in a perspective too favorably narrow, and if it were not that certain critics, though disillusioned as to the style identified with Sitte's name, have come to the master's defense with the theory that he was not really a medievalist but was actually an advocate of the now so much in vogue Baroque. These phenomena may be worth discussing, if only on the chance that they may serve as parallels to instances in less simple and less restricted fields of art history.

It is not to be wondered at that various interpretations of Sitte have been arrived at, because, for one thing, there are apparent inconsistencies in his book. The frontispiece is a view of the plaza and church of St. Peter in Rome, and a page is given to the general plan, yet in the text not half a dozen lines are given to the Piazza di San Pietro, and the only judgment expressed is that it is too large. Sitte found time to count the churches of Rome and tells

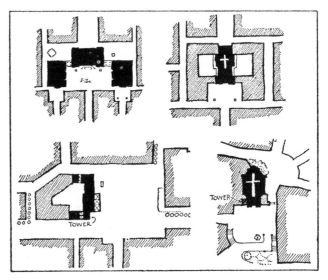

FIGURE 116. Two studies from Sitte's book, contrasted with two plazas from his plan for Marienberg, done some ten years later.

us that 110 are built against on three sides and only six stand free. But he hardly more than mentions the Piazza del Campidoglio (which enjoys the advantage of having been designed by Michelangelo) and the Piazza del Popolo, and he gives a plan of neither. It can hardly be said that Sitte shows appreciation of these three finest creations of Italian Baroque plaza design. His references to French designs are equally brief. France is now known, thanks largely to German research (the only general work on French city planning was published during the war by the Seminar für Städtebau at the Königlichen Technischen Hochschule in Berlin), as the greatest treasury of formal civic art. Sitte mentions three bits of Lyons as examples of how-not-to-do-it, and three more from Marseilles, one of which is ascribed to Nîmes. He jocosely quotes proof that the people of Rennes are unpatriotic, thanks to their straight streets. He says that the Champ de Mars and the Avenue des Champs Elysées are very wide, but has a phrase in partial praise of monumentally terminated avenues and a few charitable lines on the "transformation." Not a word about the Place des Vosges, Place Vendôme, or Place de la Concorde, not a word about the charming plazas in Bordeaux, Nantes, Rheims, Charleville, not a word about Versailles or Nancy. (In the French version Martin supplied a few of these omissions.) Sitte publishes dozens of little plans, many of them quite inaccurate, of German medieval squares which "for irregularity leave nothing to be desired" and shows that the churches and town halls follow the "good old rule" of never standing free. He condemns the checkerboard and the fanlike plan of Karlsruhe, mentions Unter den Linden but not Gendarmenmarkt or Pariser Platz, and has hardly a word to say of the fine examples of eighteenth-century planning in German cities—Erlangen, Rastatt, Darmstadt, Potsdam, Karlshafen, Ludwigslust, and a hundred others.

In many passages Sitte quite explicitly excuses and praises informality. He says that though the irregular Piazza Santa Maria Novella really has five sides, many remember it as having four. A Renaissance designer would laugh at such an idea: he would say that the plan must be so emphatically expressed that there cannot be a moment's hesitation as to the number of sides.

And yet after so many demonstrations of preference for informality and after some indications of an imperfect understanding of formal designs, Sitte calmly remarks that a whole volume could be filled with examples of fine seventeenth- and eighteenth-century plaza plans. That the designers of those plazas would have looked with no more than tolerant contempt on Sitte's medieval gems does not appear to have been a difficulty to him. Certainly the old work is beautiful in its way, and appreciation of it is not inconsistent with enthusiasm for formal Renaissance designs. But that a critic who enjoyed eighteenth-century work, desiring to improve the current city planning, should choose most of his examples from the fourteenth or earlier is not easy to understand.

There is perhaps light in the circumstance that the material of the first half of the book is almost wholly informal. The evidences of toleration of formality come later, mainly in connection with arguments against brutal geometrical planning. Perhaps Sitte discovered the possibilities of good formal work when he came to make diagrammatic plans correcting the faults of the lifeless T-square work he saw being done about him. And it is likely that Sitte felt the beauty of the old informal work and identified his personality with it before he came to appreciate in some degree the intellectual quality of the then more generally admired formal compositions. We must remember that Sitte was a painter as well as an architect and that the German architecture of the 1880's was not such that it prepared a man for appreciation of Baroque planning. Sitte hated the hard geometry in vogue at the time among the engineers who made the city plans, and he took refuge in the dear old time-unified Gothic plazas. Loving them, seeing how much more in harmony they were with the *Zeitgeist* of the decade than were the straight diagonals, he developed the enthusiasm of a worshiper and saw himself in the sweet role of revealer and prophet. He bowed distantly to the

Renaissance, but he gave his heart to Rothenburg.

The success of Sitte's book was emphatically the success of its informal medieval examples—the references to Baroque designs went unheeded. Sitte found himself leader of an eager school of designers in the archaic mode. Could he have wished a better confirmation of his natural preference?

The half-dozen plans Sitte made to illustrate ideas presented in his book are, save for a few passages, formal, but when he came to execute the commissions which followed on the success of the book, his designs were almost exclusively informal. The plan *Fig. 115* for Marienberg, made about 1900, was published in the first volume of *Der Städtebau* and can be taken as a manifesto of Sitte's principles, ripened by a decade of experience. Of some fifty new streets shown in the plan, all but a few of them quite short, only half a dozen are straight throughout. In the section intended for closely built terrace houses there are only a few arcs of long radius, most of the streets being straight save for a curve or angle at the end, to produce right-angled intersections. In the district of detached houses almost all the streets are long-radius curves. There is no example of a straight street on the axis of a building. The twenty small plazas are all informal, as are the three larger plazas and the market place. The public gardens are predominantly informal. The *Rathaus* has a tower at its *Fig. 116* corner, in line with the sidewalk of an important street. A Renaissance architect would have put the tower on the axis of the building and the building on the axis of the street. Sitte gives you a pretty picture to look at: a formal designer would have made you feel that you were in an intellectually integrated space composition. In front of the church is a little open plaza supported by a retaining wall. A ramped

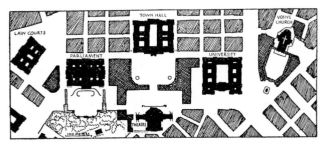

FIGURE 117. Sitte's plan for the rearrangement of part of the Vienna Ring. The black and the hatched buildings exist. The crosshatched buildings and the colonnades are Sitte's proposals. His purpose was to form settings for the buildings. The enclosed areas were probably intended to contain formal gardens, but no large trees.

drive rises across the front of the wall and turns into the plaza at one corner. In the angle thus formed stands a fountain. The entire composition contains no two objects or areas on the same axis. Sitte had not discovered that the Renaissance designers set their fountains and monuments on the axis with their buildings in order that, by the optical law of parallax, the spectator might have the means of measuring his distance from the building he was approaching and thus have a lively impression of the extent of the area and the size of the building. Neither, in spite of his book containing more than one reference to "the effects of perspective," does Sitte appear to have realized the value of perspective as a means of carrying back scale-giving dimensions from points near the eye to distant buildings.

The Marienberg plan is in many ways excellent, and a certain lucid common sense makes it superior to most of the plans done in the same style. But Marienberg certainly cannot be cited as evidence that Sitte understood or desired to emulate the Baroque designs to which he had alluded with apparent appreciation in his book.

Sitte's proposals for replanning the Vienna Ring attracted much attention and have been reproduced Fig. 117 frequently in city planning literature. In general, Sitte thought that the Ring was too open, that the monumental buildings were so scattered that there could be no logic or dignity in their situations, nor could their great size be appreciated. The Votivkirche, for instance, stands with a vast triangle before it, open to the sight and sound of busy traffic. Sitte made the excellent proposal that by putting up new (and of course fairly low) buildings an enclosed atrium be formed, corresponding in idea to the Piazza di San Pietro, though Sitte would plant his plaza with a formal garden. This atrium was to be symmetrical, but at the sides and behind the church Sitte suggested a series of very irregular openings. In this he almost certainly erred. Michelangelo, who had a godlike absoluteness of feeling in such matters, designed for his St. Peter's a plaza whose lines closely paralleled the outline of the church. When the plan of the plaza responds to the plan of the building, the walls of the plaza form a recognition of the building by the rest of the city; they mark off a logical place for the building and tie it into that place. They also form symmetrical steadying counterbalances against the mass of the building. Sitte cut off complete sidewise views of the church because it is asymmetrical lengthwise. He could have done the same with a formal plan, and in any case visual symmetry is not essential at the side or rear of a building if one has a sense of order and definite orientation. The side view of a horse is asymmetrical.

Sitte also studied the revision of the large area (some 600 by 1,100 feet) marked out by the city hall and theater, at the sides, and the university and parliament building, at the ends. This is the most sumptuous part of the Ring. It is now occupied by pavements, lawns, and informal baskets of rich foliage. Feeling the aesthetic insufficiency of this condition, Sitte ascribed it to too great openness and proposed blocks of houses so placed as to create a plaza in front of the city hall and another for the theater, the narrow row of buildings forming the separation being opened on the axis to connect the two plazas. The university and parliament were detached and given their own separate forecourts.

This plan would have the value of giving to each building an area definitely controlled by it, reinforcing its personality—a locus for its *genius loci*. But this gain is purchased at great cost. The outstanding characteristic of the Ring is its green spaciousness, so sharply in contrast to the labyrinthine old city. The Viennese greatly enjoy the Ring, and not merely as display. The Renaissance designers would certainly have said that spaciousness need not mean vulgarity and would have found a way, probably by formal gardening, to preserve and intensify the characteristic value of the site.

Paul Wolf, in his *Städtebau, das Formproblem der Stadt*, says that Sitte's value was that he took city planning out of the field of engineering and placed it again among the arts. That was a great service, and we must not lose sight of it even though we must recognize that in formulating principles for the newly restored art Sitte was the mouthpiece of his hardly blessed time. It was a time, truly, of *"Natur und den Alten,"* of picturesqueness, of romantic association. It was a time better fit to practice historical painting and to make sagas into grand opera than to formulate architectural principles.

15

Mussolini, Haussmann, and Company

Rome, 1931. Make your reservations now. For the Duke has spoken. In five years Imperial Rome must be restored. Signor Cremonesi must roll up his black shirt sleeves and seize pick and shovel. A wide avenue must open between the Piazza Colonna and the Pantheon. Thousands of monuments must stand forth in heroic, Benitoic, solitary grandeur. The barnacles of all these wasted centuries must be hewn away. A new Rome must rise in Saturnian rings around the seven-hilled city and along the sacred river all the way to Ostia. No trams in the old city, best there are in the new. One doesn't mention money on such occasions, but doubtless in due time we shall be reading typographically impressive announcements on the financial page, and editors will commend the loan on grounds of art, humanity, and sentiment.

Lovers of Rome shudder, thinking of past unsheathings of the crowbar in Rome and of past official plans. But the present danger is at least less serious than one that threatened Rome fifty years ago, when civic art knew no defensive tactic. That prodigious human steam shovel, Baron Haussmann, being interrupted in his work of digging highways for cabs and cannonballs through the maze of eastern Paris, secured a diplomatic passport and went to Italy. At Florence a great financier asked him to head a company being formed *"pour transformer Rome à l'instar de Paris."* Haussmann thought it a great compliment to be invited to join these forward-looking gentlemen. He declined, but he promised "to indicate on a map of the Eternal City the proper lines to be cut across the network of narrow, tortuous streets that covered its tormented soil."

Rome was sacked in 1527, but she should forget that calamity in giving thanks that she escaped Baron Haussmann in 1873. That gentleman ("that overgrown wild beast" was his minister of the interior's delicately appreciative description) is rarely mentioned nowadays by European city planners, but his myth is still held sacred by what may be called the American chamber of commerce school of civic art. *Wacker's Manual of the Plan of Chicago,* written to prepare the Chicago young for their future Haussmannizing, calls him "the greatest city builder of all time"—which by tonnage measurement is doubtless true.

The fundamental reasons back of the transformation of Paris are conveniently ignored by this type of city planner, because the need for public acceptance of his plans quite naturally fills his fountain pen with propaganda. Some of Louis Napoleon's thoughts were philanthropic, but not all. He wrote a history of artillery and was a student of strategy. He knew that in Paris his throne was a cannon. He knew that straight streets favor artillery, that crooked lanes favor pistols and sabers. He knew that asphalt is pleasanter to drive on than cobblestones, and not so likely to be thrown at the cops. Napoleon personally planned the first of the three groups of streets and had it well started before Haussmann was called up from Bordeaux. There was no question in Haussmann's mind that the casern on the present Place de la République and the three streets radiating from it were intended, as he says in his memoirs, "to slash the belly of Old Paris, the quarter of riots and barricades." The wide streets gave light and air to the fronts of the new houses, but they took it from the backs of the old. The area built on was increased, and the "abundance of water" came mostly from hydrants in the yards.

Airplanes and gas bombs have robbed city planning of its military value, but il Capo del Governo may have learned other lessons from Napoleon III and Haussmann. Transforming cities makes work. The riots of 1848 and the failure of the national workshops were at least the godparents of the Rue de Turbigo. "If they want work," said the head of the Liberal Empire, "let them break down their barricades and build casernes and churches." At the beginning most of the money came from the peasants of France, to whom, Haussmann says, the tranquillity of Paris is of first importance. Later the city's share increased, and the octroi was raised, but full breadbaskets don't grumble. More and more money was needed; the wily Haussmann always found a way. Minister Ollivier is a better source here than is Haussmann. He tells how the prefect of the Seine piled irregularity on irregularity, overdrawing every authorization, draining every available treasury. One of his clever devices was this: He would give a builder a contract to make a new street, houses and all, to be paid for in eight annuities. But the city had no money to buy the land, and the contractor could not condemn it. So the contractor deposited with the city the estimated cost of the land. then Haussmann's land jury condemned the property, and he paid for it out of the deposits. One imagines that under this arrangement there was not too much haggling over the contractor's price.

And Haussmann invented what was pleasantly called a veiled loan. He gave the contractors the right to issue *bons de délégation,* virtually drafts on the city. The city endorsed them, the contractors cashed them at the Crédit foncier, and the bank reimbursed itself by issuing "communal obligations" covered by the endorsed drafts. This operation made the city the bank's actual debtor, and not the contractor. Thus the city gave no money to the contractor, and the Crédit foncier lent no money to the city, which would have been contrary to a law that required parliamentary approval of communal loans. A rather thin veil, Ollivier thought. "But time pressed and the Emperor approved."

The Chicago manual draws these proceedings into the American perspective. "The people supported the men advancing the improvements because they believed that an improved city meant greater wealth for its people. This theory has been proven correct, as people from all parts of the world visit Paris in great numbers each year, and there spend large sums among the merchants and tradespeople." Yes, the people were very demonstrative along about 1871, and the bankers and contractors managed somehow to buy houses in the Etoile section without

waiting for money to be brought from all parts of the world.

What uses Mussolini will make of the political possibilities of a great construction campaign and whether he will solve the financial problems following Haussmann's example remain to be seen or surmised. That some part of his program will be carried through is sure, for the freeing of monuments has been going on slowly for several years. The little round temple of Vesta, for instance, the church of St. Mary the Egyptian, has been cut out of the hospice that concealed it. Mussolini, too, is good at finding a way. Perhaps the Black Shirts will do the tearing-down just for fun, trade oil of Ricinus for materials, and make the Masons do the rebuilding. But more likely we shall see the dignified announcements, after Mr. Morgan has listened sympathetically to a long story about classical archaeology (in which he is known to be interested) and 7 per cent.

16

The Restoration of Rome

It is a year now since Signor Mussolini made Senator Cremonesi governor of the city of Rome and commanded him to make the city a sanitary place for men to live and work in, and also to make it a more impressive visible symbol of the power and glory of ancient Rome and of the renewed Italian greatness that Mussolini promises.

That the program thus laid down was consciously overoptimistic was generally recognized. The glory of ancient Rome will need more than five years for its restoration. And there is no surplus in the Italian treasury wherewith to cut a new avenue from the Piazza Colonna to the Pantheon, to clear squares around the Mausoleum of Augustus, the Marcello Theater, and a hundred other old buildings, much less to raise a new city in Saturnian rings around the old one and along the Tiber to Ostia. These

dreams, surely, may one day come true. But it takes more than a crowbar and stonemason's trowel to rebuild cities. It takes industries, trade, transportation, inventions, and changes in standards of living.

Yet enough has been done to show that the program is still alive and that the operations under it will be a constant object of concern to all friends of Rome, all students of architecture and civic art.

For Rome is the sacred city of architecture. Sociologists who look upon the populous modern city as primarily an economic and sanitary problem are quite right. But they must have charity for the architect who sees in Rome the richest assembly of architectural beauty in the world. He insists that a way must be found to make the city livable without destroying it as a work of art. The archaeologist must also have charity, for architects know there is a Rome more precious than what has survived of the city of Augustus.

It is not, commonly, the very modern or the very ancient Rome that holds the hearts of lovers of Rome. Rather it is the city of a long middle period —let us say, not to be stingy, from Constantine to Garibaldi. That is the life span of the Rome we know, a long evolving story, various in style perhaps, but gathered naturally enough into a richly tooled binding of the Renaissance. To all but the mole-complexed teacher of classical archaeology the old ruins (always excepting the Pantheon) are not quite part of Rome. They are the incredible heirlooms of a half-mythical grandmother, their use forgotten and feeling strange to our hands. And the modern things, the Victor Emmanuel Monument, the Via Nazionale, the Palazzo di Giustizia, these unaccountable aberrations are like gaps cut in the crown of an ancient oak to let some phone wires through. But everything between St. Mary Cosmodin and the hemicycles of the Piazza del Popolo (barely a century old) is of the living Rome, the Rome we love.

This living Rome grew slowly, but not entirely by chance. Rome is a lovely picturesque landscape, but Rome is also a treasury of consciously formed works of art. Unlike Chartres and Malines, Rome is not the product of a fortunate period—her jewels were cut by particular artists at particular times. The architectural feeling of the city is essentially formal, despite the want of a general geometric framework. To the city planner, Rome is not a city of streets (though the three streets meeting in the Piazza del Popolo form the most beautiful group of streets in the world, and the Via Condotti is the most beautifully terminated street); it is, rather, a city of plazas. Most of these openings were formed during the papal period. In ancient Rome the city was fearfully crowded with high tenements. As the city grew again after the lean Middle Ages, the city planning commissioners of the popes, the *maestri delle strade*, took every opportunity to open up a little patch here and there. Nobles and cardinals, building their palaces and churches, usually cleared a space in front of them. And now, in some parts of Rome, one passes from piazza to piazza almost as in a house from room to room. Suppose you start from the little Baroque setting that is the outdoors extension of the plan of the church of San Ignazio. Fifty steps north through a crooked lane, and you are in the Piazza di Pietra, in front of the somber ancient colonnade of the Borsa. Another twenty paces, and you enter the Piazza Colonna, a large rectangular enlargement of the Corso with the column of Marcus Aurelius at its center. Go through the colonnade along its west side, turn to the left, and you are in the Piazza di Monte Citorio. Go down past the mended obelisk, turn fifty yards to the right, and you come to the little Piazza Capranica. Thence by a jagged lane in a moment, you are in the Piazza della Rotonda, in front of the Pantheon. Each of these city rooms has a feel and charm of its own, and several of them have a definite architectural organization. The essence of their charm, in most cases, is the tightness of the enframement—the contrast of the bright space of the plaza against the solid houses and dark *vicoli* around it.

Now it is through the region I have just described that Mussolini would cut his "wide avenue" opening up a view of the Pantheon from the column of Marcus Aurelius. If that is done without seriously damaging the Piazza Colonna, without ruining the Piazza della Rotondo, and without destroying several churches and palaces that lie along the line, it will be a miracle of architectural ingenuity and good taste.

The clearing of areas around old buildings is no less a knotty point among European city planners than is the cutting of new streets. Many a bitter campaign has been fought along the *dégagement* front. It seems to have been the Gothic restoration activities of Pugin and Viollet-le-Duc that engendered the idea of tearing down the little buildings that clustered against the old churches. About that time Napoleon III and Haussmann began the transformation of Paris. They took to clearing with a gusto —it just suited their desire to raise a dust and make things trim. They cleared around Notre Dame and made a square in front of it, faced with large (too large) public buildings, and a shrubbery along the river side, all quite to the taste of a time that thought the Exposition of 1869 the apogee of human civilization. The fashion spread to Belgium and Germany. Ulm cleared the foreground of the cathedral; during the past year they have held a competition to decide how to put the buildings back again. At Metz they cleared the barnacles from the sides of the soaring cathedral and proudly published a book of before-and-after pictures. The "before" pictures are now treasured as the best record of the architect Blondel's charming little buildings, an irreparable loss to the plaza with which he did sincere homage to the great mass of the church.

But in 1889 along came the Austrian Camillo Sitte and with one small book routed the advocates of clearing. He showed that all the best Gothic churches, and most of the Renaissance, were tied in with, supported by, given scale by, smaller buildings. As his trump card he counted the churches of Rome and found that there are 255, of which 41 are built against on one side, 96 on two, 110 on three, 2 on all four, and only 6 stand free. Sitte rode home in triumph—the matter was settled forever. Benito Mussolini that day studied his Caesar, pommeled his playmates, and heard nothing of the famous victory. A year ago he arose, as ruler of Italy, to command the governor of Rome to make clearings around those same churches whose close contiguity with their neighbors had been cited by Sitte to the discomfiture of the enemy. Verily, time changes many things.

As usual, the truth of the matter seems to lie somewhere between one extreme and the other. No good architect ever purposely set a variety of doll houses around a monumental building in order to make it look bigger. And no good architect, by preference, ever set his building in the midst of an unrelated formless open area, or made it the hub of a traffic center, or surrounded it with insipid unarchitectural walks and foliage. When they are quite free, all architects, classical, Gothic, or Renaissance, have sought to create harmonious settings for their buildings, to mark off an architecturally framed area for them. The Roman temples normally stood in an open space bounded by a colonnade, the peribolos. The Pisa cathedral, one of the most beautifully located of medieval buildings, rises from a flat field, between the town and a high fortification wall. Michelangelo intended his St. Peter's to stand in the center of a plaza of uniform frame, about a thousand feet square.

To us the principles applying to a monumental building, one of great historical interest, may not seem identical with those applying to a new building. But a Renaissance architect would have felt little difference. Commissioned to design a setting for the Pantheon, for instance, he would have done it in the manner of the various plans Bramante, Michelangelo, Bernini, and Fontana made for the vicinity of St. Peter's. Nor would he have stopped with the setting. He would have redecorated the Pantheon itself—"restored" it, to his own taste, without too much trouble to decide how it looked in old Roman times. That is exactly what Michelangelo did in making the church of Santa Maria degli Angeli, in 1563, out of the tepidarium of the Baths of Diocletian. If the tepidarium had not been so used, if it stood now, a red-brown ruin with weeds growing in its crevices, the suggestion that it be rebuilt, glazed, and decorated would be met everywhere with accusations of vandalism. Yet there can be no doubt that Michelangelo's church, full of archaeological solecisms though it is, gives a truer idea of the building's original appearance and a much truer impression of the spirit of Imperial Rome than could the stripped framework of ancient masonry. Ruins take on with age a simplicity and severe dignity that may utterly misrepresent the taste of the civilization from which they survive. Much of the coldness of modern monumental architecture is due to the accident that the color the Greeks used on their statues and temples was not permanent.

The modern worship of ruins seems little less than stupidity to an architect who would give his skin for a day in third-century Rome. Insofar as that worship arises from a sentiment for the picturesque and ivy-overgrown, it tends to debase architecture. But there is another way of looking at an ancient monument, a way that supplants architecture. With the passage of time a drama form grows up around the physical form of the monument. This dramatic dimension of the Pantheon embraces all the life of Imperial Rome; it reaches out into Gaul and Britain, Judea and Egypt. To eyes that can see it, all the flowing life of Rome clings to this dun mass, its grandest physical survival. Perhaps in these somewhat unarchitectural phrases I have expressed part of the Italian architect Gustavo Giovannoni's esoteric meaning when he says, *"La continuità vitale del monumento non è solo nel tempo ma anche nello spazio."* The Pantheon, to our modern culture, lives in space as well as in time. It carries with it through time something of the human goings and comings it has looked down upon. It is the stage across which forever marches for us a rich pageant of races, wars, and religions, of the flowering and withering of civilizations.

Well may Giovannoni say, then, that the art of restoration must deal with spiritual problems. It requires the most delicate good taste and imagination to conceive the full dramatic power of the monument, to create a setting that will give full effect to that power. Such art is akin to the design of stage settings, for the stage must be part of the acted play, helping producer and audience to make all the beauty they can out of the playwright's text. But the setting of the monument must not be obtrusively symbolic or historical. It must not itself pretend to be ancient. Primarily, there must be good views of the monument, against a right background. The great size of the building (I am still thinking of the Pantheon) must be emphasized, its precious quality expressed. The materials used, the forms and colors given them, must harmonize with the monument and tactfully make a virtue of its weathered gauntness. The Pantheon is doubly precious to us because it contains the tomb of Raphael. That was his own choice, made during those last calm days of a sickness that must almost have been a welcome escape from the load of toil he had been carrying. Part of that load was the direction of excavations, for Raphael was one of the first Roman archaeologists. The papal secretary Celio Calcagnini wrote of Raphael in 1519: "By digging out the foundations of ancient monuments and restoring them according to the descriptions of classical authors, he has filled Pope Leo and all Rome with such admiration that they look upon him as a god sent down from Heaven to restore the Eternal City to its former majesty." And he goes on, perhaps less closely suggesting the present distinguished Restorer—"Yet, far from being puffed up with pride, he meets others in the most friendly spirit and rejects no advice or criticism."

Raphael had in part the modern attitude toward ancient buildings, but he felt, more than we have need to, their value as teachers of architecture and as works of architecture on their own account. In these ways the harder-minded Michelangelo valued the ancient masterpieces, but of sentimental regard for the merely antique he probably had little. Lanciani says that St. Peter's is unlike the other Roman churches in that most of them were built from the ruins of a single ancient monument, but St. Peter's from a hundred. If Michelangelo had been given a free hand with the Pantheon, he would have modernized it as completely as he did the interior of Santa Maria degli Angeli. The external veneer of marble would have been restored and the dome gilded. The tympanum of the portico would have come to life with sculpture—and with such sculpture that one's heart stops at the thought of it!

If it had been objected that he was not truly restoring, he would have answered, "I have made of this dead ruin a thing of beauty and life, fit to be a temple of God. I have carved in the architrave my master's name, to his glory and to the glory of this time. I have done it as seemed to me best—if another can build better, let him do so."

Thinking of that tympanum, we cannot deny him the right to make that confident answer. We have not the right—or is there some other reason why we do not? For us archaeology must be the science of preservation. Let us hope that at Rome the science will be pursued eclectically. The beauty of the city as a whole and of the minor buildings of the Renaissance ought not to be sacrificed to reveal a few stark symbols of the virility of the *magna Mater*.

The best element of hope lies in the fact that Mussolini did not command the governor of Rome to remake the heart of the city to meet the needs of modern traffic. Save for the street to the Pantheon, primarily aesthetic in purpose, he does not suggest brutal slashings of new streets, in the manner of the transformation of Paris. The Roman plan of 1910, which was abandoned in 1916, proved definitively that these piercings are too ruinously destructive to be tolerated. Mussolini seems, rather, to contemplate making of the old city a grandiose museum, populated, of course, but not so densely as now—a kind of sanctuary from modern traffic and construction. That is an enormously difficult thing to do, for a city is a living organism whose functional membering changes only with placid slowness. Yet it is not impossible physically—perhaps not impossible aesthetically. Mussolini knows that a museum is a dreary thing unless its treasures are arranged with order and dignity and are tastefully environed.

The crucial difficulty will be the choice of architect. Few men anywhere in the world are equipped to attack this problem in civic art as Bernini in the seventeenth century and Blondel in the eighteenth were equipped. Most contemporary Italian architects do the kind of work that is liked in South America. But of late, Italian art has become both more vigorous and more refined. A few architects, freeing themselves from the French Beaux-Arts and from modern Germany, give promise of reviving the old incomparable Italian sense of form. If the right man is chosen, the miracle may come to pass: Mussolini may add to, and not destroy, the beauty of Rome.

And the new city that is to rise about the old one also will be a complex problem, of a different sort. The economic basis of Rome is not broad, and only industry will build a great modern city. There is no empire now to send galleys of grain to Rome. But perhaps Mussolini can create the industries and can take the people of Rome out of their insanitary tenements. His new city will have still to be Roman, to recognize the Roman love of company, delight in crowds. And the architectural form of the city ought also to be Roman, not a copy of Parisian *faubourgs* or of English garden suburbs. There is a golden tradition of civic art in Italy. The new Rome could be its greatest creation.

17

Williamsburg

While the United States Government has been destroying and plotting to destroy in Washington, Mr. Ford has been collecting old buildings for his museum at Dearborn, and Mr. Rockefeller has gone him one better by collecting an old town—and not only an old town but an old state capital, complete with history, traditions, a college, numerous firsts, oldests, and uniques, and a live population, including several rare old ladies who would grace any museum in the world.

Williamsburg has, of course, close relations to the city of Washington. L'Enfant knew the town. It was admired by Washington and other men who influenced the design of the national capital. The similarity of the plans is obvious, though I trace the resemblance to the common style and common requirements, and I do not suggest that the older plan was the principal model for the later one. But the fact that Williamsburg was part of colonial culture must have facilitated L'Enfant's work.

The town plan of Williamsburg probably derives from a sketch by a skilled architect, imperfectly worked out on the ground. Incomplete though it is, the town has the good order and managed emphasis that mark a good Renaissance design. People go to Williamsburg to see the sumptuous and beautiful buildings and gardens that have been restored or rebuilt, but I am sure that the basically good plan is a factor, whether consciously or not, in the invariably pleasant impression of the place.

The restoration has hardly affected the plan except in the shopping center that has been developed at the College end of Duke of Gloucester Street. The necessary parking accommodations are managed *Fig. 118* tactfully and are neither conspicuous nor offensive. The store groups themselves, however, that have been built (there was some remodeling) at each side of Duke of Gloucester Street constitute a preposterous travesty on eighteenth-century planning. The stores are frantically picturesque and various; the fronts are parallel to the curb but are set back at random distances from it. Only the post office setback is sufficient to produce a satisfactory area. Often the offset, between one store and another, is so slight as to be without plastic value. In one case a store with a bow window is set back from its neighbors just about the amount of the window's projection, the total result having less vigor than no variation at all. There is no design value in these weak deviations from alignment, merely an affectation of unmechanicalness which, since we know it is not modern, we are intended to assume is colonial. Emphatically, it is not. The southern planters laid out their slave quarters on axes and cross axes and made dignified symmetrical courts out of their barns and stables. Williamsburg is not a medieval town, formed by centuries of accidents. It is a product of seventeenth-eighteenth-century rationality. If the restoration is intended to give us a true picture of the culture and the architectural ideals of colonial Virginians, this shopping district is a gross misrepresentation.

Furthermore, for the truth must be told, the place smells strongly of landscape architecture. Sitting on one of the pleasant sidewalk benches to have my shoes shined, I counted nine different species of trees (two of them dead) within the distance of a peanut toss. There were tall holly trees, fresh from the woods, planted within a foot of the store fronts and leaning away from the wall, as if they had

FIGURE 118. Williamsburg, along the Duke of Gloucester Street.

grown there from babyhood. It was a naturalistic planting of street trees, to go with the naturalistic planting of shops. Nobody but a landscape architect could have thought that all out.

From the sumptuous way in which the buildings and formal gardens are carried out, I judge that there was no wish to understate the quality of the old designs or the skill of the colonial craftsmen. I believe that strict archaeologists will agree that many parts of the work represent what the early Virginians would have liked to do rather than what they actually did do. The same attitude might well have stimulated the town planning work. Take for example, the Palace Green, lying between the Governor's Palace and Duke of Gloucester Street. The man who made the plan (in England, doubtless) assumed that this mall would be level and that it would afford a perfect view of the Palace from the street. As it happened, there is a little rise of ground at the middle of the mall that cuts off the lower part

Fig. 119

of the building, spoiling this all-important view. A few hundred dollars' worth of grading, before the young trees were set out, would have remedied this patent fault and would have brought out the true quality of the design.

This Palace axis continues on across Duke of Gloucester Street, the main axis of the layout. South of Gloucester Street, as it is at present, there is a field opening up a view into the country. So casually is the whole thing handled that from the upper front window of the Governor's Palace you see practically nothing but grass and trees—there is nothing at all to indicate that the main street of the town, the main axis of a design to which the Palace is related by perpendicularity of axes, runs across your vista. In the distance a hill slopes sharply across the view; beyond that, woods. This failure to develop the design architecturally, as the designer must have intended, contrasts sharply with the very elaborate development of the garden axis north of the Palace. A very modest amount of "expression" of the intersection of axes (at Duke of Gloucester Street) and the continuation of the cross axis toward the south would satisfy the minimum needs of the situation. Some grading, a few whitewashed posts or stone piers, some white fence, possibly a pair of sheds or summer houses, would serve to "render" this important part of the plan. The "Frenchman's map," showing the town in Revolutionary times, indicates that some sort of formal development marked the mall axis south of the main street.

The view of the Capitol from the College gate is already partly obscured by the shade trees on Duke of Gloucester Street. That is the American spirit to a T. Spend a million dollars to create a beautiful perspective, and then let it be overgrown with thick foliage for fear of inconveniencing a squirrel.

Williamsburg is a huge success. People are flocking there; they love it. They love the quaint buildings, the old cooking things in the Governor's kitchen, the pillory, the old box bushes, the powdered ladies in farthingales; they love the Governor's coach and cocked-hatted coachman driving through the streets, just as in ye olden tymes. The architects of the frigid Washington Triangle, when they go down there, must wring their hands and say, "Alas, why didn't we think of this?" There will never be another Triangle, but there will be other Williamsburgs.

And why? Is it the vogue of antiques and our delight in being able to collect with Mr. Rockefeller a colonial town when in the past we have been able to collect, or read about collecting, only door knockers and spinning wheels? Is there a vein in us of nostalgic patriotism, a hungry love that we cannot feel for this harried present time but can freely give to that simple and beautiful and unworried golden age? Is it the smartness of knowing about the past, a phase of the world interest in archaeology? Is it merely that men still long to go on pilgrimages?

One thing is fairly clear, that Williamsburg is largely a phenomenon of sentiment. The management recognizes this in such details as the costumes of the guide ladies and similar affectations. Reports of "Ye Olde A. & P. Foode Shoppe" are exaggerated but not untrue in essence. The grossly picturesque store center is certainly a surrender of architectural sense to sentimental antiquarianism. And the point I have mentioned about the Palace Green where the visual spacial composition is spoiled by a few feet of earth: so obvious a blunder can be ac-

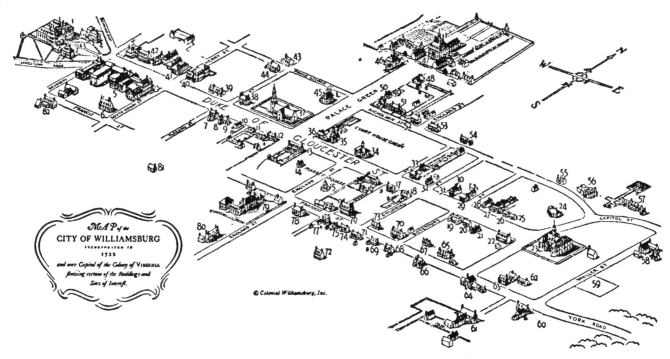

FIGURE 119. Williamsburg. The store groups referred to in the text are at numbers 5 and 41.

counted for only by supposing that the architects looked at the Green through some sort of magic glass that made of it a sentimental value in which formal perfection would be a redundancy. To people whose perception of pure proportion, formal relation, and the modeling of space is an infinitely more exciting experience than their sentiments, this typically American (and English) substitution of sentiment for sensation and perception is a constant distress. It runs all through our art, of course, but the loss seems greatest in architecture and civic art, where the formal values are so simple and evident and where they can be kept relatively pure of dis-

tracting meanings—as they cannot, for example, in literature.

I associate this sort of feeling with the wide and deep popularity of informal landscape gardening. No art style is more widely accepted. And the basis of "landscape" is a sentiment, a feeling that nature's art is better than man's. Three generations of infiltration of landscape conceptions have insidiously corrupted our architects, making them tolerant of "informalities" that actually negate essential objectives in their designs. This atmosphere, incidentally, is a dangerous one for the evolution of "modern" architecture, for it encourages a general softness and mere avoidance of "artificiality," usually taken to mean the absence of axiality and defined pattern.

Much of the popular acceptance of "landscape" —the word has come to have a meaning far removed from the landscape gardening of Humphry Repton's time—is due, I believe, to a dim feeling that this way of arranging things is opposed to art and is a new demonstration that intuition and the heart are, after all, superior to the arts that require genius and training. This kind of antiart is a very deep-lying element in American thought and feeling.

In any case there is no question that the kind of thinking that produced the plan of Williamsburg and the plan of Washington is not the kind of thinking that has meaning to most of us today. The severely rational and formal type of art is apparently fundamentally irritating to people who are dimly conscious of a basic irrationality and inconsistency in their own thought. Our efforts to retain religious and patriotic conviction while constantly surrounded by evidences of irrationality in nature and human conduct necessarily destroy the easy mental balance which alone takes pleasure in a rationalized art. A kind of sadism impells people who are conscious of their own uncertainties to hate minds, and creations of mind, which have the sense of order they cannot understand. When people of this type can ascribe emotional meaning to a work of art, they are avid to substitute this intelligible

meaning for the formal organization which disquiets them. They look at the Lincoln Memorial and see a symbol of a tragic life. Perhaps they also see a demonstration of accepted propriety in the choice of materials and architectural style. These are values they can accept and share, but any exhibition of purely rational design unsupported by sentiment arouses the antagonism which is part of uncertain comprehension. There is something very deep in human nature which makes failure fully to understand equivalent to fear, and fear equivalent to hate. Hence the invariable success of the ridicule of poets and artists and hence the delight of visitors to Williamsburg in the purposed disorder of the quack-colonial shopping center. Freed from any burden of necessity to observe and understand an organized unity, they can freely enjoy the toy-town prettiness and the lush sentimentality.

Is there perhaps a compromise? Can civic artists whose ill-judged time and place of birth throw them into a civilization of word worship, sentiment seeking, and minute counting—can they find some way of expressing space and mass and area that *will* have meaning to crowds of people, as L'Enfant hoped his plan would have? There is no more reasonable place to look for the answer than at one of the big fairs where designers are free from conservative restraints and where the popular response can be closely gauged.

18

The Century of Progress

City planners have one bond with the landscape architects, that they become very charitable of architecture. They lean heavily upon a gracious law by which a large collection of bad architecture may become very tolerable civic art, or charming scenery. And their constant solace is the happy accident. They feel (let us suppose) an active thirst to experience the coming to life of space in unexpected perspectives and in spirited conjunctions of silhouette. Thus it happens that they find crumbs of nourishment even in badly baked bread.

The Chicago Century of Progress was mixed—to continue our homely figure—in a hundred-million-dollar bowl but was baked, alas, in a thirty-million-dollar oven. The bakers did their best, but the loaf fell. The Fair had no general plan and at a dozen points no perceptible local plan. The mixture of chic science, architectural bontonism, architectural jazz, big-shot advertising, Coney Island entertainment, and sentimental archaeology caused the physical and emotional collapse of all but the sturdiest visitors. The confusion was complete. The incidental buildings were more looked at than the "dominants," oversubtle compositions of architectural plan failed to carry in the normal view, the intended spirited variety became a monotonous incoherence, and the color seemed always tentative.

Yet I spent a dozen Saturday evenings at the Fair and enjoyed them all. What was irrational by sober daylight became at the day's end a fairyland for optical adventure. The arbitrary bulks and colors of the buildings were subjugated by the sunset's warm light and long shadows; they were drawn into a single picture with the lagoon and its moored and moving boats. The pale-dark towers of tragic Chicago and the leaden lake seemed more unreal than these meaningless but hypnotizing shapes when familiarity had drawn them together.

If in its totality the Fair became a landscape rather than a work of art, its details could not be dismissed as valueless to architecture. The designers of the Fair, or some of them, were experimenting with abstract sculpture and with the correlation of forms that were alike so obscurely that their order could be sensed only by some sort of metaphysical touch. It is in this direction that the postarchitectural art seems to seek esoteric rationalities to take the place of those primitive conceptions of mass in stability and well-knit membering that have been enervated by our modern structural systems using concealed steel and large sheets of rigid materials. One suspects that some of their constructions were intended to find something responsive in the hazy physical meaning we give to such phenomena as ether waves and cosmic rays. Since radio waves are tossed back and forth by the earth and some layer of the stratosphere, why shouldn't their vibration be symbolized by two parallel planes, which they are imagined to animate, much as the constant threat of movement is the energy that gives tactile animation to a stone arch? Forming one of the minor gates of the Fair there was a construction of steel pipe and orange canvas that fascinated me deeply. There was something Japanese about it, and a reminiscence of kites. It worked somewhat (in addition to the muscular appeal of the strong posts) as if the tactile meaning of surface were intensified, in some such symbolical way as I have tried to suggest, by an atmospheric pulsation playing between close and parallel planes. Things of this sort, construction for the beauty of

construction, are needed in civic art, particularly in civic garden art. They can have so much more vivacity than the conventional earth furniture of stone.

In their civic art—their planning of open spaces and building groups—the designers of the Fair obviously adhered to the slogan that guided their architectural work: Don't bore. They therefore avoided anything so hackneyed as a general plan of organization. Only in a few passages did they suffer strict axiality to appear, and they billowed the ground surface almost as industriously as the landscape architects do when they want to justify winding walks on a terrain that nature made flat. In their planning they used freely what the painters call the *imprévu*. In fact, there is a general impression that the correct type of planning for the arrangement of buildings in nontraditional styles is necessarily an informal one. The reasoning seems to be that since axiality is obviously an art value, functionalism (which was named and advocated for modern man as a better guide than art) must give us a different result—asymmetrical forms.

Many passages in the Century of Progress plan had much resemblance to the style identified with the name of Camillo Sitte. That style was developed from the accidental or in part accidental medieval civic art. It was influenced by both informal gardening (which has always been conceived of by its practitioners as functional art) and the formal architectural planning it sought to displace. In Sitte's plans the streets were usually straight and at approximately right angles. But they were asymmetrical in plan and elevation, and the terminal or "closing" element normally was of informal, pictorial character. The open places set with fountains and statues in informal relation to the area were

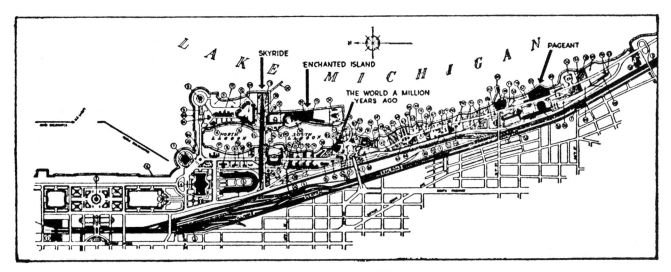

FIGURE 120. The Century of Progress Exposition—the Chicago Exposition of 1933.

asymmetrical and as closely enclosed as practicable. Like the *Sittesche Stil,* and like, one supposes, all young art movements, the modern style has in it a lively element of sadism, directed against the old way. That which pains the old teacher delights the rebel pupil. The feeling of being wayward, destructive, lusty, unlike, and superior is a rich reward for the perils of insurrection. This stimulating sadism, this antiart, is experienced also, though not so sharply focused, by the public. They learn that it is smart to destroy, that it is chic to know the proper object and means of destruction. Of the modern style few people can perceive what it *is,* but anyone can see what it is not. "Familiar" and "different" are the aesthetic scales of most minds. The familiar is beautiful until it becomes chic to prefer the different.

There was the further effort, at the Century of Progress, to exploit the chic of science. The rape of science by the modern style in building and decoration is one of the entertaining elements in what our literary friends call the contemporary scene. The reasoning runs in the following syllogism: Science is destructive of old ways; the modern style of architecture is destructive of old ways; therefore the modern style is science expressed in architecture. The fact that some kinds of scientists are more fanatic worshipers of symmetry, as in the cutting of a cogwheel, than ever were the architects of the Renaissance is just as easy to ignore as the fact that the old ways destroyed by science and by the new art are not ways of the same order.

Though they had to renounce any general organization—beyond the psychological dominance of the lagoons—the planners of the Fair were fertilely experimental in their detailed planning. The great circle of flags at the main entrance to the Fair and the avenue of sloping flagstaffs with their enormous banners were moving and beautiful things, rich in suggestions for serious civic design. Piers, stele, and lighting standards were used to define and give plastic depth to open spaces in ways that recalled the sculptural enrichment of French plazas and Italian gardens. The Baroque planners sought always to make their work sociable and friendly and cheerful, touched with humanity. The Fair was free to seek the same expression of life, unhampered by the conventional concrete, granite, evergreens, and grass that make so many American civic centers a pall upon the imagination.

The Fair planners wrestled with plaza design, though rather in terms of courtyards and gardens than as monumental assemblages of buildings. The court of the science building—a high mass with arms extending to the shore of the lagoon—was well proportioned and vivaciously modeled, the sort of thing that ought to be studied by those architects whose only rule for creating an ensemble is to enforce a uniform cornice height.

Of the technical aspects of the Fair construction every city planner must have been struck by the success of the pedestrian pavements. A bituminous pavement covered with fine crushed stone is easy on the feet and easy also on the eye, since it is dark and cannot glare. It makes an infinitely better foil against vertical masonry walls than does concrete, because the slick and usually overscaled slabs of a concrete pavement hide the mother earth on which buildings stand and men walk. The low-set flood lights on the lawns were distinctly worthy of restrained emulation in public gardens.

A big exposition is a fairyland, a museum, a bazaar, and a carnival. At the Century of Progress the bazaars and the carnival shows had several centers of intensity; there was no such complete segregation as at the Columbian Exposition. And the Century of Progress, particularly in the second year, carried to an unprecedented development that old entertainment motif, the village, which has the charm of combining the four delights of the fair. Here was the most ironical part of a highly ironical whole. Alongside the boldly forward-looking modernism of the Fair's main buildings flourished the lush antiquarianism of the villages. The customers, it is embarrassing to confess, seemed definitely to favor the medievalism—with music. No doubt, they considered the modern buildings very smart, but they spent their quarters to see the Belgian Village and the Black Forest.

There is no denying that several of the villages were fetching places. They were small, close, harmonious, of human scale, bearing plainly the human mark. It was pleasant to walk in any direction free from traffic danger—for the constant noise and constant peril of traffic in our cities is a heavier nervous burden than most of us realize. The villages were small enough to be sensed as a whole, they were places of escape from worry and boredom—escape into a simple physical and emotional unity made pleasant by a hazy familiarity. There was the flattery of being asked to be at home in Belgium, Italy, or Tunisia. And there was the crowd, the sociability. Say what you will, it is sweet and sanitary, at carnival time, to sink one's personality in the thought and feeling of a crowd.

I recollect an architectural cocktail party where at one point the conversation touched the Chicago villages. What was their charm? Among the theories advanced were infantilism, grandmotherism, peasantism, snobbism, and agoraphobia. The last, at least, is not wholly inconsistent with aesthetic perception. Even when we have no dislike for open places, most people have a liking for safe havens such as a quiet cloister or a sunny clearing in a woods. Far be it from a lover of old civic art to say the villages were all silly. They had in various degrees something of the composition of solids and voids, narrow streets and open plazas, that endear to us Venice and Rothenburg and Ghent.

City planners must deal with the vest-pocket village—and must have a care lest it make fools of them. The shopping center at Williamsburg is a fair warning of the spiritual swamps into which a jolly Puck of this sort can lead an artist. It should be possible to discover the sound values of the villages and to reject the oversentimental elements. Suburban shopping centers of the "park and shop" type are being built around many cities. These could profit by a close study of the Fair villages. An understanding of marketing customs, traffic, and parking, for work of this kind, must be supplemented by an understanding of the history of towns, which will suggest the means of adding deep aesthetic values to practical convenience.

One went to Chicago in 1933 and 1934 to experience three-dimensional space mastered in terms of modern architecture. One found delightful *jeu d'esprit* in the furnishing of open spots; one found architecture to please every taste save that of the professional critics, who know a happy land where there is no *so what?* in *à la moderne;* one delighted in lagoons that seemed lately to have been borrowed from the wild ducks and to have been surrounded temporarily with Gargantuan colored playthings in place of willows. One found lush sentiment enshrined in medieval villages made old with painted weathering, made wonderous with icicles of glass. But one found no civic art that revealed so much intellectual conviction as laid down the stern and hated gridiron of Chicago.

Part V

On Domes and Water

19

The Reign of the Masonry Dome

If you wish to measure the revolution that steel, the elevator, and desk worship have caused among architectural values, nothing will help you so much as to know what the full meaning of the dome was to Michelangelo and his time. For the dome reigned over architecture during the generations that built St. Peter's—became, indeed, the center of a school of architectural effort striving to realize an ideal that was more clearly seen, one must think, than any other that has given energy to art. That ideal was the perfect dome-centered building.

We now can quite easily reproduce the shapes of domes by bending a few steel beams or by cementing together a few layers of hard thin tiles. But we have lost the desire to know the dome as a perilous heroic adventure in building. Engineering has so far outdistanced daily experience that it has be-come a sort of magic that will protect us and serve us, though we cannot understand it. We enter the Woolworth building without any sense of fear. But in the living days of stone-arch building, a kind of fear was part of the beauty of architecture. Burke was right, joining awe and sublimity. The people of Rome who walked under the dome of St. Peter's in 1590 did not lightly accept the ceiling above them as a pretty surface held up there by some clever mechanical trick. They and their fathers and great-grandfathers had seen the ox teams pulling creak-ing cartloads of great stones up through the Borgo, and they repeated stories of the oak forests cut for scaffolding. The Oriental proverb that arch and dome never sleep was more to them than a pretty saying. The cultivated among them, at least, felt that enormous mass of stone as a membered whole alive with symmetrical thrusts, frictions, compressions, and coherences.

And it was this sublime monster, the masonry dome, that Bramante, Leonardo, Michelangelo, and Vignola dreamed of raising to a kingship over architecture more absolute than it had ever had in Rome or in Byzantium. Their ideal was a building whereof every stone should serve the dome that crowned it. They wanted to embody in a building —in a whole city if you would let them—the complete unfolding of the mechanical and formal significance of the dome principle. They saw in the old long-naved basilicas and Gothic churches merely a practical housing for congregations; each bay of them was a unit, but there was no inevitable structural law that fixed the number of bays. Identical bays, too, performed different functions, and identical functions were performed by dissimilar members—these being the very errors most hated by architectural logic. Brunelleschi's fine dome at Florence has for supports three compact apses and an arch of the wide high nave. Clearly, the mass of the dome bears down equally on all four sides: would it not then, if freed from arbitrary human interference, create for itself exactly equal supports, identical in form because equal in strength? The supporting members, to be sure, might be grouped and modeled so that they could do their work better or in order to honor the dome, both inside and out, with a series of contrapuntal echoes interpreting or completing its form. But every section taken through the vertical axis of the dome must be symmetrical.

Gothic architecture is constantly spoken of as spiritual, and the taste of the Renaissance is called sensual. That is in part because the barbaric splendor of the Gothic has worn or been torn away and in further part because modern eyes see the color of Renaissance interiors but not their structural and formal unity. The Gothic is rich in the vertical lines which by a crude symbolism we call spiritual. But the popes and architects of the Renaissance, masters of geometry and formal logic, made for their spirituality a symbol in harmony with their intelligence, planning churches that would draw the whole earth up to a single point, huge complexes mastered by a single law. They must have smiled at the Gothic builders who laid their churches upon a line drawn from the cross in the market square to the Holy Sepulcher in Jerusalem and, it is said, sometimes bent their main axis to symbolize the bent body of the crucified Christ. Bramante and Michelangelo built St. Peter's on a line running from the center of the earth to the zenith of the heavens. They sought to symbolize, by incarnating it, the absolute truth of the syllogism that was the core of their art: "If the functions are the same, then the forms are the same."

The unity that I am ascribing to the dome-centered building was not a requirement of clerical mysticism—its great enemy and final victor, in fact, was the Latin cross and the traditional processions of the Cult. The architects of the sixteenth century strove for the perfect solution of the dome composition because that was the great professional problem that history and the thought of the time assigned to them, just as the most vital work of our architects is being put into the solution of the tower office building. It was the good fortune of the sixteenth century that artist and engineer were still one man and that, further, the technical and aesthetic command over the sole material, stone, was so complete that only ultimate problems remained for solution.

Such a problem was St. Peter's—the attainment of structural-formal perfection in a domed building so large that human beings, even in great crowds, could not sense the actual size of a larger one.

Michelangelo was the most skillful worker in stone of his time. So he built St. Peter's. He built it as a demonstration of absolute logic and unfettered skill in stone building. When he walked, in imagination, through his design, as an architect loves to, he felt the separate existence of every member, felt the relation of each member to all the rest, the economy and sufficiency of its form, its part in the work, what forces bore upon it, how they were met. He read the whole building, solid and surface and void, as we read a lyric, with, instead of the approximate likeness of rhyme and meter, the abounding floods of symmetry in his church, and instead of the poem's charming play of ideas, some thousands of tons of stone hanging, in an intricate equilibrium, over his head. But how can you set down precisely the meaning to the human mind and body of participation in the phenomenon of an ideally organized mass supported equally by four ideally suitable and ideally placed supports? That might be the formula for a sawhorse—to Michelangelo it meant a universe in which accident had no part, a tangible rendering of man's greatest aesthetic creation, the concept *law*. For law in the abstract he substituted the laws his hand and eye could know: gravitation, the coherence of stone, geometry. Set in play, these laws produced a vast masonry dome crowning a building devoted wholly to the dome's physical support and formal amplification. And so was fulfilled the desire of the Renaissance for absolute law in the disposition of space-enclosing stone—for absolute dignity, mastery, amplitude, elegance, and reason in the shaping of stone-surfaced space.

These skyscrapers we see springing up around us are sometimes lovely, and in groups they often have a rugged alpine picturesqueness. But they know as little of Michelangelo as a vaudeville theater knows of Sophocles. His titanic logic is forgotten, the materials and forms he struggled with have become ridiculous toys. Well, our task is to form ideals for steel and to realize them. Perhaps it is in self-defense that we prefer not to think of other labors. But whoever wishes to know the heights of the human mind must try to know Michelangelo's vision, a huge dome-centered building, as simple and as clearly formed by law as a sunflower or a snowflake.

20

The Cleveland Reservoir

Our drinking water, in Cleveland, is stored in a covered reservoir. The reservoir keeps the water clear and cool, and to do that as effectively and economically as possible is its only reason for existing. Quite incidentally, it is an architectural masterpiece.

It is called the Baldwin Reservoir. (Actually there are two, but I shall use the singular number because they are exactly alike.) It is a subterranean room about five hundred feet square, surrounded by concrete walls, paved with concrete and covered with a roof of intersecting flattened barrel vaults of concrete carried on round concrete piers. The crown of the vaults is forty feet above the floor. The piers, which are thirty inches thick, are about twenty feet apart both ways. The only openings are a few small manholes in the ceiling.

The beauty of the Great Hall of Cleveland is first of all in its vast extent—its six hundred columns, its fifty aisles. But it has delicacy, too. The aisles are pleasantly proportioned in cross section. The columns are spread conically at the floor, an unpleasant shape but at a distance softening into a simplified diagram of an architectural column base. At the top there is a rather bungling transition from round to square to meet the square springing of the vaults, but here again, with almost pathetic lack of affectation, the aesthetic function of a capital is expressed.

There is nothing quite like it anywhere. Each aisle has about the proportions of the side aisles of a moderately high Gothic church, Winchester Cathedral for example, though the flattened vaults remind one of later Gothic buildings such as St. George's Chapel, Windsor. But for the great area,

FIGURE 121. Cross-sectional view of the Cleveland Reservoir.

the forest of equispaced columns, the precedents are ancient. That is a hot-climate Mediterranean idea. The great hall in the temple of Ammon at Karnak was 160 by 320 feet and contained 134 columns. The Hall of a Hundred Columns at Persepolis had just a quarter the area of the Cleveland hall, but its ceiling was twenty feet higher.

For the "public inspection" in 1925, before the reservoir was flooded, a few aisles along the west wall were lit by hanging an electric bulb close to the ceiling in every fourth or fifth bay. The rest of the hall was dark save for a few "Jove's eyes" where manholes had been left open. The warm yellowish electric light spread out from each of the lit bays and laid a net of radiating column shadows on the floor. The curved shapes of the springing vaults, caught by the shadows of the vaults nearer the lights, produced a fantastic mosaic of interwoven spots and lines varying from bright gold through every shade of warm gray to deep soft black. The columns were halved and quartered by the shadows of other columns or were picked out of the darkness by narrow tangent strips of light.

In search of new aspects I wandered out from the lit bays into the dark forest of columns. A dozen bays deep in it, when I looked back along an aisle, I saw a bluntly bullet-shaped area of warm gray concrete wall, streaked with vertical shadows and framed by the lighter lines of the more directly lit columns near it. Nearer me the columns became

less and less light. There was a similar gradation of light in the ceiling, not uniform but flecked with light and dark as rays or shadows caught the surfaces of the groined vault. Across the bottom of this deep stage setting moved a line of little people silhouetted against the bright wall, so far away that I could not hear their voices or tell whether they were looking out into the darkness toward me.

Another fine view was from north to south along a dark aisle in which there was an open manhole in the top of the last bay. Everything around me was jet black. In the distance again the bullet shape, this time not of warm light but cool silver, the white light streaming down through the manhole and along the gray columns, spreading out on the floor to form a white line from one base to the other.

The view which had most of "art" in it was a concrete standpipe, seen from about two hundred feet away, along the aisle in which it stood. The front of the enormous pipe was lit by an open manhole just above it. The white light flooded down along the gray cylinder, broken only by the black drooping shadow under a flange offset ten feet from the top. Each side of the cylinder darkened into shadow, but just at the turning was a pale line of ruddy light from the electric bulbs. On the floor some ponderous valve affair served as altar, and a dark crowd of pigmy worshipers stood with heads uplifted as the high-priest chanted "Ten million cubic feet, two million dollars. . . ." Everywhere I was surrounded by a star of diagonal vistas, narrower, more sharply crowned, more Gothic than the full views down the aisles.

No architect ever lived who would not stand in silent wonder in this Hall of Six Hundred Columns. It is an abstraction, a song in some nameless mother language that everyone understands. It is the work of a law, of a formula ruling over space and mass—rather, perhaps, a law brought into the range of our feelings by being stated in the most fundamental, simplest terms of human need for formal perfection. It is the product of man's desire for order, freed from the old conventions of architecture by the new conventions of engineering.

The great beauty of the reservoir is its simplicity and purity. Nothing is petty, nothing is irrelevant, nothing is boastful, nothing tells a story, nothing mumbles the names of gods, men, or races—nothing is human. There are no windows, no doors, almost no light, no sign of human use, not even a stone cut small so men could lift it. And yet it is superbly human. Beside it the formless jumble of nature becomes a congeries of willful antics. It is so human that in an hour it became very dear to me. Its floor's level firmness gives my body the safest and most assuring relation to the earth; the solid ceiling, curving from pier to pier, does not weigh upon me and yet protects me from all the unknown things of the air. The strong round columns seem human, make me feel taller and stronger. My eye follows them as they march away into the shadow, and I actually touch and measure and embrace the space that surrounds me. I live at last in a cosmos.

And we built it to cool our drinking water.

Part VI

Critiques of Landscape Architecture

21

Central Park

It is obvious enough that Central Park is a bit out at elbow. Its trees are stagheaded, and its lawns are spotty. But tradition survives soil depletion, and tradition is very firmly convinced that all Central Park needs is a hundred thousand loads of manure and a flock of newly bathed sheep to make it again what it was in the days of Lily Bart, the best of all possible parks. That proposition I rise to question, to deny. I rise in behalf of the Geometric Park Movement (the capitals are mine), which, though still in its cradle, has its grip on a serpent or two and promises some time, with the help of no Atlas messenger, to have its way amid the gardens fair of Hesperus.

Why, we of the movement ask, should a public garden in an unusually unrustic city be contrived out of billowy meadows, rocky hills, labyrinthine lakes, and tufted shrubberies? Since we don't shape

our doorways like the mouths of caves or carry crooks for canes, why must Central Park be the amalgam of a Herefordshire sheepwalk and the location for a movie version of *Hiawatha?* We know the answer: Central Park is Nature, and Nature is man's Great Solace, the only sure antidote to hurdy-gurdies, poolrooms, factories, tenements, and all the other vicious influences of a great city. Such eighteenth-century scientists as Thomson and Cowper discovered this quality, and the sociologically enlightened American of the 1850's confirmed their researches. F. L. Olmsted, codesigner, with Calvert Vaux, of Central Park, was convinced that "the town" had a deleterious effect on "the mind and the moral strength" and that only "green pastures and still waters" could restore those members to their primitive health. The way it works is apparently by

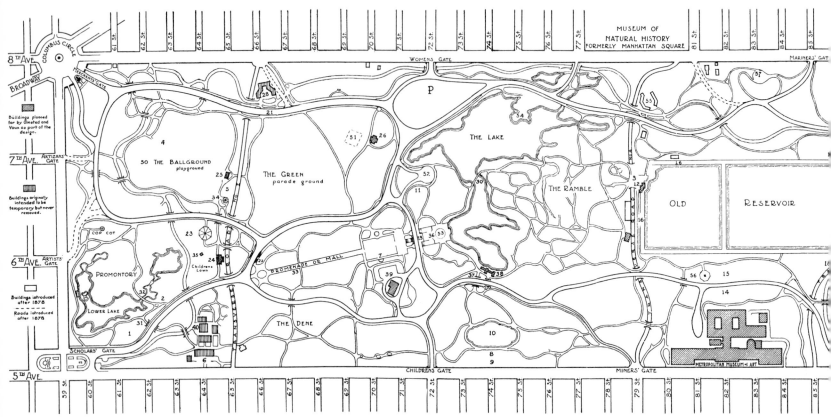

FIGURE 122. Plan of Central Park. From "Central Park Key Map," prepared by Gordon J. Culham.

association. You go to Central Park, you have memories of the little farmhouse on the hill, you think of the old oaken bucket, you resolve to lead a better life. But suppose you come from the Warsaw ghetto? Do not despair: the message of peace will come to you nevertheless, and in Nature's Universal Language, which Central Park speaks most fluently!

To all this the Opposition answers that the formal Grand Parc at Versailles expresses repose just as clearly. In art, as in nature, straight lines, level planes, balanced forms, dark colors, and slow rhythms produce in us emotional states which we associate with physical rest. For a fact, Versailles and Hampton Court are far more restful than Central Park. Many passages in Central Park are not merely not quiet—they are actually exciting. Great rocks dotted and piled all around, little hills crowned with rustic shelters or leaning trees, lawns fantastically shaped and modeled and dotted with explosions of rock and shrubbery, deep-set ponds of contorted outline, a network of drives, walks and bridle paths sinking, rising, twisting, interlaced, leaping over and diving under each other, trees of every shape and size, stone bridges, iron bridges, lamps, signs, and every kind of human sound and movement—what sort of lullaby is that?

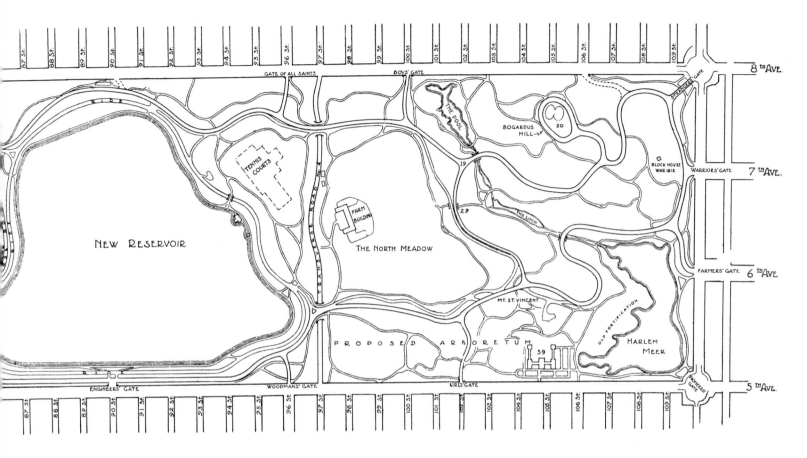

Central Park, indeed, cannot hide behind nature's skirts, and its design cannot be justified by alleging an exclusive restorative charm, physical or moral. Olmsted's claim that only his true counterfeit of nature's bosom could compensate the city dweller for the nervous irritations that harass him is only another proof that love will find a reason. He knew and loved the style he worked in. He identified it with nature, the holy word of his time, and so made of it a religion. Ruskin (who, inevitably, was Olmsted's favorite prophet) made a religion of Gothic architecture. Our present separation of nature and art from morality, our attitude toward art form and

the form-will, leaves to the ideas of Olmsted, as to those of Ruskin, little but their historical interest. Central Park is an effort to attain beautiful form. Its style is no more sacred than other styles. We must accept it as the expression of a sincere faith, but that is no reason for fatuously believing that it presents the best and only way to handle the area it occupies, and still less an excuse for setting it up as a model which all other large city parks must follow.

As form, then, I shall consider it. And first as part of a larger form, the city of New York. Civic art has for its ideal the aesthetic unification of the entire city. This can be done by applying such basic architectural principles as axiality, radiation, and proportion. There must be also, as in every work of art, a uniform style; the city must express a harmony of form-will. And a city park must be integrated with the city in both these ways. The park at Versailles inevitably expresses the same type of pleasure in form that the town of Versailles expresses. They could be reversed, the park being built up and the town planted, without striking incongruity. But that sort of thing was fundamentally impossible to Olmsted and his associates because they thought of the city as the enemy of the country. The country was sacred, the city profane. They could make suburbs into pretty imitations of the country, but it never occurred to them that parks might be made beautiful versions of the city. They made Central Park a sanctuary to preserve a piece of country from its enemy, the city. There was no compromise. The park announces its hatred of the city in every line. It refuses to integrate its plan with the city plan. Its style is the exact antipode of the style of the city.

The park's most conspicuous contact with the city plan is that it stops Sixth and Seventh Avenues. These streets have developed into powerful walled vistas. They shoot at the park like two huge cannon-shots of space, capable of dominating the entire lower half of it, and in winter they come near doing so. But the park ignores them. At Seventh Avenue two big sycamores rise like a spite fence across the line of the avenue, stopping the view in both directions. All the streets that enter the park are forced at the gate to renounce everything they have been. Just inside, most of them are pulled sharply to one side, down, then up again.

The Plaza and Columbus Circle were conceived

FIGURE 123. A winter view of Central Park from the RCA Building, looking north.

as vestibules to the park, but neither can be thought of as part of it. They are contiguous to the park, but not articulated with it. The Plaza is now a charming feature of Fifth Avenue, but its function of gateway to Central Park is so obscure that one may easily fail to notice it. The only recognition of the park in the Plaza design (and perhaps its only fault) is the substitution of posts and chains for balustrade at the north end. Along with this denial of the streets of the city must be cited Central Park's lack of connection with the Hudson and the East River. This may not be charged, perhaps, against Olmsted and Vaux, but it is the sort of fault the style they worked in is constantly committing. A strip one block wide running to each of the rivers would not have added one twentieth to the area of the park. And when the park was built, the tidal marshes touched Fifth Avenue.

The saddest aspect of its failure to integrate with

the city is that it occupies the very area from which should rise the city's acropolis. The idea of the city crown, a center of the city plan, raised high at the heart of the city, is one of the oldest and finest principles of city planning. The plan of Manhattan is the most orderly plan of its size in the world, but it is not organized. The company is perfectly formed, but there is no standard bearer at its head. Within the area of Central Park a standard could have been raised, a rallying point for all Manhattan. The basic formal elements of Manhattan are straightness, uniformity, long vistas, a general rise toward the center of the island. These elements exist imperfectly, unimpressively. Freed from practical limitations, in Central Park they could have been expressed with ideal beauty and intensity. The park could have fulfilled the function of art, to create forms into which the imagination of a period could enter with pleasure. And what our imagination wants is usually the purification, the sublimation, of our practical activities. Does someone say that Central Park is now a true embodiment of New York's form-will? Then we must regret that the rest of the city is not a maze of zigzag Rothenburg *Gässchen* and curved St. John's Wood drives lined with shrub-embowered villas.

The park denies the city; it also denies to man the fundamental satisfactions of architecture and gardening—the clear perception of space and mass. Landscape gardening, we are told, is "the art which conceals art." Its aim is *rus in urbe,* a means of saving travel when you want to walk or drive in the country. But nowadays we ask for art that insists upon itself and drives its form home to us as emphatically as our senses can bear it. Art can improve on nature, can make simple and intense the expression of nature. In Olmsted's day a stage setting for a forest scene was crowded with fat tree trunks painted with ivy and owl holes. Now we see some dark vertical strips against a light sky and have a cleaner feeling of the form-character of a forest. Central Park gives us meadows, foliage, and hills in their natural form. Park designers of the geometric school believe that feel of ground, extent of area, height of hill, the physical relation of trees to air, soil, and each other, the mass and strength of rock are demonstrated much more vividly by the forms of art, by planes, walls, rows, regular shapes and balanced masses. Above all, they feel that only by a geometric relation of geometric parts can the ruling feature of a design establish its dominance over a large area.

The Central Park one can imagine, a glorious revelation of the beauty of New York, may never exist. Yet the form-will of a people is a mighty force. New York has created the Grand Central and the prodigious street north of it, the Bush Terminal, the Shelton, the interior of the Bowery Bank, Geddes' Inferno, and the majestic rhythm of traffic in Fifth Avenue. Eyes fed on the great scale of these masterings of space must someday penetrate the fog of inherited sentiment through which we now look at the prettiness of Central Park. New York has unequaled material power, a desire for large size ruled by simplicity and order, a healthy confidence in man and his work. Some time, whether in the area of Central Park or somewhere else, these forces will create a huge formal park.

22

The Landscape Priesthood

There is in this country a fairly numerous group of persons called landscape architects. They range from Tony Piccolo, a suburban artist of the spade with a front yard full of tagged retinosporas, through the service departments of the big nurseries, up to the true Olympians, the fifty Fellows of the American Society of Landscape Architects. There is, also, an order of lay sisters who serve tea on the lawn when their Kelway hybrids are in bloom and applaud briskly at the end of an informal talk on the culture of Alpine bog plants. There is, again, a mixed group of publications, from the quarterly that does not utter the name of Repton, Olmsted, or Eliot without a prayer of thanks to Allah, down to the police-dog-and-motorboat type of garden magazine that publishes a calendar telling one when to rake the leaves off the tulip bed. Finally, there is a burgeoning system of instruction in landscape architecture, a Mother School adjacent to the Mecca of the art (and of the cod industry) with numerous offspring at the state universities. And yet, in spite of all this pomp and noise, I quite seriously believe that the sacred art of all these busybodies has made the visible face of this continent somewhat less beautiful than it would otherwise have been.

I say this without denying that landscape architects have formed many beautiful compositions and have saved from destruction many areas of fine natural growth. The Middlesex Fells are delightful, indeed, and I envy the squirrels that play all day in the Ramble in Central Park. Charles Eliot was, to be sure, a highly useful citizen. None the less, the introduction of the English landscape style of gardening was a calamity of the first magnitude. One does not blame the mid-nineteenth century for having its wallow in the pool of nature sentiment. But why do landscape architects of today continue to resort to that pool and form nationwide organizations for its pious protection, when to the nose of every intelligent contemporary the place is obnoxious? American landscape architecture is now a huge joke. It has produced a few pleasant reproductions of Surrey landscape and a few charming Italian gardens. But as a vital, evolving art it is dead.

The story goes back to the inspiring era of George I, when one Kent leaped the fence and discovered that all nature was a garden. It was already known in his day that nature was either the principal proof of divinity or God's favorite residence. The gardeners in the new natural style thus acquired a sacerdotal distinction which they have never wholly got rid of. The landscape garden was in the beginning (see *Paradise Lost*) and ever shall be. Other arts reflect human vagaries, but this one has an unchanging norm. The Abbé Delille's rule was simple: "Worship the genius loci and consult God." Edward Young said that nature was Christian. That, like Christianity, it was surely most to God's taste in the home counties of England, was not doubted. Such were the roots of the fanatic identification of gardening with nature, and of the fierce denial of the capacity or right of any but the initiated themselves to judge their work.

This confidence in the Heaven-willed eternal verity of informal gardening sat heavily on the revered Olmsted, the St. Peter G. Eddy of American landscape architecture. He loved to quote—the Psalmist's words were his divine authority—"He maketh me to lie down in green pastures, He leadeth me beside the still waters," and doubtless there came to his mind an English meadow and millpond. That many-sided strong mind of his deserves an exploring Gamaliel Bradford. Does it mean anything that he loved buggy riding and hated cities? That he was an Anglophile, and that his "real prophet" was Ruskin? Olmsted saw himself as a pioneer in a cultural wilderness, but whatever tool he used, that wilderness supplied. He did not invade—he answered a Call.

New York wanted Central Park and wanted to be told that it was the best antidote to her slums. The gentlemen who profited by those slums were not surprised when they found the antidote well laced with bridle paths. New Yorkers wanted to be told, as Olmsted roundly told them, that "the average amount of disease and misery and vice and crime has been much greater in towns," and that the remedy was to make in Central Park "the greatest possible contrast with the streets and the shops and the rooms of the town." It was such a pleasant remedy! It was God's wish, or Nature's, and if the Irish didn't walk three miles for the still-water cure, or if it didn't cure them, well, it is not our fault that Nature prefers carriage-owning Protestants of English ancestry.

There was the usual progression in Olmsted's faith, from the external to the internal. In England, five years before Central Park was planned, he saw the public garden at Birkenhead. "I cannot undertake," he exclaimed, "to describe the effect of so much taste and skill as had evidently been employed; I will only tell you that we passed by winding paths, over acres and acres, with a constant varying surface, where on all sides were growing every variety of shrubs and flowers, with more than natural grace, all kept with the most consummate neatness." The young Yankee saw a neat job. Two decades of success fixed the creed of the winding path and made defense of it superfluous, as witness this pronouncement of his: "Whether the contemplation of natural scenery is practically of much effect in counteracting and alleviating these evils [of urban crowding] . . . I do not propose to argue, . . . for if the object of parks is not thus suggested, I know of none which justifies their cost." And that was that. Twenty years more of honors and reading Ruskin made of him a mauve-decade Isaiah: "Nature is the shape and image of right reason—reason in its highest sense embodied and made visible in order, stability, in conformity to eternal law." And, one might add, also in conformity to the soul need of Frederick Law Olmsted, a New England Puritan doubting the creed of his fathers, seeking in benevolence and the love of nature substitutes for the harsh religion that was their substitute for art.

For fifty years Olmsted preached and practiced, and his faith has now spread to every corner of the country. His disciples have almost as tight control over American gardening as the Klan once had over Indiana politics. Large estates, though they have their formal gardens, are mainly in the landscape style. Every suburban lot breaks out in scalloped borders and specimen plants as naturally as a Plymouth Rock hen lays a brown egg. No park board would dream of employing a designer who questioned the validity of the landscape postulate. Cemeteries, as everybody knows, are always landscaped, and so are all the Floral Heights. It is truly pitiful to see normally straight-edge-minded engineers trying to equal the trick streets and "yawpy"

intersections of the initiates. Even when landscape architects do not get the job, the landscape idea usually does, though it be a Scotch gardener that incorporates the tradition. It is not only in Mr. Babbitt's Zenith that landscaped lawns are standard equipment. The Colleoni statue in Newark is landscaped, the Lincoln Memorial is landscaped (a classic Greek setting based on data from the paintings of Puvis de Chavannes), the Toledo art museum is landscaped, the Los Angeles Automobile Club is landscaped—nothing, indeed, has escaped the blight.

Chance has given the priests of the inner temple a firm hold on the training of the novices. In the 1870's Olmsted moved from New York to Brookline. He built up a large practice, and dozens of men got their training in his office. One of these was Charles Eliot, son of the president of Harvard. When, about 1900, after Charles Eliot's death, Harvard began instruction in landscape architecture, it was natural that the new department should become practically a branch of the Olmsted office. F. L. Olmsted, Jr., was made an instructor and, later, Charles Eliot professor. At present the three principal teachers are old Olmsted men. The school is both orthodox and eclectic. Two of the instructors are Italian-garden fans, and the student work is touched with reminiscences of Lante and Gamberaia—but only at one side of the house. There is a chaser of wild garden close at hand, and the principal view is valed and shrubbed and clumped in the established camouflage mode. A professor and the school librarian have published a bulky textbook on more than one page of which the eighteenth century returns to life, as for instance: "A landscape of rocky upland country about a mountain tarn might be mysterious in a day of low-drifting clouds, stern or desolate in a storm, and perhaps on a bright breezy Spring morning even gay." They say also that a composition of two trees is difficult to manage. The instructor in planting design is a botanist who has ventured to write a book on *Man's Spiritual Contact with Nature.* One of the illustrations in it has this legend: " 'And God reveals himself in many ways.' Here are two—a tree and a church." He also quotes this remark by Ruskin: "What a thought that was when God thought of a tree!" It is minds freighted with such lovely but sterile ideas who are training the men who will make America's contribution to an art practiced by Raphael, Le Nôtre, and Wren! And as long as they are at Harvard, they must continue to teach this sort of stuff—they cannot deny the Logos incarnated in Olmsted and Charles Eliot. The late President Eliot's bequest to the school is only the most recent of many chains that tie them to the traditional faith.

Very few of the students there are drawn from Harvard College. Most of them are graduates of state universities where undergraduate instruction in horticulture and ornamental gardening is given. Of these many go back to their old schools or to others as instructors, on the recommendation of the Harvard faculty. This interchange of personnel produces a strong spiritual connection between the Olmsted-Harvard tradition and hundreds of men and women who go from the state universities with a smattering of garden design, enough to get them jobs as draftsmen, or with a general impression to guide them in forming the settings of their own homes or as members of city-beautiful committees.

Plant breeders, to induce variations, force their seedlings into rampant growth. Exactly that is what the moribund garden art most needs. Students of garden design, instead of being held down by traditional tastes and conceptions of practicality, ought to be encouraged to commit every sort of imaginative indiscretion. One of the programs should begin thus: "The Italians of America wish to build an enormous garden in honor of Michelangelo (or Mussolini) which shall do the utmost possible violence to the teachings of Humphry Repton." The impression that fancy will flourish when you simply refrain from laying obvious bricks on it is an illusion. A child of six twists his tongue and draws unheard-of dragons, but candidates for degrees play safe. The chairman of the Harvard School of Landscape Architecture points with pride to the maturity of his pupils. The average of their ages is twenty-eight. That is a catastrophe. The brain of such a student is a terminal moraine pushed into his skull by the academic and professional glaciers that have moved over it. Only pedagogical dynamite, not abstention from repression, can open up those minds and start them reworking the treasures of accumulated aesthetic form.

Not merely by the deadfall of professional education does the landscape tribe trap its victims. Its hardy braves hunt far afield. In Massachusetts the assistant extension professor of landscape gardening lectures to you, shows you lantern slides, and makes plans for planting the school grounds. In Iowa a landscape extension specialist shows you a demonstration farmstead. In Georgia he is a field agent in landscape gardening. The federal Department of Agriculture has its county agents on your trail and sends you a bulletin on beautifying the farm, art at its government best. Agricultural institutes, normal schools, farm papers, and county fairs do their bit.

Garden magazines furnish plans and planting lists. The lists may vary, but the same plan goes to Maine and Texas. Nursery service departments, run by young fellows who have studied at the state college under Harvard graduates, gladly make plans for planting their shrubs in the corners of your lawn. Garden clubs invite lecturers to tell you how to do foundation plantings of mixed evergreens.

A few years ago an issue of the official organ of the American Society of Landscape Architects was devoted to extension work along landscape lines, as one says. There were reports from all the fields. The Department of Agriculture man sent a photograph of a previously gaunt farm home beautified with a curved walk and flocculent shrubbery. A southern horticulturist told of his booklet, entitled *Beautifying the Rural Home,* and of his summer teaching at a college in Tennessee. The editor concluded the symposium, pointing out matters that might better be left to private practitioners. Now, several of these "symposing" professors are friends of mine, and I regret to report that some of them are fitted to teach no art higher than pitching horseshoes. Yet the editor—a man of sense off duty—cast not one suspicious glance at the *quality* of all this busying. In the true gospel, it seems, there is no varying quality. A shrub planted is a soul saved.

The American Society of Landscape Architects, unlike the corresponding architectural organization, has enlisted almost all the practitioners in its field. Membership is essential to respectable professional standing—and helps get jobs. Admission to the lower ranks of the society is easy. Given the necessary diploma or a certificate of service in an approved office, all one needs is a slight competence in drafting and facility with the established clichés.

Since junior members are taken directly from the colleges, proved power of design would be an absurd requirement. Fellowship and high office follow upon professional success and conformity to ethical standards.

Every royal academy has its chorus of ancients. In the A.S.L.A. it is the Boston crowd. Olmsted men are preponderant in the society, if not numerically in the majority. The present head of the Harvard school is quite actively a past president. The official organ is edited by a Harvard professor, a member of the Olmsted firm. The western members occasionally rebel against the eastern control of the offices and committees, but they do so very cautiously. There is apparently no protest against the academy's fundamentally conservative attitude toward design. Naturally, the leaders in the A.S.L.A. do not openly influence the members to use one style of design rather than another. They have little need to. The society has never heard of Kirschville, Pennsylvania, and Kirschville has never heard of the society. But when the directors of the Angels' Rest Cemetery ask young Mr. Strauchenpflanzer to draw an extension plan, they know it will be formed in pleasing pretzel curves. Anything else would offend their intelligences. Anything else would, of course, be stiff, formal, unnatural, inappropriate, undemocratic, un-American, irreverent. As long as these sturdy words walk the ramparts, the burgher landscape architect may sleep serene. His stock in trade is safe.

And yet not quite. A prowling foreign fancy, the vogue of formal gardens, lately waylaid some of the best customers. Faced with this condition, the profession showed subtle tact. It made the thief a salesman. It became eclectic: it designs formally or informally as is most functional, a phrase safely construed as meaning according to the wishes of the client's wife. Will the guild adapt itself to the trend of taste and slough off naturalism entirely? Alas, it cannot! The somewhat delicate reason had best be expressed from within. Hubbard and Kimball of Harvard, in their book on landscape design, define the profession's catchment area thus:

In producing the formal setting of a palace, the landscape architect's equipment may indeed differ from that of the architect only in his knowledge of plants and what effects can be secured with them; in reproducing or intelligently preserving a natural woodland, however, the landscape architect must have a knowledge of nature's processes, a familiarity with nature's materials, a sensitiveness to the natural beauty of rock and wood and water, which does not form the professional equipment of any other artist.*

No extraordinary knowledge of cerebral ecology is needed to suggest that under this foliage of logical distinction will be found the fungi of economic interest. If all land arrangement were formal, the landscape architects would soon sink to the level of horticultural assistants to the architects. Not until the osteopath, seduced by pills, gives up his vertebral lesions, will the landscape architect forswear his undulating shrubbery.

The last competition for the Rome prize in landscape architecture illustrated this regimentation of ideas in the profession very well. The program—unlike many other competitive programs that have required dominantly informal layouts—fixed no style of design. The small memorial park was to be built on an irregular terrain with a hill in its midst, which the builders of the Parthenon would have lusted to shape into a great rectangular terrace overlooking the town. Yet all the competing designs were in the informal park style. One of them was full of walks in commas and ovals, French curves as dashing as any in the Parc Monceau. In the winning plan the principal entrance drive split a rectangular intersection of the boundary streets and, just within the park, impinged against the point of a triangular island of lawn. On the hill was a timid touch of informal formality, quite impotent to master the design—a passage that could be called formal, if that is what you want, but not formal enough to suggest that an architect did it.

These men may honestly not like that sort of thing. But as students and as competitors they were browbeaten by the landscape atmosphere. They were intimidated by the topography, they had no convictions capable of standing up against what happened to exist, they all knew that the landscape creed holds trees and ground forms sacred. These restraints were just as effective as if the program had explicitly said, "No masculine rendering of the hill-overlook idea, such as you may shortly be going to the Pincian Hill to study, is permitted." The Pincian Hill and Hadrian's villa may save one of these men. The others will go back to their proposed contours in full line, existing contours in dotted line, and the annual banquet of the A.S.L.A. This society's fundamental purpose, apparently, is to keep its art separate and distinct from the contiguous arts. It is an antisocial purpose. The arts were better off when the chance of genius might make of one man architect, goldsmith, and engineer. Specializing is in part responsible for the conspicuous inconsistencies

* H. V. Hubbard and T. Kimball, *An Introduction to the Study of Landscape Design* (New York: Macmillan, 1917).

of phase among our arts. He is a lucky architect who on successive days works on a factory, steel bridge, lunchroom, church, skyscraper, and country villa. He is more likely to make architecture the true fruit of our culture and genuinely enjoyable to us than a specialist is.

When it comes to making a beautiful country, no professional art can take the place of mellowed folk art. Italy was not made beautiful by artists so much as by peasants and laborers. The garden architects of the Renaissance did not create things wholly new; they built more dramatic versions of the old courtyards, gardens, and grape arbors. A peasant thought the master's garden fine, but he did not think it strange. Artists and peasants could work together to make the country beautiful, because they used the same form language. There is a tiny plaza at the edge of Orvieto, a few feet of parapet wall, a bench, four trees. But the art of the place, it will be noted, is exactly the art of the Villa d'Este.

The landscape style does not speak the folk language and cannot be harmonized with folk art. There is a brief essay by Olmsted in which he contrasts a white picket fence with a picturesque stone wall of varied texture, planted with rock plants and sketchy vines. The wall might be pretty, but Olmsted's choice shows that he was blind to the beauties and the limitations of folk art. Go to New Bedford: the town is full of charming garden motifs, bits of box parterre, granite gate posts, buckthorn hedges looking over stone walls, low terraces and steps, and balanced lilacs at the gates. Out at Padanarum there are great cedar hedges and green piers twelve feet high and eight feet through that would be famous in garden lore if they were at Hampton Court. Now go to the Stetson estate, nearby, planned by

Charles Eliot. In whole effect and in every detail it is as much unlike the fine garden tradition of New Bedford as it could possibly be made. The entrance drive would not be more exotic to the local culture if it were planted with palms. The same sort of thing can be seen in any part of the country. In California the early settlers from the East applied their old ways to the new materials and made the beginnings of a charming indigenous art of the land. The stunning clipped Monterey cypresses in the Odd Fellows' cemetery at Salinas, the occasional old velvet-soft cypress hedges, the lofty green arches over front gates, the eucalyptus lanes, the houses set in orchards—in the face of all this enormous wealth of suggestion, landscape architecture has produced what? The Angeleno's pride, the atrocious East Lake Park!

The landscape style is irremediably toxic to the good taste of the countryman. It is nature-imitative, informal, antigeometric, opposed to the display of craftsmanship, which no genuine folk art can be. Especially in building and the surroundings of the home, folk art has always formed simple symmetrical arrangements. Only such rudimentary principles of design as straightness, uniformity, economy, and equal balance can be understood by the simple minds who do the great mass of building and gardening. The illiterate Italian peasant or the art-fearing New England farmer, left alone, will make for his house a charming setting of stone walls, terraces, walks, hedges, arbors, and rows of trees, handled with pleasant characteristic touches in each locality. But give him new materials and new ideas, and he contrives a display of inane ugliness. Ornamental landscape gardening, standardized and nationally advertised, is wiping out whatever there is still left of the beautiful folk types of garden art.

The landscapers need not all hang. Many of the younger men see the tangle of myth and vested interest that binds the profession, and are slowly cutting their way toward the light. They are looking for inspiration, not merely in the national styles of gardening, but in every sort of space and ground arrangement, in Renaissance plazas and Mayan temple groups. They are groping toward new forms in land design, with as yet nothing agreed upon except that there are aesthetic motives and mechanical means in our huge gridiron cities, in our love for height and size, in the Wilson dam and the Yale Bowl, in concrete mixers and steam shovels, and in booster energy and national highways. They see that gasoline has changed the design and location of parks. Observing the Sunday crowds lying two deep on Revere Beach, they doubt that only hilly lawns and trees in groups of three or five can rest the city soul. They see that the current American is not a gardener, that he does not care for plants as plants, though he loves grass, trees, sunlight, and panoramic views as much as ever. I know of one young landscape architect, in charge of a nursery, who is simplifying his plant lists so that a person of ordinary intelligence can look at his catalogue without getting dizzy.

It is true that Americans, even such as care for art in one way or another, are barely interested in garden and park design. That is because we do not know what we are missing. As an instance: there are few things that have more of both charm and dignity or make a stronger appeal to human form feeling than a fine avenue of trees—not mere street trees, but straight walls of foliage with a broad carpet of grass or gravel between them, like the avenues in St. Cloud. American landscape architects have been busy three quarters of a century, but where in any of their public parks is there a really fine avenue? We have suffered so long from the incredibly narrow taste of our park designers that our imaginations have no measure with which to assess our loss. That loss is virtually a whole art, an art that Apollo seems somehow to have inspired with breadth and dignity and also with the fancy and friendliness that make it a joy to every mind.

But ideas do change—in time. New work will be done, new words will become the nuclei of new values, and appropriate disguises will be found whereby the new ways can penetrate even into the heads of the professors. The benevolent analyst whose name is hereto superscribed will then be tendered honorary membership in a reformed A.S.L.A. And at last the Anglo-natural style of garden will be laid away in the God's acre of eighteenth-century metaphors.

Part VII

Residential Site Planning

23

The Neighborhood Concept

Silly talk and make-believe plans should not obscure the fact that the neighborhood—in some forms and degrees—is a very useful planning motif.

It is, indeed, an almost inevitable result of planning for specific functions, which is the first principle of modern urbanism. Streets, for example, are designed for the special purposes they are to serve. Residential streets are planned for local use only— for movements from the homes to shops, schools, transportation. Efficiency is gained if the same line of movement affords access to several objectives. Thus, by simple planning logic, a service center is formed, with residential streets that tend to spread from the center, though not beyond its operating radius. This is the diagram, subject to infinite variations.

It is incomprehensible to me that any planner should wholly reject so plastic a planning motif as the neighborhood since that is equivalent to saying that no amount of imaginative adjustment in plan, composition, scope, or size can make a useful approach to the design of residential areas. Though well aware that it is not often possible to assemble the elements of an ideally appointed neighborhood, I find that the concept has value even when imperfectly realized.

It is regrettable that we cannot know all our neighbors, but the essential thing is that each person shall have a few friends. Even in large cities, the best friends of a middle-aged couple are quite often persons they knew in school or as young married people, as a result of a few years of residential proximity. If the neighborhood favors the formation of such bonds, it is worthwhile. And it can provide a satisfying physical environment for persons whose social contacts are scattered through the city.

It is obvious that the neighborhood—like the endless gridiron of Chicago—can be used for racist "protection." But I know of a group that is planning a neighborhood in order to enjoy freedom from racial, religious, and economic snobbery. Reginald Isaacs's attitude on this point is too much like reform by prohibition.*

* *Editor's note:* Reginald Isaacs caused considerable debate and discussion as the result of his refutation of the neighborhood concept. A number of responses to Isaacs's challenge were published in the December 1948 issue of *The Journal of Housing*, including that of Peets.

It would be relevant, perhaps, to repeat the common saying that it is not so much what you do as how you do it. If we take the word "how" to mean in how many skillfully studied ways, each adapted to its purpose and situation—then I would say that the best "substitute" for the neighborhood concept is newly and more intelligently designed neighborhoods. That, I think, will be the answer—quite probably under a new name, so everybody will be pleased.

24

The Orientation of Row Houses

The orientation of buildings is always a compromise between varying, often opposed, factors. This study of the orientation of row houses is a discussion of those factors with the purpose of assisting architects to work out the orientation that most fairly compromises between the conditions that have to be met on a particular site.

Orientation involves convenience of access, relation to topography, interest of outlook, direction of wind, and various seasonal relations to sunlight. It is mainly with the last of these factors that these notes are concerned.

Sunlight has different values at different times of day and of year and at different places, indoors and out. The various roles played by sunlight in and around our homes may be grouped under three headings:

1. Sunlight inside the house

Though no longer considered to be important therapeutically, sunlight has great psychological and aesthetic value and has an incidental sanitary effect from the fact that well-lit rooms are more likely to be kept clean. In winter, sunlight is wanted whenever and wherever it can be had. At all seasons, morning sun is welcome in the kitchen and dining room, which are usually one room in low-cost housing—and in the bathroom and bedrooms. In the afternoon, sunlight is wanted in the living room except in hot weather. And in hot weather, the afternoon sun is not welcome in bedrooms.

2. Sunlight on the exterior walls of buildings

Generally speaking, as a matter of human comfort, the sun is wanted on all walls of residential buildings except in hot weather; but in moist hot weather, sunlight may have value to the structure of a building even though it may render the building less comfortable to live in. The sun keeps walls dry and free from moss, melts snow and ice on roofs and window sills, dries gutters, and retards the decay of woodwork.

3. Sunlight on the ground around buildings

In winter it is advantageous to have the sun strike the ground all around a house, but it is especially useful in the street, where it melts ice and piled snow and dries sidewalks after rains. Sunlight is necessary to the garden and to the laundry drying area, and all ground near buildings should receive sufficient sun to maintain grass and prevent the growth of moss. During summer afternoons, however, people want on one side of the house to find shade—preferably in the shadow of the house itself.

For the location of row houses, at least in the northern states, the orientation which most fairly compromises between these positive and negative factors seems to be that which places the length of the building along a line running northeast and southwest, at an angle of 30 to 45 degrees from the north-south line.

In the discussion of this statement the phrases "effective sunlight," "summer sun," and "winter sun" will be used. Effective sunlight here means, as bearing on sunshine in rooms, such rays of the sun, between one hour after sunrise and one hour before sunset, as strike the wall of the building on the side in question, at an angle not less than 30 degrees— that being the angle at which a beam of light that enters a room through an opening three feet wide in a wall eight inches thick will have a width of about one foot. A beam smaller than one foot wide,

entering a room at a horizontal angle less than 30 degrees, is of such slight value that it can be ignored in practical calculations. By summer sun is meant the position or course of the sun on August 1; by winter sun is meant its course on February 1.

The purpose of these phrases is to simplify the comparison and evaluation of building orientations. Some treatises on the subject fail to distinguish between sun that strikes a wall and sun that enters a room. Most diagrams, as they appear on building plans, indicate the position of the sun at sunrise and sunset at the summer and winter solstices, in spite of the fact that these dates are representative of only a few days and the further fact that from the first-floor windows of the typical city house the sun cannot be seen when it is less than an hour or two from the horizon. Some analyses of orientation for sunlight, on the other hand, stress the factor of intensity and hence give very reduced value to a low sun. Intensity is very important if one is seeking the sun for its antirachitic value, out of doors, but the cheering effect of sunshine, as it is diffracted by a lace curtain or falls across a breakfast table, may actually be greater if its intensity is low.

The dates arbitrarily chosen to represent the range of position of the sun in summer and in winter have the advantage of being more representative because they approximate the length of the average day above and below, respectively, the twelve-hour days of the equinoxes and also because they fall at times of the year when the position of the sun is more important in our lives than it is just at the solstices. On the first of February the sun has more psychological value than it has late in December, and it is in very early spring that the thawing and evaporation action by the sun is most wanted.

The hot afternoon sun of summer is not so disliked on June 21 as it is at the end of July and early in August, though the sun is not then so high and does not set so far north of west.

The orientation of row houses on a line running northeast and southwest is preferred because, in brief, it captures morning light and avoids the entrance of early afternoon sun into the rooms, gives sunlight on all four walls of the building on all but the shortest days, and also good sun on the ground and in streets running either parallel to the rows or perpendicular to them. It aims at a compromise between the two buildings that normally face each other along a street or other access lane. If, in this pair of rows, the living rooms of both rows are on the street side, it is only the easterly row that gets sun on the kitchen–dining room side in the morning and in the living room in the afternoon. This is the ideal sequence. The houses on the westerly side of the street have morning and noon sun in the living room and afternoon sun in the kitchen. This is not ideal, but it is better that each unit should have sun in some of its rooms at the time when the sun is most welcome—from early morning until noon, and especially in the winter—than that all the units should be robbed of light during the middle of the day, as happens when the rows run due north and south. If the site plan can be arranged so that all units look in one direction, as they frequently do in modern European plans, it ought of course, to be the kitchen–dining room that has the easterly aspect. In that case the larger angle from north, say 45 degrees, may be advantageous, while the smaller angle, about 30 degrees off north, is preferable when half the kitchens face west.

The 30-degree-east placement gives the easterly windows a beam of light a foot wide until noon. From noon until about two o'clock on the first of August (in the northern states) the sun's rays will strike the long walls of the building at less than 30 degrees—measured in plan, which, of course, is greater than the actual angle against the vertical wall. This means that the rooms will escape hot sun during these hours.

25
Residential Site Planning Texture

By texture I mean here a residential planning scheme—the relation of house to lot, of lot to street, and of street to city plan. There are many such schemes; in this country the commonest is our familiar grid of streets lined with curbs, street trees, sidewalks, and lawns; the houses are usually "singles," each with a drive to a garage in the rear yard.

For several decades this "American street," as it might be called, has been under critical attack. Strictly, it is not a *residential* street but an all-purpose street that happens to be used for housing. It carries much casual traffic, and the city's growth may make it a crowded thoroughfare. This possibility, or the tradition of it, explains the excessive width of right-of-way and building setbacks. The costly frontage development tends to make the lots narrow and deep; they are therefore unfavorable to sensible house planning and ill adapted to use as outdoor living space. Views from the front windows are dominated by cars, moving or standing, yet the house is not conveniently related to the automobile. The family car usually travels an excessive distance on the lot; visitors come and go across a public sidewalk.

Perhaps the first alternative solution to present itself—other than the millionaire suburb—was the English garden city. Within a few years, planners were talking about superblocks; using this concept, Clarence Stein and Henry Wright designed a "town for the motor age." With half an eye on Radburn, the greenbelt towns were built, and many private developments. A vista toward more likable planning textures began to open up.

In the same period, however, another planning movement was under way—a gathering indignation against exploiters who chopped up farms into 30-foot lots improved only with corner stakes and cinder sidewalks. To cure this disease, civic leaders drafted subdivision codes and zoning laws, and they kept up their demands for wider streets, larger lots, more complete improvements. These measures quite successfully keep out the predacious subdividers—but unfortunately they also keep out everything except the American street. Are new suburbs charming with Radburn's courts and inner parks or with Greenbelt's shady superblock? No. The only apparent change since the 1920's is that the houses are smaller and the streets are wider.

City engineers and zoning officials are the most conservative group known to anthropology. Still, a few cities have amended their ordinances to give large developments some degree of release from the codes. These breaches in the zoning laws, it must be noted, are due not so much to the new site planning as to the federally financed housing projects and the big apartment developments. But they are a welcome beginning; one purpose of these studies is to present some of the planning techniques that should be made permissible under special zoning paragraphs—or, better still, should be recognized in the general provisions of subdivision codes, zoning ordinances, and master plans. The studies were all made in connection with the design of Green-
Fig. 124 dale, Wisconsin, in 1936–1937 for the United States Public Housing Administration.

Fig. 125 The Greendale plans, only part of which are reproduced here, used three scales—20, 100, and 400 feet to the inch. A first study, on a 400-scale topographic map, laid down the main circulation lines.

The housing areas also were outlined and assigned tentative densities. Next, the 20-scale schematic *Figs. 129-141* studies were worked out, without reference to any particular site. These schemes, sometimes in combination, were then applied to appropriate building areas in plans drawn over 2-foot-interval topographic sheets at 100 scale. Reduced to 400 scale, these area plans were traced to make the tentative general plan reproduced here.

The program of the studies, in addition to the basic purpose of reconciling a large development

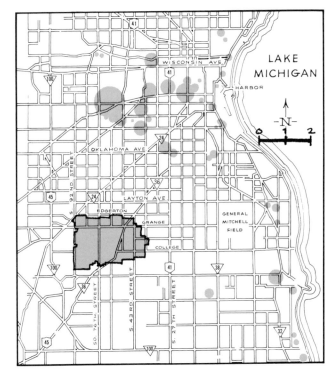

FIGURE 124. The location of Greendale, Wisconsin, in relation to Milwaukee.

consisting predominantly of mass housing with the social-aesthetic standards of the greenbelt towns, included two practical objectives: first, to spend as little as possible on streets and utilities; and, second, to hold down the municipal operating costs, a high tax rate being the town's great competitive handicap. The raw land cost was not high enough to be a determining element in fixing densities. Total occupancy was set at about 3,500 families, the estimated limit of the market; this figure represents a gross density of about one family per acre. A development plan based on acre and half-acre lots was rejected because it would destroy the regional recreative and aesthetic value of the land—in an urban region the greenbelt is a factor of regional texture, not of town planning—and because the site and municipal costs would be more than most of the customers could afford.

The general plan is therefore grounded on the principle that a low gross density justifies a relatively high average net density. There is, however, a wide variation of density among the different housing groups, and there is a considerable range of lot sizes within most of the groups. The very scenic west part of the village is expected to attract high-income families. This area, like several other housing groups, is laid out with streets of conventional type.

The planning textures presented here as substitutes for conventional street and lot arrangements all propose a separation of the pedestrian and vehicular channels of movement, the vehicular channel being in most cases at the rear of the houses. That, of course, is the scheme of Radburn and many housing projects. The Greendale studies differ from Radburn in the use of looped service streets instead of cul-de-sacs, in the franker recognition that visitors will approach the house from both front and rear, and in more detailed accommodations for owners' and visitors' cars.

The two channels—service street and center walk—will be described briefly; the plans and captions show some of the different forms they may take.

The service street is narrow—say a 40-foot right of way—but is planted with trees and shrubs to prevent it from looking like an alley. The traffic pavement is 20 feet wide, of good concrete for low maintenance. It has a **V** section, making its edges comfortable for walking and curbs unnecessary, and permitting the pavement to serve, often, in place of a storm sewer.

The functions of giving access to garages and of providing car parking are also performed effectively. A garage or covered carport can be built at the right-of-way line, requiring only a 10-foot apron to connect with the pavement. Additional parking is provided in the lateral strip between pavement and lot line, or on the lot. Definitely, this lateral parking must not be continuous—it must be broken by patches of grass, shrubbery, and trees. If the parking were made continuous, it would be used by moving traffic and would ultimately require heavy pavement. Separated bays can be paved with a light material such as broken stone or gravel, with grass as a binder. The plan should permit car parking on one side of the concrete pavement at points not used for access to parking berths.

At each house there should be one berth for casual parking, and it should be at the disposal of the abutting owner. Some provision of this kind is necessary for the full utilization of the two principal advantages of the service street scheme—elimination of the public sidewalk as a physical and psychic barrier between house and street, and proximity of the service street to the kitchen side of the house, where the natural affinity of the family car lies.

Shifting now to the pedestrian channel, the center walk should be abundantly designed; while it goes without saying that active adults and older children will use the service streets when their direction of travel makes it convenient, nevertheless the center walk is a necessary symbol of propriety and completeness in the organization of the home. From the walk, people will see the petunias in the garden and the pretty glass oddments in the living room windows. It will be an ideal place for the play of the young and gossip of the old; serving twice as many families as a convential sidewalk, it should be a more effective instrument of sociability among neighbors. It must therefore be wide, say six feet of concrete with a good grass strip at each side for snow plowing and clearance from shrubbery. Where it branches off from the sidewalk of the big traffic street will be a good place for a seat or two; at the farther end the walk ought to lead out to open recreation space. As far as possible, of course, walks through green areas should be used for access to schools, shopping, and work.

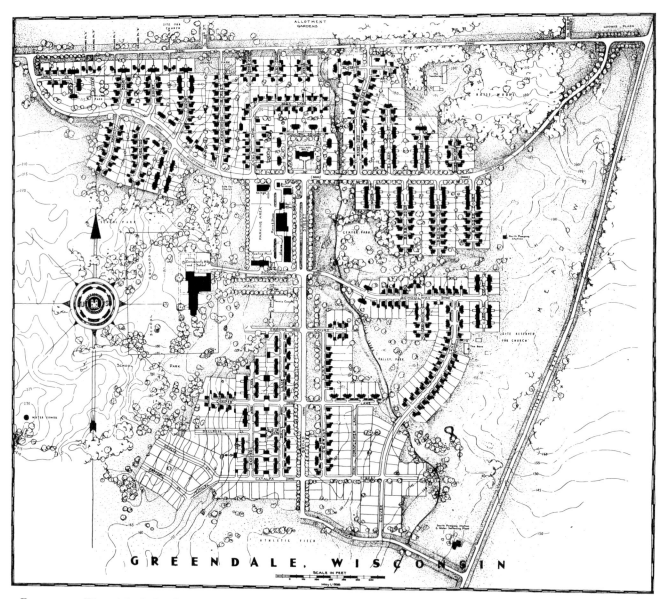

FIGURE 125. The original plan for Greendale, dated 1938, was designed between 1936 and 1937 by a staff headed by Jacob Crane, Elbert Peets, Harry Bentley, and Walter C. Thomas. The north-south axis is Broad Street, which meets the east-west curvilinear Northway. It is the locus of the civic center.

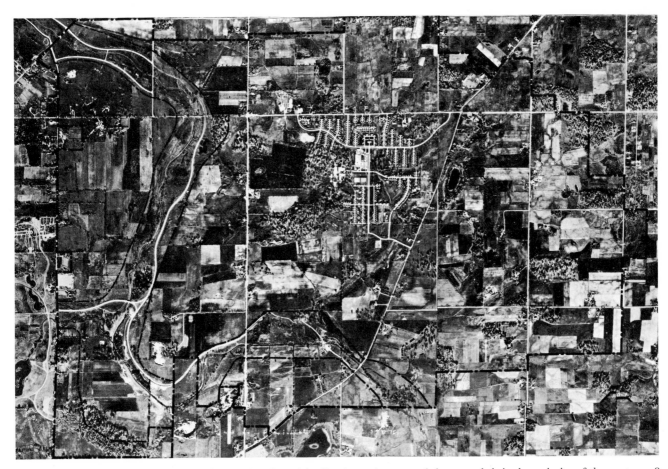

FIGURE 126. Air photograph of the site showing the originally planned town and the extended site boundaries of the 1947–1948 plan for enlargement. The portion planned in 1938 is clearly visible in the upper center. The scale of this air photo is about one fourth that of Figure 125.

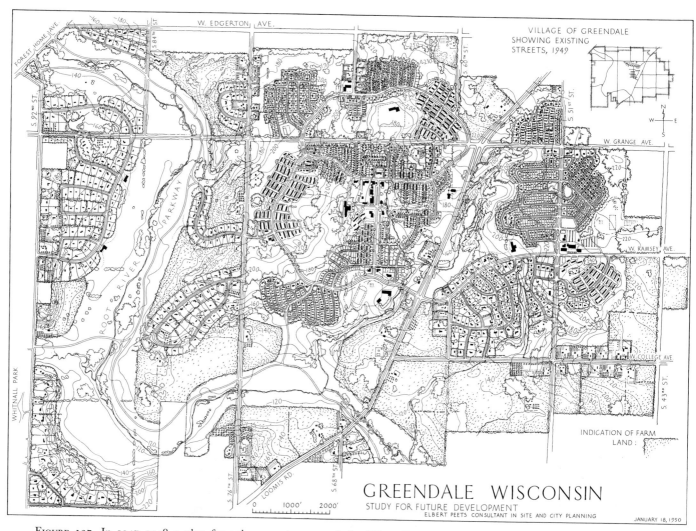

FIGURE 127. In 1947-1948 a plan for enlargement was made by Elbert Peets, for the U. S. Public Housing Administration. This plan covers about five square miles, shows existing village roads on half-mile squares, and diagonal state highway 36. Upper Northway (curvilinear) was proposed to complete the irregular oval, and a curved street west of the original center would extend to the north-south street at the east side of the site. Many of the patches discernible in this version of the plan can be identified in the detail site plans following. This plan proposes a sharp differentiation of circulation routes and residential streets. In general, through streets are straight; long curved streets facilitate on-site movement; and small curved streets serve the housing groups. The plan stresses a union of a simple basic structure with emphatic modulation and variety in its component parts.

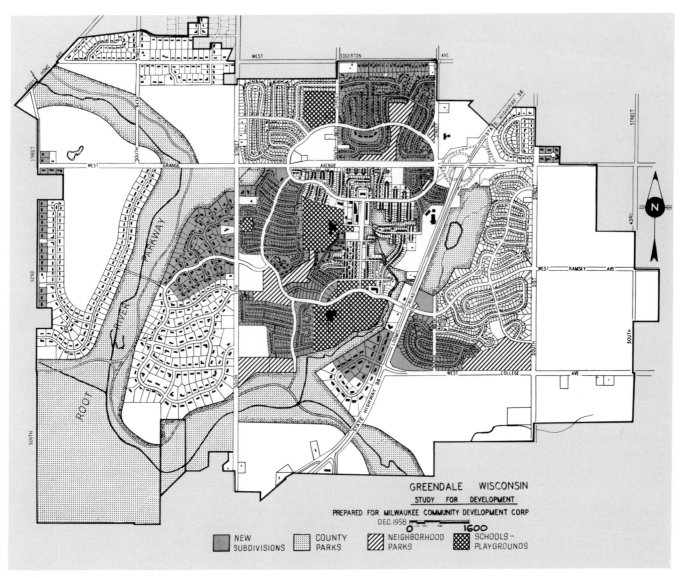

Within the figure:

GREENDALE WISCONSIN
STUDY FOR DEVELOPMENT
PREPARED FOR MILWAUKEE COMMUNITY DEVELOPMENT CORP
DEC.1958

NEW SUBDIVISIONS

COUNTY PARKS

NEIGHBORHOOD PARKS

SCHOOLS - PLAYGROUNDS

FIGURE 128. A 1958 version of the plan, by the Milwaukee Community Development Corporation. Compare this with Figure 125.

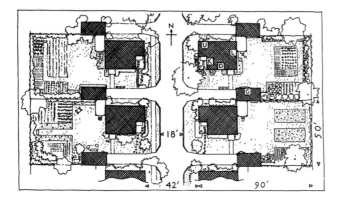

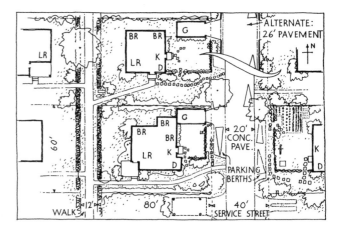

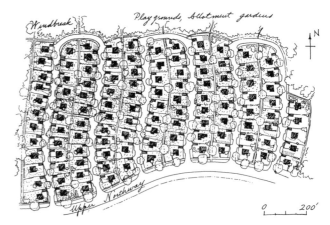

FIGURE 129. The typical Greendale house. In the present Greendale village about half the families live in single houses, most of them arranged as shown in this schematic plan. The cul-de-sac runs north and south, the houses facing south, parallel to the street. A car entering the side court stops within easy reach of the kitchen and living room doors. The garage helps to enclose the neighbor's porch and protects it from north winds. Thus placed, the garages create a semi-enclosed lawn for each house. The lot is small but efficient; there is space for vegetable gardening. The narrow street makes utility connections very short. There are several negative factors: children must play in the street; the sidewalk, not in the original scheme, is too narrow; there is no through street for a Sunday promenade; and few people see the pretty gardens. The house type shown here is rental housing.

FIGURES 130–131. One-story houses in 60-by-80-foot lots. These plans show the elements of the center walk scheme. The house lots are relatively wide, side yards are emphasized, the front door is convenient to both center walk and service street. The garage, at the northerly edge of the lot, helps enclose a small but useful kitchen yard. Off-street parking berths are shown in various forms.

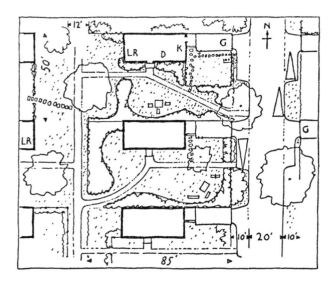

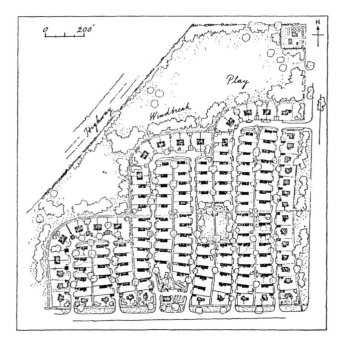

FIGURES 132–133. Solar house, lot, and street. The word "solar" is used here in a meaning broader than usual—in fact, the center of interest is the lot rather than the house. The lot is considered to be one of a series of lots, so that a group of families may co-operatively enjoy the full advantages of sunlight orientation. In these two-story houses all rooms but the bath have south windows—large or small, as suits the architecture. It is also part of the plan that there are no windows in the north wall, though there will be glass blocks and ventilators. This makes the yard usable right up to the neighbor's house and, with the help of tactful planning, gives unusual privacy to yard and house. Nothing is less private than the back yards of ordinary two-story houses. The front door could be at the north corner, but the south location gives a traffic-free living room and joins outdoors to indoors with dramatic effectiveness. The off-street parking shown here is most economical and practical. Solar houses work best, of course, on a south slope and where service drives can run approximately north and south. The light effects in a north-south street are superior to those of an east-west street, in summer and winter. The group in Figure 133 comprises 98 solar houses with a fringe of 26 one-story singles and 26 units in two-story twins. The fringe is both aesthetic and practical in purpose: the one-story houses are a better buffer against the traffic streets, and the twins can take advantage of northerly views across the greenbelt, which would be wasted on the solar houses; they also make a more pleasant picture from the highway. The net density, omitting traffic streets and greenbelt, is 6.7 families per acre. Looped drives are preferable to dead-end streets. One reason is that they can be longer. The use of short cul-de-sacs so increases the expenditure for collector streets as to make it a heavy construction and maintenance burden—and the increase in the number of collector streets tends to cancel the safety and convenience that are the justification of the special residential street.

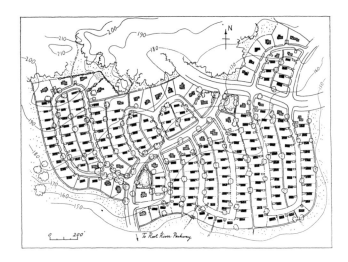

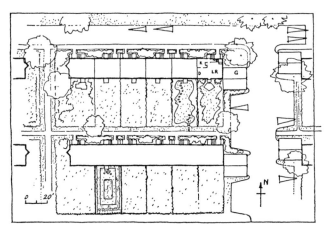

FIGURE 134. Solar houses on 60-foot lots. This plan was studied in relation to the topography of an outstanding section of Greendale, the "south hill." An earlier study was based on half-acre lots and custom-built homes, but the strong south slope pointed to a solar house layout. The hill commands a long vista over a river valley. This type of plan requires careful checking on the ground to determine whether the open channels might be straightened to preserve the good views. Certainly, some of the houses in the south fringe should be re-sited because they block vistas along the center walks. Tree planting should be done with the same point in mind. The section illustrates the importance, architecturally, of high fences as a bond between house and site.

FIGURE 135. Row houses, common orientation. This is a variation of the plan in Figure 136. It is adaptable to sites which permit southern orientation for the garden front. A southerly slope is desirable because the lower end of the yards is the best direction for the flow of surface water. The unit and yard scheme—a single door as service and social entrance, living room at the rear, and all buildings facing the same way—derives from Neubuhl, the famous housing group near Zurich. The FHA has recommended it, and a version of it won a New York State housing prize. About 22 feet wide, it is a luxurious two-bedroom unit. This scheme is not used in the general plan; it could be substituted, in the right locations, for solar houses or standard row houses.

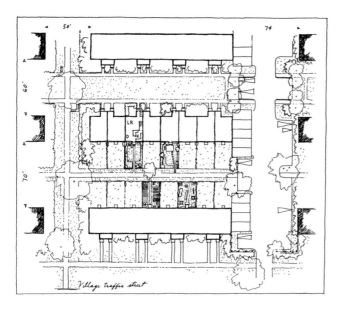

Village traffic street

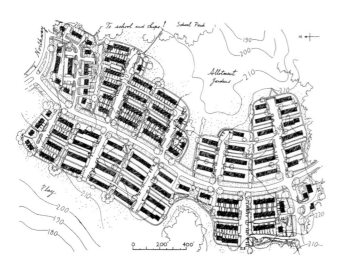

FIGURES 136–137. Site plan for row houses. The row house, once common in the Middle West, was made obsolete there by the balloon frame and streetcars. The later demand for higher density was met by the "flat." Now reintroduced by government projects, row houses are gaining acceptance. The family car and the garbage can are the twin dragons that must be overcome by the row house site planner. Shall the front area be desecrated by cars, or shall the vehicles be at the back, the visitor finding the front door if he can, stumbling through the kitchen if he must? The currently smart solution is the dual-purpose door (Neubuhl again?). The car is parked at the curb —which is virtually at the door—and the garbage can is obscured by concrete. So it is at Fresh Meadows, Long Island, where the front area is a vast lawn. That is satisfactory for New York City, but citizens of the United States proper yearn for yards. In USHA days, the Technical Division favored "end space parking" to keep the car out of the domestic picture, front and rear; this is the solution on which the studies in Figures 138 and 139 are based. The housing is assumed to be for rent—or the houses, with yards, might be owned by individuals, the rest of the land being maintained by a group agency. The service lanes are normally connected to form loops; in a few cases short extensions are treated as cul-de sacs. The parking, in garages or parking bays, should be one space per dwelling unit. In addition, there should be a few berths reserved for visitors and placed near the walks giving access to the front doors. The circulation system includes walks in the end spaces not used for parking; these walks give access to the village traffic street and to the greenbelt space. This project plan contains 500 units with an average frontage of 20 feet. The net density is about 12.5 families per acre. The "dogleg" street in the upper left corner was necessitated by the surface drainage situation.

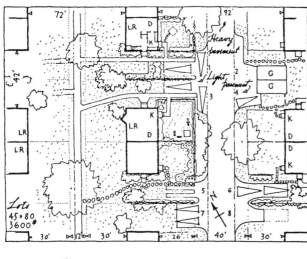

FIGURE 138. Twins—but not necessarily identical. Except around Wilmington, Delaware, and Chester, Pennsylvania, and in scattered mill towns, twin houses—officially known as semidetached dwellings—do not seem to be established as a traditional dwelling type. During the "defense" period many thousand one-story twins were built; they saved plumbing materials and were not as regimented as rows. A few commercial developments have used them, selling the units separately. It is a type that should be studied; besides saving on construction cost and on heating it reduces site costs and is very efficient in the use of lot space. In the plan (Figure 139) each lot is one twelfth of an acre, yet the spaces between the 24-foot by 48-foot buildings are 42, 72, and 92 feet. To avoid an excessively symmetrical look, twins should be designed to stand back to back rather than side by side. That favorite sadism of public housing, the common entrance walk, must, of course, be avoided. Inequality of orientation is inevitable, but by special features such as the use of bay windows the disadvantage of a northerly unit can be reduced. An important item of construction design is suggested by the war-housing story of the man who called out "What time is it?"—and the neighbor's wife answered "Seven o'clock."

FIGURE 139. Town site plan. In this patch of town plan, the looped service streets are bent zigzagwise by 10-degree angles at 300-foot intervals, that being the standard spacing of sewer manholes. The ground here has a moderately uniform slope. This method of breaking straight streets is considerably cheaper to build than are curves. The execution is also more exact—it is very difficult to get a walk built with really smooth long-radius curves—and reversed bends are more convincing architecturally than reversed curves. In "Old Greendale" the cul-de-sacs are mostly bent rather than curved, and they look quite good.

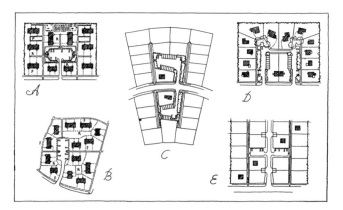

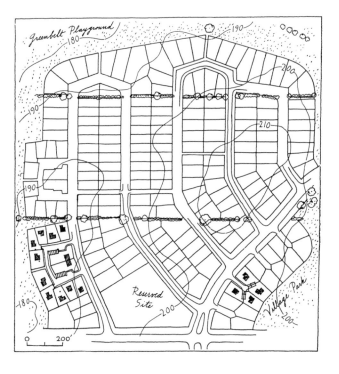

FIGURE 140. Park and walk in. A few planners and architects are asking if it is necessary to bring the car up to the house. Why can't a single garage compound serve a dozen houses, each standing in its own garden, with a pleasant walk connecting it to the compound and the street? In the past, fuel delivery has been the obstacle; oil, gas, and electricity now make the scheme technically feasible. The big garden apartment groups —the FHA permits a 250-foot walking distance—are preparing the way for its acceptance. As a crude *parti*, the idea was used in many war projects. Sketch plans *A* and *B* are from Pensacola. Plan *C* is an early schematic study, not used, for the American Community Builders' development, Chicago. Study *D* is an effort to correct the vulnerable points of *C*—distance from car to house, fire protection, waste collection, access to lot for heavy repairs. Plan *E* is merely a double-frontage street, an idea all planners have played with. The park-and-walk scheme is the most plastic planning motif imaginable; unquestionably, it has value in certain situations such as shore lines, park boundaries, fine wooded areas, rough topography, and odd-shaped building sites. Any pattern that is not linear in character, however, will almost certainly increase utility costs; a pattern limited by the fire-fighting distance does not develop utility spurs of sufficient length to justify the cost of the collector street. As will be noted in the version of plan *D* used in Figure 141, residents of the group must turn an additional corner to get to their homes. Street corners symbolize wasted utility lines; the cheapest town to build and operate would be one in which no resident turned more than one corner in going from his home to the shopping center.

FIGURE 141. Mostly conventional lots. This plan is a research study for the subdivision of areas at Greendale that may be laid out in substantially conventional streets and lots. Two old hedgerows traverse the site; street and lot lines have been adjusted to save them and to feature large trees. The angular treatment of the loop-ends facilitates drainage and makes a definite point at which the street names change. All residential streets branch from a main village traffic street—to simplify finding addresses. The little-court schemes are used to develop building sites not reached by normal lot depth.

26

Greendale

A sampling of the American civic art of these days obviously must comprise some notice of the New Deal's town planning.

Following the financial occurrences of 1929, it became a matter of general agreement that a housing program ought to be undertaken, with some kind of federal help. At the beginning slum clearance seemed most promising, probably in part because the destruction of old buildings and the construction of new ones for (presumably) the same low-income tenants appeared likely to sustain urban land values and not seriously to affect rentals. A considerable amount of this rebuilding has been put through, but it has become evident that it is impossible without a large subsidy to bring the old slum tenants back into the new apartments, even when the doubtful expedient is used of increasing the population density of the rebuilt area. In some instances, furthermore, it appears that the slum environment—the smoke, for example, and the square-mile overcrowding, which is still a burden after room overcrowding has been relieved—survives the rebuilding and diminishes its social value.

Experience may show how these handicaps can be overcome, but the theory is spreading that cities are fated to spread centrifugally, that it is futile as well as antisocial to try to maintain the present density of population. Some take it to be a necessary corollary that this tendency renders the low-rental apartment obsolete both in the blighted districts and in the new land on which the city is spreading.

The subsistence homesteads experiment was a fruit of the growing belief that industry ought to decentralize. The experiment was at least not a clear success, mainly for the reason that the provision of an appropriate industry could not be made a part of every project plan. The next step was to test a European device, the colony town outside the large city but within range of existing employment. For this purpose the Division of Suburban Resettlement was set up, under the Resettlement Administration. Suburban Resettlement is at this writing building three suburban towns at Washington, Cincinnati, and Milwaukee.

Greendale, the Milwaukee project, enjoys the spiritual advantage of being born poor. Its planners aimed at a population of a thousand families with incomes of twelve hundred dollars a year or a little more; their calculations soon showed that only with money at nominal interest could such a town pay its way and amortize its cost within sixty years, the estimated life of the contemplated plain but sturdy houses. In a big city, people of this economic stratum live in a kind of partial poorhouse. Their homes are old buildings the value of which has been written off by more prosperous occupants. The small taxes they pay, concealed in rent and other living costs, may not meet the cost of schooling one child. Practically all of the enormous capital and maintenance cost of public utilities, streets, police and fire protection, libraries, schools, parks and playgrounds, hospitals, courts and prisons is paid for in taxes—to view the situation diagrammatically—by the workman's employer, and is reflected in the factory's accounts as an increase in the price of its product and a reduction in its wage scale. In simple truth, the cost of the city comes mainly out of workers' wages. This is the "concealed subsidy"—it might be called a concealed wage—of which housing experts talk. Now when a workman goes out to

the suburbs and buys a home in a town where there are no factories or hotels or rich people to pay this subsidy, and the workman still draws his pay from a factory in the city, he automatically loses most of this concealed wage. The man will be paying (in the form of a reduction of money wages) part of the cost of police protection and schools enjoyed by his friends in the city, while at the same time he will be paying (in taxes) the cost of the protection of his home and the education of his children. That is why the well-to-do live in the fresh-air suburbs and that is why laborers live in city slums or in smoky factory towns. All this discussion may appear to have little to do with civic art, but it has had a great deal to do with the plan of Greendale.

The program, the skeleton of ideas and facts, on which Greendale is being planned is something like this: Automotive transportation makes it possible for men to live a considerable distance from their work; pure air, rural surroundings, and contact with the ground are physically and psychically good; life is better in a small town where social co-operation is possible; by eliminating inflated land values, by appropriate planning, by large-scale construction, and by taking advantage of every reasonable means for reducing living costs, working-class families can afford to live in small special-built suburban towns. The plan of Greendale has been directed toward making these statements true—particularly the last of them.

A large area (about five square miles) of rolling farm land, eight or nine miles from Milwaukee, was bought. Near the center of it a compact town, planned for an ultimate population of about four thousand people, is being built. The farm land will

Fig. 124

FIGURE 142. Air view of the center of Greendale, looking northwest. In the foreground is diagonal Route 36.

mostly remain farm land, in close economic connection with the town, probably through correlated cooperatives. It is intended that another compact group of houses, and a number of looser groups, will eventually bring the number of families up to about three thousand.

When it came to the location of the first compact town, a site was chosen that was not cut by existing roads. The site is near main highways but does not actually touch them. In the design of the plan, the first principle determined upon was that the streets *Fig. 125* should be divided into two types: traffic streets and residence streets. The traffic streets are wide, follow easy gradients, are planned to avoid their being used as trunk highways but rather to form convenient channels of traffic flow from highways to the town and within the town, and they are not used to create lot frontage. The residence streets are narrow, sometimes are rather steep, normally short, and normally dead-ended. In fitting this scheme to the irregular and partly hilly site, an intermediate type of street developed, a kind of collector street giving access to several cul-de-sacs, and itself carrying abutting lot frontage.

Along with the street plan had to be met the questions of row house versus single and of private yard versus community block interior.

Row houses—officially rechristened group houses —have in late years been accepted as the necessary form of low-cost suburban housing, just as multi-family dwellings, formerly thought of as apartment houses, have been accepted as necessary in cities. In the latter case the controlling factor is the land "value"; in suburban housing the land cost factor is usually not sufficient to force housing into apartments, but it reinforces the cheaper-construction argument in favor of row houses. Rows are somewhat cheaper to build than detached houses, and the saving in street and utilities costs is considerable. Commercial low-cost housing projects have usually adhered to local customs, rows being much used in Eastern cities. The sophisticated town planners, largely on the authority of English precedent, have accepted the row house—in short rows—as desirable, or perhaps rather as unavoidable, even for work in districts where it is not traditional. The planners of Greendale, under pressure of a limited budget, accepted the row house for about half their housing units, but they set out to find a way to place and build single houses economically enough to justify using them for the other half.

How that was done is to town planners the interesting part of the Greendale story, but a discussion of the other factor I named—the handling of the block interiors—is a prerequisite to it.

That "front yards" could be left unfenced was a discovery of the 1890's. A studiously planned community near New York, some ten years ago, boldly did away with the ancient and beloved back yard. Radburn, "the town for the motor age," was an ex-periment in several ways of much value to town planning. The basic principle of the plan is the division of the land into "superblocks." An area of perhaps one thousand by two or three thousand feet is surrounded by wide traffic streets; from these, dead-end lanes run into the block, giving wheeled access to a dozen or more single or twin houses, mostly with incorporated garages. Alternating with the lanes are footways, corresponding—but in location only—to the old-time alley. The houses front toward these footways, and the entrance walks diverge from them. There are no fences: the space between the rows of houses is developed in the manner known as parklike. Perhaps it will make this description clearer if I say that strangers do not quickly perceive which is the front of the houses and which the rear. Even on Monday, I understand, there may still be uncertainty. Actually, social visitors are intended to park their cars on the traffic street and walk in, via the footway, to the house they have in mind. It should be added that a strip of private park runs through the superblock, with walks that pick up the ends of the footways and form, with the help of underpasses beneath the traffic roads, a safe route to the school. This last feature has been much acclaimed; actually the underpass is used only when it is convenient, and there is competent doubt as to whether it will really lead to the survival of the Radburn young to be thus protected during the habit-forming years.

The planners of Greendale liked the Radburn lanes, but they could not accept, for a town of Middle Western workingmen, the parked yards. They accounted for this aspect of the town of the motor age by thinking of Radburn as a Riverside Drive apartment house taken apart, set down on the ground, and environed with one of those interior gardens the Phipps apartments have made the cynosure of all apartment eyes. The human elements in this transaction have no hankering, in spring, to plant a row of cabbages, nor have they formed the habit of pitching horseshoes on Sunday morning. No, it is overdoing it to let the motor age deprive us of personal relationship with the "ancient mother." The Greendale plan started with the premise that every house should have its patch of ground, with a fence around it.

Our old conception of a town street was that it should be a sort of public garden upon which it was pleasant to have an outlook from the living room and the porch. Suburban residence streets, in those days, were intended to attract admiring pleasure drivers. This conception is changing, thanks to gasoline and to a growing appreciation that the front lawn was a very expensive thing in land, in cost of utility connections, and in upkeep. It had to be paid for by crowding the houses into a disgracefully close row; the side yards were so narrow as to be useless.

The special way of putting together street, house, and lot that distinguishes the Greendale street—as, in the spirit of the advertising age, its begetters have christened it—appears most novel to those whose knowledge of town planning history is least. The type of house it implies is much like the side-garden house of our colonial towns, a house built on the street and along one side of the lot, with a garden between it and the neighbor. Even more it resembles the ancient and universal arrangement of the houses in farm villages, where one does not enter the house directly from the street but through a court around which the buildings are grouped. Not

FIGURE 143. A construction view, showing the extremely economic construction.

unexpectedly, visitors to Greendale—the town is under construction as this is written—have sometimes found an Old World flavor in its residence streets. They are narrow, for one thing. That was done to reduce the cost of grading, drives, and the utility connections: sewer, water, and electricity. It is the end of the house that touches the side of the street—there is no "front yard"—and the entrance is in the longer front, facing on the *Hof.* The lot is quite wide for a poor man's town, at least fifty feet. The court comprises all the room between one house and the next, because each house lies on the side line of the lot. This is not a serious matter since all the houses are rented: the town, in effect if not in form, will own itself and rent its houses to its people —but that is another story! There are few windows —on the first floor none—in the house wall abutting on the neighbor's court.

FIGURE 144. The same construction, but with the benefits of real site planning. Today the trees shade the site.

The street, then, consists of two rows of houses facing parallel to the street, not perpendicular to it as is the common scheme. It is obvious that orientation becomes important in such a plan. Almost all of the residence streets at Greendale run north and south; the houses face south, and the width of the courts is sufficient to ensure winter sunlight in the living rooms. The garage is at the rear of the court. With the neighbor's garage it serves to enframe a little lawn that is just behind the house; and beyond this lies the garden or recreation area of the rear yard.

This plan conceives of the house, the car, and the garden as together comprising the "home." It was worked out as a correlation of the house with the community and the world on one side and the privately held bit of land that is the garden on the other. The motorcar is the link between the house and the world: the court brings the car into the home complex—one can go from the car to the house as directly and with almost as perfect privacy as one goes from room to room in the house. One's friends drive in; they are not forced to stop in the street, to walk across a public sidewalk, and to remain in public view until the street door of the house is opened. The court is a harbor in which the family car may anchor and unload in safety after its journey on the high seas of the traffic roads.

This Greendale type of house and lot planning brings the residence street back into civic art—it

FIGURE 145. Groups of back-to-back or duplex houses, sited to save trees.

FIGURE 146. View of a park in the village center, looking eastward.

rescues the street from the street trees and the front lawns. The street becomes a defined channel of space, as it was in the old town plans. It is a plan well suited to substantial uniformity in the houses; they stand far enough apart to have personal identity, yet they are, together, an entity of a higher order than each is separately. Because the houses form directly the street walls, they can be manipulated for plastic effect; a setting-back of the houses at the entrance to a street, or a pinching-in of the plan at its end, has value that tells in the modeling of the designed space of the street. The entire street, too, is often so short that within it can be compassed

the completion of a simple rhythm, from the portal to the terminal members. When the ground is favorable, a symmetrical pattern works out naturally; if an irregular space must be divided or if the lay of the land and existing trees affect the layout, the result is inevitably an informal grouping that Camillo Sitte —or the modernists, if the houses had that cast— would find more charming than the other. The whole scheme, to the present writer's great contentment, is conducive to straightness in the streets.

And it is not quite an accident that in its skeleton organization the plan of Greendale is much like the plan of Williamsburg.

27

A Concluding Thought

When Werner Hegemann and I were writing our book on civic art, we talked often of the future of civic art, not the window-box type of civic center and that sort of thing, but city and art of the same meat, the intended beauty of cities as places of commerce and life and government, beauty built into streets and open squares that are the daily gathering and passing places of men. We had to say that no more towns like Nancy and no more plazas like the Piazza del Popolo would ever be built.

And we had to say, further, that if an effort were made to attain the old civic beauty, it could not be done in the old forms, for the automobile has taken the city unto itself, destroying the possibility of any full human experiencing of the city as an aesthetic whole. We studied old plans, sketched the fair sights that would appear as one walked in those streets.

But we knew that modern traffic would leave little pleasure in such a town.

Traffic, however, is not the only enemy of civic art. Modern cities are so large and so richly built, with every building doing its best to detach itself visually from the rest, that they become an intolerable burden upon the various elements of our minds and bodies that react to mass, form, and color. The buildings vary also in height, and the high ones rise far above the power of the street to control them. This competition within the street wall is another factor in the destruction of the street as a perceivable whole. The plain fact is that our cities have architectural indigestion—they would be better architecture, as cities, if the fronts of buildings were in the same style as the rears, which are usually simple, harmonious, and uniform in scale and material.

The hope for beautiful cities as architectural ensembles lies in the direction of the new towns which must grow up in response to the distributive factors in our mechanical and economic evolution. In some of these towns, as in the Resettlement Administration projects, budgetary limitations will compel the architectural abnegation which competitive commerce does not permit. Some will test new ways of sparing our days the burden of traffic noise and danger. Something resembling the traffic-free villages of the fairs may be evolved as the form of the town business centers. A firm separation of residence streets from traffic streets will give some peace and beauty to the homes in future towns and suburbs.

But there is no need to abandon existing cities to the dragon Traffic. Architects must fight against the growing theory that traffic volume is a phenomenon of nature which man may not deny. Traffic engineers often work on assumptions that are at least unphilosophical. People to whom there are finer values in life than getting from one noisy place to another in five minutes instead of ten, or adding a million dollars to the land values in this street rather than in that one, must learn to fight for their faith. In Washington, for example, there were other possibilities than the slashing of the broad traffic route of Constitution Avenue diagonally across Pennsylvania Avenue. The traffic roadways within the avenue of the Mall are wholly unnecessary and are obviously destructive of the intended simple grandeur of this monumental composition.

In little bays from the traffic stream, minor passages of civic beauty may still be attained. The plaza of the Rockefeller Center will have its imitators and rivals. And in successive regional, national, and world fairs many beauties of civic art will be given us, beyond the power of cities to compass.

Exceeding these possibilities, the student and lover of the old civic art must dream of a public garden art in which the rare essential glories of old cities—and of old and new town plans that have never been built—can be translated into forms realized in tree masses, hedges, walls, green and paved areas, and water surfaces. In such gardens an easy state of mind is possible, a calm reaction to verticals and horizontals, nears and fars, such as our cities will not tolerate. And in them people can meet and talk without keeping one eye on a traffic light. There is more to be learned about garden designing from the study of Renaissance town planning than in any other way, and I believe that the facts about solids and voids, masses and supports, that can be learned from civic art must be the basis for effective garden planning in whatever architectural styles the future brings. It must not be supposed that a mastery of the means and purposes of Renaissance city planning is easy or commonly encountered. The numberless confusions as to what is important in the L'Enfant plan, failures even to perceive what that plan is, demonstrate how much we need still to know about this elusive art.

But surely it is not possible to be wholly pessimistic about the future of those kinds of aesthetic creation which we may group in the phrase civic art, when the last year has given us so fine a thing as the Mall already is. It is true that I must go there at dusk when the bunglings of L'Enfant's modern successors are charitably obscured in order to get the feeling of perfection. Well, that is an easy price to pay, here in the soft afterglow of a summer evening.

APPENDIX A

Other Articles by Elbert Peets

I   On L'Enfant's Plan for Washington

1. "The Geneology of L'Enfant's Washington," in three parts, *Journal of the American Institute of Architects:*
   Part I, April 1927, pp. 115–119.
   Part II, May 1927, pp. 151–154.
   Part III, June 1927, pp. 187–191.
   (This is Peets's most scholarly writing on the subject, tracing roots and similarities.)

2. "An Accurate Re-Drawing of the Central Part of L'Enfant's 'Autograph Plan,'" *Architectural Record*, September 1932, pp. 158–160. (This is the article wherein Peets's oft-reproduced drawing of central Washington was first published— see Figure 39.)

3. "L'Enfant's Washington," *Town Planning Review*, May 1933, pp. 154–164. (See Chapter 3.)

4. "The Original Plan for Washington," *House and Garden*, July 1940, Section I, pp. 16–18, 57, 61.

5. "The Geneology of the Plan for Washington," *Journal of the Society of Architectural Historians*, May 1951, Volume 2, pp. 3–4.

II   Critique of Planning in Washington

6. "Current Town Planning in Washington," *Town Planning Review*, December 1931, pp. 219–237.

III   Site Planning

7. "Post-War Use of Temporary Sites," *American City*, November 1943, pp. 49–50. (An ingenious proposal for converting World War II housing sites into peacetime housing sites.)

APPENDIX B

Biographical Résumé of Elbert Peets

Elbert Peets was born in Hudson, Ohio, on May 5, 1886. He was graduated from Central High School in Cleveland in 1905 and from Western Reserve University in 1912, *magna cum laude*, Phi Beta Kappa, and with First Scholarship Honors. While in college he worked for H. U. Horvath, a landscape architect and nurseryman. He entered Harvard University's School of Landscape Architecture, where he earned the degree of Master of Landscape Architecture in 1915. While at Harvard he taught horticulture.

After finishing his studies at Harvard, he worked for the firm of Pray, Hubbard, and White, landscape architects, making plans for land subdivisions. In June 1916 he started to work with Werner Hegemann, the noted German planner, on the town of Kohler, Wisconsin. With Hegemann he designed subdivisions, parks, playgrounds, and cemeteries.

From January 1917 to December 1918 he worked as a civilian Planning Engineer with the U. S. Army, Camp Planning Section of the Construction Division. He made plans for hospitals and movable military facilities. In January 1919 he returned to work with Werner Hegemann, principally on the design of Washington Highlands in Milwaukee.

From April 1920 to March 1921 he toured Europe on a Charles Eliot Traveling Fellowship. During this time he visited London, Paris, Rome, Vienna, Berlin, and Amsterdam. In April 1921 he rejoined Werner Hegemann and collaborated on the preparation of the book *Civic Art, the American Vitruvius*. This work was published in 1922 and is regarded as a monumental classic. Between June 1922 and June 1923 Peets worked on the design of Wyomissing Park, a suburb of Reading, Pennsylvania. In this, too, he collaborated with Hegemann. Henry Vincent Hubbard, later a distinguished teacher at Harvard, also worked on this plan.

In July 1923 Peets started an independent practice in Cleveland, which he maintained for about a decade. His work involved private gardens, parks, and land subdivisions. It was in this period that he began writing his essays. In July 1933 he joined the Cleveland City Planning Commission, where he designed parks, playgrounds, and other civic improvements.

November 1933 marks his debut in the service of the federal government. He went to Washington to do site planning and road layout of the town of Beltsville, Maryland, for the U. S. Department of Agriculture. In this capacity he represented A. D. Taylor, president of the American Society of Landscape Architects. He returned to private practice in Cleveland in November 1933. He also continued his writing. However, this interlude in Cleveland did not last very long, for in November 1935 he returned to Washington to work with the U. S. Farm Resettlement Administration as the principal town planner of Greendale, Wisconsin.

During February and April 1938 he developed plans for the future development of Santa Catalina Island, including the town of Avalon, for the Wrigley estate. His recommendations were documented in the *Preliminary Report on a Planned Development of Catalina Island,* March 10, 1938. He then became Chief of the Site Planning Section for the U. S. Housing Authority. The following year he wrote a report on housing and city planning for San Juan, Puerto Rico. He continued work in Puerto Rico with a report for the National Resources Planning Board entitled *An Interim Program of Planning Studies for the Physical Development of Puerto Rico.* His coauthors were Hale Walker and Tracy Augur.

Peets lectured at the New York Museum of Natural History on aerial urban reconnaissance and site recognition in 1944. At the end of the war he became a consultant for the Federal Planning and Housing Authority and for the Public Housing Authority. From 1945 to 1948 he prepared plans for the extension of Greendale, as well as drafting a zoning ordinance. In this same period, and through 1951, he served as a housing consultant and site planner for the Municipal Housing Authority of San Juan, Puerto Rico.

From 1946 to 1947 he was a designer and consultant to Mr. Phillip Klutznick of American Community Builders, developing plans for the town of Park Forest, Illinois. From 1950 to 1954 he served as a member of the Fine Arts Commission in Washington, D. C. He was also a consultant to the National Capital Park and Planning Commission.

Between 1950 and 1960 he lectured at Harvard and Yale, at the latter school through the invitation of Christopher Tunnard. With the sculptor Felix de Weldon he developed designs for a number of monuments, including World War II battle memorials. He also worked as a consultant to: Harland Bartholomew, planner of St. Louis; McGaughan and Johnson, architects, Washington, D. C.; and Donald Marshall Call, landscape architect. In the early fifties he coauthored a design concept for Southwest Washington with Louis Justement in which a preservation and restoration approach was suggested.

By the early 1960's, illness began to limit Elbert Peets's professional work. In the summer of 1965 he left his modest apartment in Washington to retire to the home of his sister, Mrs. Blossom van Bergen, in the town of Austinburg, Ohio.

Index

Academy of Fine Arts (France), 9
Adams, Henry, 57
    house of, in Washington, 56, 64, 73
Aldobrandini
    gardens of, 116
    plan of, 22, 24
Alexandria, Va., 5
Alphand, J. C. A., 138, 139
American Institute of Architects, 89
American Society of Landscape Architects,
    186, 190
Ammon, temple of, at Karnak, 177
Amsterdam, map of, 13
Anacostia, Md., 62
Anacostia River, 70
Annapolis, Md., 3, 13, 27
Aosta, plan of, 22
Arc du Carrousel, Paris, 134
Arc de Triomphe, Paris, 97, 134
Architektura von Festungen (Speckle), 117
Arlington Memorial Bridge, Washington,
    107–112 *passim*
Athena, statue of, Parthenon, 104
Avila, Spain, 64

Baily, Francis, 15, 18
Baldwin Reservoir, Cleveland, Ohio, 176–178
Baltimore, Md., 27, 29, 145

Bangkok, Thailand, 64
Barillet-Deschamps, 139
Baroque art, 131, 132, 145–149, 155, 168
Barrière de la Trône, Paris, 134
Bath, England, 58
Baths of Diocletian, Rome, 157
Belgium, 115, 156
Bell, W. G., 124n
Bentley, Harry, 206
Bernini, Lorenzo, 66, 120, 121, 157, 158
Birkenhead, England, garden of, 187
Blondel, Jacques François, 20, 23, 131, 140,
    156, 159
Boboli gardens, Florence, 115
Bordeaux, France, 13, 148
Borghese gardens, Rome, 116
Borghi, 121
Borsa, Rome, 155
Bramante, Donato, 157, 174
Bridges, in planning, 110
Brown, Glenn, 89
Brunelleschi, Filippo, 174
Brussels, Belgium, 145
Building regulations, early, 8
Burnham, Daniel, 16, 47, 54, 70, 72, 89

Cabin John, Md., 62
California, gardens in, 192

Campo Marzo, Rome, 24, 117, 121, 122
Canals, in plans, 27–29, 79, 127, 137
Capitol, Washington, D.C., 8, 12, 14, 17, 18,
    20, 23, 24, 28, 30, 32, 42, 43, 45, 69
    Hall of Statuary in, 32
    view of, 67, 79, 94, 110
    and White House, 48, 53, 61, 89
Caprarola gardens, 116
Cascades, in plans, 45
Cassiobury park, 117
Castle Howard, 17, 35
Centers of radiation, 15
Central Park, New York, 45, 181–185
Chamber of Deputies, Paris, 85, 86
Champ de Mars, Paris, 85, 134, 148
Champs Elysées, gardens of, 138
    see also Paris, streets and boulevards
Chantilly forest, France, 52
Charleroi, plan of, 68
Charleville, France, 148
Chartres, France, 155
Checkerboard (chessboard) plans, 7, 15, 19,
    21, 25, 37, 41, 68, 116, 124, 145, 169,
    198
Chevy Chase, Md., 62
Chesapeake and Ohio Canal, 27
Chicago, Illinois, 16, 135, 198
    Court of Honor, 1893, 69, 72

Chicago Exposition of 1933, 165–169
Chicago Fair of 1893, 68, 89, 168
Cincinnati, Ohio, 217
Circles, in plans, 34, 40
City plans, early, 13
Civic art, 107–112, 131, 183
Civic centers, 28, 29, 48, 75, 168
Cleveland, Ohio
  civic center in, 48
  reservoir in, 176–178
Colonnades, 156
Columbia Historical Society, 89
Comité des Artistes, Paris, 134
Commission of 1901, *see* McMillan Commission
Company of the Potomac, 4
"Congress House," 43
Copley Square, Boston, 56
Court of Honor, Chicago, 1893, 69, 72
Courts, *see* Plazas
Craalinge of Amsterdam, 124
Crane, Jacob, 206

Darmstadt, Germany, 148
Deschamps, Paul, 138, 139, 140, 142
Diagonals (streets), 7, 15, 19, 37, 41
  in London, 117
Domes, masonry, 173–175
Doornick of Vygendam, 124, 125
Downing, Andrew Jackson, 68, 89

Edinburgh, Scotland, 68, 143
Egypt, 96, 97
Eliot, Charles, 186, 188, 189, 192
Ellicott, Andrew, 4, 6–8, 11, 16
Encroachment laws, 77
English influence, 143, 145
  see also London
Equestrian statues, 107–112
Erlangen, Germany, 148
European influence, 16
Evelyn, John, plans of, for London, 13, 14,
  20–22, 25, 115–132 *passim*
Exposition of 1869, 156

Fairmount Parkway, Philadelphia, 48
Federal buildings, design of, 61–66
Federal Hall, N.Y.C., 4, 10
Federal house, *see* Capitol
Fifth Avenue, New York, 38
Finnish art, 65
Florence, Italy, 13, 115, 151, 174
Fontainebleau forest, France, 52, 115

Fontana, Domenico, 128, 157
Ford, Henry D., 160
Forest Hills Gardens, Long Island, 145
Forests in plans, 52
Fort Washington, 32
Fountains, in plans, 18, 28, 83
France and French influence, 18, 25, 51, 115,
  129–131, 144, 147, 159, 168
Frankfort, Germany, 13
Fraser, James Earle, 108–110
French, Daniel Chester, 102
Fresh Meadows, Long Island, 213
Friedlander, Leo, 108–110
"Fumifugium" (Evelyn), 116

Gabriel, A. J., 89
Garden cities, 202
Gardens in plans, 24, 25, 51, 52, 91, 92, 115,
  116
Garnier, Tony, 138, 139
Genoa, Italy, 115, 120
Georgetown, Va., 5, 13, 27
German influence, 143–145, 148, 156, 159
Ghent, Belgium, 169
Gilbert, Cass, 54, 89
Giovannoni, Gustavo, 157
Goecke, Theodore, 146
Gold in statuary, 104, 107–112
Gothic art, 146, 148, 156, 174, 176, 183
"Grand Avenue," *see* Washington, D.C., Mall
Grand Canals, 23, 45, 46
Greenbelt towns, 202, 203
Greendale, Wis., 203, 204, 206–222
Greenwich park, England, 21, 117, 118
Gridiron plans, *see* Checkerboard plans
Guerin, Jules, 92
Gwynn, John, 122, 123, 124n

Hamilton, Alexander, 5
Hampton Court, England, 18, 90, 94
  park of, 21, 116–118, 182
Harrisburg, Pa., 29
Harvard School of Landscape Architecture,
  188–190
Haussmann, Georges Eugène, Baron, 16, 133–
  142, 156
  financial strategy of, 137, 152
  memoirs of, 137, 139, 142
  Mussolini and, 151–153
Hegemann, Werner, 223
Holland, 115
Hollar, plan of London, 123, 127n

Hooke, Robert, 124–127, 128n, 132
Hubbard, H. V., 191
Hunting forests, plan of, 22, 24, 25, 122

Ideen-Wettbewerb, 66
Independence Hall, Philadelphia, 3
Isaacs, Reginald, 198
Italy and Italian influence, 115, 129, 130, 144,
  147, 168
Ivry, Contant d', 72, 74

Jefferson, Thomas, 5–7, 9, 13, 16, 21, 37, 54,
  64, 68
Jefferson Memorial, Washington, 105–106
Jones, Inigo, 72, 123, 127n, 130

Karlshafen, Germany, 148
Karlsruhe, Germany, 13, 45, 139, 143, 148
Kimball, T., 191
Kingston, N.Y., 3
Kite shapes, 117
Knight, Valentine, 126–129, 132

Lancaster, Pa., 3
Lanciani, Rodolfo A., 158
Landscape architecture, 143, 181–193
La Roche-sur-Yon, France, 143
Latrobe, Benjamin H., 56, 64
Leghorn (Livorno), Italy, 115, 127n
L'Enfant, Pierre Charles, 3, 8, 9, 12, 16, 18,
  26, 34, 68, 86, 160
  architect of Federal Hall, 4, 10
  arranges N.Y. pageant, 10, 27, 97
  designer of plazas, 29
  difficulties with commissioners, 7, 11, 45
  genius of, 35, 42
  life story of, 9–12, 23, 40
  plans for Washington, D.C., 6, 7, 12, 14, 19,
    21, 22, 27, 28, 30, 32, 37, 38, 54, 78,
    143, 224
  mutilation of, 79–87
  revival of, 68, 69
  and the White House, 17
L'Enfant association, 87
Le Nôtre, André, 51, 115, 130, 141, 189
Leonardo da Vinci, 174
Lincoln Memorial, Washington, 50, 74, 90,
  101–104, 107, 110–112, 164, 188
  statue in, 101–103
London, England, 5, 20, 24, 51, 126
  plans of, 13, 15, 20–25, 38, 116
  rebuilding plans of, 115–132

London, England (*continued*)
  streets and areas of
    Aldersgate, 132n
    Berkeley Square, 117
    Billingsgate, 127
    Blackfriars, 120
    Bloomsbury, plan of, 68
    Bow Lane, 120
    Cannon Street, 120
    Charterhouse, 127n
    Cheapside, 120, 122
    Cornhill, 120
    Covent Garden, 32, 115, 120, 122, 123, 127n
    Cripplegate, 132n
    Embankment, 120
    Exchange, 122, 123, 124n, 128, 132n
    Fleet area, 117, 120, 122, 123, 124, 124n, 127
    Great Eastcheap, 120
    Guildhall, 132
    Hatton Street, 124
    Holborn, 127, 127n
    King Street, 132
    Ludgate Hill, 123, 124n, 128
    Moorfields, 127n
    Pall Mall, 38
    Physicians' College, 120
    Poultry Street, 132
    Queen Street, 132
    Queen Victoria Street, 120, 124n
    Regent Street, 38, 139
    Royal Exchange, 20
    Russell Street, 122
    St. Dunstan's, 117, 122, 124, 124n
    St. James's Square, 120
    St. Martin's lane, 116
    St. Mary Woolnoth, 120
    St. Michael's, 122
    St. Paul's, 20, 117, 120, 121, 122, 123, 124, 124n, 128, 132
    Smithfield, 124
    Temple Gardens, 124
    Thames Street, 132
    Tower Hill, 123, 124n
    Tower Street, 120
    Watling Street, 120
    Westminster, 124, 127n
    Whitehall, 124
  London Bridge, 20, 128
London Society of Antiquaries, 20, 22
Louis Napoleon, *see* Napoleon III

Ludwigslust, Germany, 58, 148
Lyons, France, 13, 147

McKim, Charles F., 47, 70, 72, 89
McMillan Commission, 47, 50, 54, 56, 61, 62, 64, 69, 70, 81, 88, 89, 92, 93, 105, 106, 110
Madrid, Spain, plan of, 13
Malines, France, 155
Manila, Philippines, plan for, 16
Mannheim, Germany, 146, 147
Mansard (Mansart), Jacques, 120, 141
Marienberg, Austria, plan of, 145, 147, 149
Market places in plans, 27–29, 32, 84
Marly-le-Roi, France, 47
Marseilles, France, 43, 147
Martin, Camille, 144
Maryland, 3, 6, 8, 9
Mayan art, 65, 193
Merceria, Venice, 40
Meštrović, Ivan, 108
Metz, France, 156
Michelangelo Buonarroti, 67, 147, 150, 156–158, 173–175, 189
Milan, Italy, map of, 13
Mills, Robert, 48, 72
Milwaukee, Wis., 217
  see also Greendale, Wis.
Montpellier, France, map of, 13
Moore, Charles, 89
Morris, William, 144
Mount Vernon, Va., 5, 65
Mount Vernon Place, Baltimore, 29
Mussolini, Benito, 151–155, 158, 159, 189

Nancy, France, 47, 58, 65, 143, 148, 223
Nantes, France, 148
Napoleon I, 134
Napoleon III, 134–142 *passim*, 152, 156
National Capitol Park and Planning Commission, 61, 62, 74, 76
Neighborhood concept, 197, 198
Neubuhl, Switzerland, 212, 213
New York
  Central Park, 45, 181–185
  Federal Hall, 4, 10
  Fifth Avenue, 38
  plan of, 13, 185
Nîmes, France, 147

Ollivier, O. E., 137, 152, 153
Olmsted, Frederick L., 47, 72, 89, 94, 181–192

Olmsted, Frederick L., Jr., 188
Orléans, France, map of, 13

Palladio, Andrea, 126
Pantheon, Rome, 151, 154, 155, 157, 158
Paris, France, 13, 26, 46, 58, 82, 85, 97, 122, 138
  Arc du Carrousel, 134
  Arc de Triomphe, 97, 134
  buildings
    Carnavalet Museum, 139
    Chamber of Deputies, 85, 86
    Ecole Militaire, 134
    Halle au Blé, 142
    Hotel de Ville, 135, 137
    Invalides, Les, 18, 83, 85, 134
    Louvre, 85, 135, 140
    Madeleine, the, 48, 85–87, 134
    Notre Dame, 142, 156
    Opera House, 85
    Palais d' Industrie, 142
    Palais Royal, 134
    Panthéon, 32, 139
    Sainte-Chapelle, 139
    Tribunal de Commerce, 139
  Colonne de Juli, 139
  parks
    Bois de Boulogne, 138
    Buttes Chaumont, 138
    Luxembourg gardens, 115, 134, 142
    Monceau, 138, 191
    Tuileries, the, 45, 48, 115, 134, 137
  rebuilding of, 133–142, 143, 148, 152, 156
  St. Denis, gate of, 134
  St. Martin, gate of, 134
  streets and boulevards
    Avenue Alexandre III, 18
    Avenue des Champs Elysées, 83, 85, 88, 89, 90, 91, 92, 97, 134, 148
    Avenue de l'Observatoire, 134, 139
    Avenue de l'Opera, 82, 85, 86, 137, 140
    Boulevard des Capucines, 137
    Boulevard Henry IV, 139
    Boulevard Magenta, 137
    Boulevard Malsherbes, 134
    Boulevard St. Germain, 138
    Boulevard St. Michel, 139
    Boulevard de Sébastopol, 139
    Boulevard de Strasbourg, 134
    Boulevard Voltaire, 137
    Champ de Mars, 85, 134, 148

Paris, streets and boulevards (*continued*)
    Cours-la-Reine (Cours de la Reine), 90,
      115, 134
    Etoile, 85, 138–140
    Faubourg St. Antoine, 137
    Place du Carrousel, 134
    Place du Châtelet, 140
    Place de la Concorde, 18, 33, 45, 48, 72,
      89, 97, 131, 134, 148
    Place Dauphine, 134, 142
    Place de l'Etoile, 85, 138–140
    Place Louis XV, 33, 48, 134, 143
    Place de la Nation, 137
    Place de l'Opera, 140
    Place de la République, 137, 152
    Place Royale, 30
    Place St. Sulpice, 134
    Place Vendôme, 134, 148
    Place des Victoires, 134, 142
    Place des Vosges, 30, 134, 148
    Rue des Ecoles, 134, 138
    Rue du Faubourg Saint-Honoré, 89
    Rue de Rivoli, 30, 134, 135
    Rue Royale, 33, 85
    Rue Soufflot, 32
    Rue de Turbigo, 137, 152
Parthenon, 104, 191
Patte, Pierre, 88, 89
Patte-d'oie, 14, 18, 24, 51, 94, 111, 128
Peabody Institute, 21
Peets, Elbert, 36, 206, 208
    biographical résumé of, 226–227
Persepolis, Hall of a Hundred Columns, 177
Persigny, Duc de, describes Haussmann, 133
Philadelphia, Pa., 3, 5, 9, 11–13, 48, 68
Piazza San Marco, Venice, 29, 40
Pisa cathedral, 156
Place de la Carrière, Nancy, France, 47
Plazas, 18, 28–30, 34, 39–42, 63, 89, 117, 124,
    128–130, 144, 148, 155, 156, 168, 224
Poëte, Marcel, 134
Pompeii, 58
Pope, John Russell, 71, 105, 106
Porter, Kingsley, 83
Potomac River, 4, 5, 27, 32
Potsdam, Germany, 148
President's house, *see* White House
Princeton, N.J., 3
Public Buildings Commission, *see* McMillan
    Commission
Pugin, Augustus W., 156
Puvis de Chavannes, Pierre, 74

Radburn, N.J., 202–204, 219
Rainaldi, Carlo, 120, 122
Ralph, James, 128n
Raphael, 158, 189
Rastatt, Germany, 148
Reading, Pa., 29, 68
Rectangular plans, *see* Checkerboard plans
Renaissance art, 128–131, 139, 148–150, 155,
    156, 160, 174, 175, 192, 193, 224
Rennes, France, 148
Repton, Humphry, 164, 186, 189
Resettlement, suburban, 217, 224
Residence Law, 5, 8, 9
Rheims, France, 148
Richardson, Henry H., 56, 64, 73
Richelieu, France, 58, 115
Ringstrasse, Vienna, 145, 149, 150
Rockefeller, John D., Jr., 160
Rockefeller Center plaza, 224
Roland Park, Baltimore, 145
Roman Forum, 85
Rome, Italy, 15, 18, 21, 25, 52, 58, 83, 85, 90,
    97, 117, 128, 130, 140, 157–159
    Borghese gardens, 116
    buildings, 147
      Baths of Diocletian, 157
      Borsa, 155
      Marcello Theater, 154
      Palazzo di Giustizia, 155
      Pantheon, 151, 154, 155, 157, 158
      St. Mary Cosmodin, 155
      St. Mary the Egyptian, 153
      St. Peter's, 67, 121, 147, 156, 157, 158,
        173, 174, 175
      San Ignazio, church of, 155
      Santa Maria degli Angeli, 157, 158
      Trinità de' Monti, 18, 121, 122
      Vesta, temple of, 153
      Victor Emmanuel Monument, 155
    Forum, 85
    fountains of Lepidus, 115
    Marcus Aurelius statue, 155
    Mausoleum of Augustus, 154
    Monte Cavallo, 115
    Mussolini and, 151–153
    plans of, 22, 24, 111
    Pincian gardens, 90, 191
    restoration of, 154–159
    Spanish Steps, 122
    streets and piazzas
      Campo Marzo, 24, 117, 121, 122
      Corso Umberto I, 83, 85, 155

Rome, Italy (*continued*)
    Piazza del Campidoglio, 140, 147
    Piazza Capranica, 155
    Piazza Colonna, 151, 154, 155
    Piazza di Monte Citorio, 155
    Piazza Navona, 142
    Piazza di Pietra, 155
    Piazza del Popolo, 18, 24, 52, 85, 120–
      122, 147, 155, 223
    Piazza della Rotonda, 155
    Piazza di San Pietro, 45, 147, 150
    Piazza Santa Maria Novella, 148
    Piazza di Spagnia, 85
    Piazza di Venezia, 83, 85
    Porta del Popolo, 21, 24, 83
    Porta Pia, 21
    Via Condotti, 18, 83, 85, 122, 155
    Via Felix, 115
    Via Merulana, 21
    Via Nazionale, 155
    Via Nuova, 38
    Via Pia, 115
    Via Sistina, 21
Roosevelt, Theodore, memorial, 105
Rothenburg, Germany, 146, 149, 169
Row houses, orientation of, 199–201, 212,
    213, 219, 221
Royal Society, England, 20, 115
Rueil, France, 115
Ruskin, John, 183, 187–189

St. Cloud, France, 115, 117, 193
Saint-Gaudens, Augustus, 47, 89
St.-Germain forest, France, 52, 115
St. Mark's, Venice, 104
St. Paul's, London, 20, 117, 120, 121, 122,
    123, 124, 128, 132
St. Peter's, Rome, 67, 121, 147, 156, 157, 158,
    173, 174, 175
San Francisco, Calif., plan for, 16
San Francisco Fair (1915), 65, 66, 72
San Giorgio Maggiore, Venice, 126
Santa Maria della Salute, Venice, 126
Satellite towns, 217
Savannah, Ga., 13, 22, 68, 143
Sayes Court, England, 116
Scamozzi, Vincenzo, 126
Schoenbrunn, Vienna, 90, 94
Site planning, residential, 202–205
Sitte, Camillo, 130, 135, 143–150, 156, 166,
    167, 222
Sixtus V, Pope, 21

Slum clearance, 216
Society of Antiquaries, London, 117, 118, 119
Solar houses, 211, 212
Speckle plan (1590), 22, 117, 122, 123
Spengler, Oswald, 106
Squares, *see* Plazas
Städtebau, Der, a journal, 146, 148
Städtebau, Der (Sitte), 144, 148
Städtebau, das Formproblem der Stadt (Wolf), 150
Stein, Clarence, 202
Strada Nuova, Genoa, 115, 117
Strasbourg, France, map of, 13, 131
Swedish art, 65
Sylvestre's engraving, 117

Tapered avenues, 32, 34
Thomas, Walter C., 206
Thornton, William, 5
Turin, Italy, 13, 116
Twin houses, 214, 219

Ulm, Germany, 156
U.S. Public Housing Administration 203, 208
Unter den Linden, Berlin, 148

Vanbrugh, John, 35
Vasari plan (1598), 22
Vaux, Calvert, 89, 181, 184
Vaux-le-Vicomte, France, 90
Venice, Italy, 13, 29, 169
  Merceria, 40
  Piazza San Marco, 29, 40
  St. Mark's, 104
  San Giorgio Maggiore, 126
  Santo Maria della Salute, 126
Versailles, 18, 23, 26, 45, 67, 90, 91, 94, 141
    148
  canal at, 23, 47
  parks of, 117, 182, 184
  plans of, 13, 15, 20, 24, 25, 46, 68
Vienna, Austria, 90, 94, 144, 150
Vienna Ring, *see* Ringstrasse
Vignola, Giacomo da, 174
Villa d'Este gardens, 116, 192
Vincennes, France, 137, 138
Vinci, Leonardo da, 174
Viollet-le-Duc, Eugène E., 156
Vistas, 80–83, 92, 106, 120, 121, 128, 139, 185
  see also Patte-d'oie
Votivkirche, Vienna, 150

Wacker's Manual of the Plan of Chicago (Moody), 135, 152, 153
Walter, Thomas U., 67
Washington, George, 4–9, 16, 21, 26, 32, 45, 52, 54, 68, 160
  proposed statue of, 4, 14, 23, 48, 79
Washington, D.C.
  Arlington Memorial Bridge, 107–112 *passim*
  buildings
    Archives building, 68–71, 81, 83, 84, 105
    Arlington Hotel (old), 56
    Bureau of Standards, 76
    Capitol, 8, 12, 14, 17, 18, 20, 23, 24, 28, 30, 32, 42, 43, 45, 48, 53, 61, 67, 69, 79, 89, 94, 110
    Center Market, 27, 79, 80
    Corcoran house, 56, 64
    D.A.R. building, 74
    Decatur house, 73
    District Building, 39
    Dolly Madison House, 56, 73
    Federal Warehouse, 70
    Hay, John, house, 56, 64, 73
    House office building, 18, 45
    Interior Building, 74
    Justice Building, 39, 70, 80, 82, 83, 86, 87
    Library of Congress, 69
    Pan-American building, 74
    Patent Office (old), 32, 69, 71, 72, 79, 84
    Post Office (old), 39
    Public Library, 79, 84
    Red Cross building, 74
    St. John's Church, 56, 64, 73
    Scottish Rite temple, 105
    Senate office building, 18, 45
    Smithsonian, 54, 89
    Southern Railway Building, 39
    State, War and Navy Building, 73, 87
    Stockton house, 64
    Sumner, Charles, house, 56
    Supreme Court Building, 69
    Treasury Annex, 57, 73
    Treasury Building, 18, 39, 50, 53
    Union Station, 89
    U.S. Chamber of Commerce, 57, 64
    U.S. Court of Claims Building, 57
    Webster's home, 56, 64, 73
    White House, 7, 8, 14, 17, 18, 20, 23, 24, 32, 34, 35, 42, 43, 47, 48, 49–55, 61, 64, 72, 73, 79, 89, 105
  Capitol Hill, 27, 28
  Commission of Fine Arts, 71, 105

Washington, D.C. (*continued*)
  commissioners for planning, 5–9, 11
  Federal Triangle, 23, 40, 67, 69–77, 81, 86, 89, 162
  Fine Arts Commission, 83
  Garfield Park, 28
  Jefferson Memorial, 105–106
  Lincoln Memorial, 50, 74, 90, 101–104, 107–112, 164, 188
  Mall, 23, 32, 42, 43, 46–48, 54, 58, 61, 64, 68–70, 79, 80, 82–84, 88–90, 92, 224
    plan for, 50, 62, 88
    rebuilding of, 88–97, 107, 110, 112
  Navy Yard, land for, 9, 28
  "Pantheon" (proposed), 28, 79, 80, 82, 83
  plans for, 22, 23, 27, 36, 37, 53
  sale of lots, 5–9, 16
  streets and squares
    B Street, 61, 96, 97
    Capitol Avenue, 54
    Capitol Square, 18, 30, 31, 43–45, 58, 89
    Connecticut Avenue, 51, 55
    Constitution Avenue, 70, 71, 72, 95, 96, 97, 106, 224
    Dupont Circle, 51
    East Capitol Street, 69, 70
    Eighth Street, 28, 32, 33, 46, 69–72, 79–82, 84, 86, 106
    Eleventh Street, 41
    F Street, 72, 82
    Farragut Square, 52
    Fifteenth Street, 64
    Fifth Street, 27, 41
    Fourteenth Street, 39, 41, 46, 71
    Fourth Street, 64
    Grand Fountain Plaza, 32
    Judiciary Square, 69
    L Street, 41
    Lafayette Square, 52, 55–58, 61, 63, 64, 69, 72, 73, 77
    Louisiana Avenue (old), 70, 81, 82
    M Street, 41
    McPherson Square, 52
    Maryland Avenue, 89
    Massachusetts Avenue, 21, 41
    Mount Vernon Square, 84
    New York Avenue, 21, 41, 52, 54, 55
    Pennsylvania Avenue, 14, 17, 18, 21, 23, 32, 33, 38, 39, 42, 43, 50, 52, 53, 54, 55, 61, 64, 70, 71, 79, 80, 81, 82, 89, 97, 224
    Rock Creek Drive, 108, 110, 111, 112

Washington, streets and squares (*continued*)
  Scott Circle, 55
  Sixteenth Street, 50, 54, 55, 56, 64
  Sixth Street, 28, 39
  Thirteenth Street, 39, 71
  Thomas Circle, 40, 41
  Twelfth Street, 32, 39
  Vermont Avenue, 41, 55
  Virginia Avenue, 74, 75

Washington Monument, 23, 32, 47–50, 54, 67, 68, 70, 72, 74, 75, 80–82, 90, 94, 103
Watergate, Washington, 110–112
White House, 7, 8, 14, 17, 18, 20, 23, 24, 32, 34, 42, 43, 73, 105
  and Capitol, 48, 53, 61, 89
  setting of, 32, 35, 47, 49–55, 61, 64, 72, 79
Williamsburg, Va., 3, 13, 22, 68, 124, 160–164, 169, 222

Wolf, Paul, 150
World's Columbian Exposition, 73
Wren, Christopher, 20, 24, 38, 66, 115, 119, 120, 128, 130, 131, 189
  plan for London, 121–123, 125–132
Wright, Henry, 202

Zoning, 75, 77